VIA FERRATAS OF THE ITALIAN DOLOMITES

VOLUME 2: SOUTHERN DOLOMITES, BRENTA AND LAKE GARDA AREA

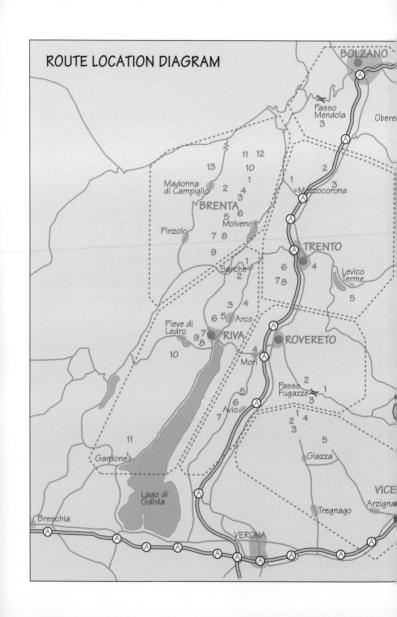

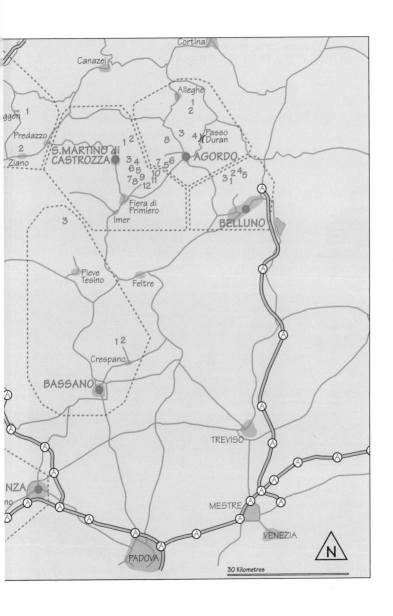

Cortina

Canazei

Alleghe

ggen 1

Predazzo

2
Ziano

S.MARTINO di
CASTROZZA

1 2

3 4

6 5

7 8 9

12 11

1
2

8 3 4 Passo
             Duran

7

10
5

6

AGORDO

3 2 4 5
   1

Fiera di
Primiero

Imer

BELLUNO

3

Pieve
Tesino

Feltre

1 2

Crespano

BASSANO

TREVISO

A

A

NZA

no

A

A

A

A

MESTRE

A

VENEZIA

A

A

PADOVA

N

30 Kilometres

Campanili Basso seen from Sentiero Brentari (BREN 8)

VIA FERRATAS OF THE ITALIAN DOLOMITES

VOLUME 2: SOUTHERN DOLOMITES, BRENTA AND LAKE GARDA AREA

by
Graham Fletcher and John Smith

CICERONE

2 POLICE SQUARE, MILNTHORPE, CUMBRIA LA7 7PY
www.cicerone.co.uk

© Graham Fletcher and John Smith 2003
Revised and reprinted 2005
ISBN 1 85284 380 2
Photographs: © Graham Fletcher and John Smith, unless otherwise indicated

A catalogue record for this book is available from the British Library.

DEDICATION

We want to dedicate this guidebook, and give special thanks, to all the people we have met in carrying out our research. Their friendliness and helpfulness, especially in the face of our limited Italian language skills, has been a very warming experience. We give particular thanks to the Trentino tourist offices and their people, without whose help and information this book would have been a lot more difficult to produce. Many thanks to everyone.

DISCLAIMER

Most routes in this guide will be found on Tabacco or Kompass maps of the respective areas, with either walking or mechanical access as explained in the guidebook. However, inclusion of a route in the guidebook does not automatically give right of access or freedom to climb.

Climbing via ferratas involves many dangers. There is no substitute for mountain experience and sound judgement; this book is not a substitute for either.

The guidebook writers, publishers and distributors do not accept any liability for injury or damage caused to, or by, climbers, third parties, or property arising from the guidebook's use.

The decision to climb a via ferrata is entirely yours and you do so at your own risk.

Front cover: *Crossing the Passagio dei Diedri on Monte Albano above the town of Mori (ROVER 4)*

CONTENTS

ROUTE LISTING

KEY TO DIAGRAMS

	Land below 1000m
	Land between 1000m and 1500m
	Land over 1500m
)(	Significant ridge with col/forcella
△	Summit
	Lake & river/stream
	Glacier
—Ⓐ—	Autostrada, with access point
SS12	State road, with reference number
	Provincial road
	Minor road
- - - - - -	Road not useable by general traffic
Ⓟ	Recommended parking area for route
	Cable car or other lift
- - - - - -	Footpath
▬ ▬ ▬ •	Via ferrata
BOLZ 1	Route reference number
■	Rifugio/hotel with overnight accommodation
☒	Bivouac
☐	Cafe/rifugio without overnight accommodation

ABOUT THE AUTHORS

When **Graham Fletcher** started climbing, you had to file the threads out of nuts to make running belays and Bonington was clean-shaven. However, the demands of an academic life and, later, a busy professional career took care of the next 30 years. After rediscovering his sense of priorities, Graham took early retirement and took up where he left off. He's still trying to figure out how Friends work.

John Smith has been walking and climbing mountains around the world for about 30 years, but his first visit to the Dolomites was not until 1998, when he fell in love with the mountains, culture and Via ferratas. In ticking off routes with a growing passion, he recognised the need for an up-to-date English-language guidebook, and also found that many routes existed which had not been published at all in English. Researching the new routes for this second volume has provided many more enjoyable and exciting days in the Dolomites.

PREFACE

Over the past few years via ferratas in the Italian Dolomites have become more and more popular, with new routes developed and old ones improved. This guidebook is the second in a series of two published by Cicerone Press which covers the whole area of the Italian Dolomites.

Volume One takes in the Eastern, Northern and Central areas of the Dolomites. Volume Two covers via ferratas in the Southern Dolomites (with routes on the Civetta, Schiara and Pala mountains) as well as the Brenta in the west. Additionally (and not, as far as we are aware, previously published in any English-language guidebook) routes are included around the northern end of Lake Garda and the Piccole Dolomites north of Vicenza. Here the mountains are generally lower and you can enjoy ferrata climbing over a much extended season, with some routes climbable for most of the year.

Graham Fletcher and John Smith, 2003

This climber is clearly unaffected by the exposure on VF Stella Alpina (AGORD 5)

INTRODUCTION

In volume one we asked the question 'Are the Dolomites the most beautiful mountains in the world?' Well, after four years' research in putting these books together, we still think so. With explosive shapes and unique colours the Dolomites can be regarded as the crown jewels of the European alpine range. Via ferrata climbing is a way of enjoying the sheer magnificence of this awesome mountain environment, where you will be stopped in your tracks by amazing views and mountain situations.

Many via ferratas were originally built to aid the movements of alpine military units during the First World War, and now they represent one of the major attractions in the Dolomites. They are, in effect, a range of protected routes, with fixed cables, ladders and even gorge-spanning bridges, which aid ascent to places normally reserved for expert rock climbers.

In recent years, old wartime routes have been restored and many new routes added to give a network of routes around the whole Dolomite region. Some of the new ferratas are 'sport routes', often technically quite hard, as you will see from our assessment of the grades.

Routes are regularly checked, maintained and waymarked by the Italian Alpine Club, the CAI (Club Alpino Italiano). You will also see reference to SAT (Societa degli Alpinisti Tridentini) which is the CAI's largest section, with more than 20,000 members in 76 sections. SAT has 39 refuges and 12 bivouacs, and maintains over 6000km of paths, including via ferratas, and thus plays a major role in maintaining the Dolomite environment.

HOW TO USE THIS GUIDE

This guide departs from the usual convention of listing routes by reference to the geological group in which they lie. Instead routes are grouped according to the best point of access to help you decide where to set up base. This has inevitably involved a few fairly arbitrary judgements, and many of the valley bases are sufficiently close together to enable you to tackle several different groups from a single location. Information is also included on the availability of cable cars and jeep taxis, which can make getting to the start of the route considerably easier and conserve your energies for the climb.

The availability of maps is covered in 'Map Availability and Place Names' below. Most via ferratas are indicated on the maps in popular use, although errors in location and naming are not unknown. You should also note that as the Dolomite mountains are characterised by such swooping, vertical faces, maps can only give a fairly diagrammatic impression of topography. This means that it is not always easy to visualise the vertical dimension of a route, especially the gradient to be encountered, nor is it easy to visualise the exposure involved until confronted by it! Even some of the

The lovely town of Arco is dominated by its castle

technically easier via ferratas will take you into some extremely exposed situations, as indicated in the route descriptions; this has been taken into account in the assessment of grades.

The route location diagrams for this guide are just that – diagrammatic. Their purpose is simply to help the reader locate the route on the appropriate map. Note that their scale varies, depending on whether it is more helpful to place the route in its wider context or to give more detail. The diagrams are not a substitute for a properly detailed map for use on the hill.

The times given in the guide assume a reasonable level of fitness on the part of the climber and, just as important, no undue congestion on the route. However, these timings are for guidance only, so whilst a fit and experienced via ferratist will frequently complete a route

more quickly than the guide time, it is possible that the busier and more accessible routes will require twice as long as the guide time.

The expression 'via ferrata' tends to be used as a generic term relating to any protected route. However, there is other nomenclature used locally which you will come across. 'Sentiero', 'sentiero attrezzato', 'sentiero alpinistico', 'percoso attrezzato' and 'cengia' (Italian for 'ledge') are some of the other terms in common use. To avoid confusion, this guidebook has adopted the terms used locally. You will, incidentally, often find that routes called 'sentieros' are easier than those referred to as via ferrata routes. Whilst some sentieros are fully equipped with cables, ladders and stemples, many are little more than extended traverses of mountainous areas, involving less challenging terrain. Here, the need for protective cables is limited to the more exposed passages encountered. Nonetheless, you should note that even though some of the easier sentieros have limited hands-on climbing, they often have considerable exposure! (**Note:** while the plural of 'via ferrata' is, of couse, 'vie ferrate', this guide uses the anglicised form, 'via ferratas'.)

ROUTE GROUPINGS

Several foreign-language guidebooks exist to via ferrata climbing, using slightly different approaches to grouping routes, although most are based on geological groups. This book, however, organises routes around the most convenient valley bases in which to stay, or from which to approach the routes (although routes are cross-referred to mountain groups in Appendix 3). As with all systems this leads to some anomalies or overlaps. It is important to stress, however, that this is a **guide**book: given a map, some local knowledge and, most importantly, some time to spend enjoying the Dolomites, you will work out your own itineraries for your via ferrata days. We hope you have as much fun in the Dolomites as we have, and are sure you will enjoy poring over your maps and working things out for yourselves! **For a detailed description of the grading system used in the guide, see the 'Safety' section.**

WHEN TO GO

There is no ideal time to go to the Dolomites, as there are a number of factors to consider; although, as with any mountain area, good luck with the weather is critical.

A number of the routes in this volume are at lower altitudes, especially those around Lake Garda. Consequently many of these routes are climbable at almost any time of the year. They are also easily accessible from several airports to the south (e.g. Venice, Verona, Brescia), making ferrata climbing a short-break (even long weekend) option. Such routes are, however, perhaps best avoided in the heat and crowds of high summer.

The season for via ferrata climbing in the higher mountains is, of course, greatly dependent on the extent of snow fall in the previous winter and the timing of the first snows of autumn. Generally speaking, mid- to late June until the end of September is the period you should consider for your trip. Lower south-facing routes will be in condition for the longest period. Like all mountain areas, though, the weather can be unpredictable, and snow is not unknown even in August.

Climbers on VF degli Alleghesi, Monte Civetta (AGORD 1 and 2)

Rif. Torre di Pisa (see BOLZ 1)

August is an extremely busy month, when all Italians head for the beach or the mountains. On the plus side, all the summer lift services operate in August, as do the bus services. The downside is that the popular via ferratas will be very busy, and the cost of accommodation will be at its highest. Mountain *rifugios* are also busy, so a phone call to book beds in advance is advisable in high summer.

TRAVEL TO THE DOLOMITES

The quickest way to get to Italy is to fly, with Venice, Treviso, Bolzano, Verona, Brescia, Munich and Innsbruck all providing speedy access to the region. Budget operators currently fly into Venice, Treviso and Brescia. Bus services run from all airports into the Dolomites, but frequency is often poor, even non-existent on Sundays (see below, 'Local Transport').

While cars can be hired at any airport, rates are cheaper in Germany, so the extra drive from Munich may be worthwhile if time allows. Although not essential for many of the popular via ferratas, a car is certainly very useful in getting around: dependence on public transport takes a sizeable chunk out of your climbing time. The European motorway network is now so good that it is possible to drive from the channel ports into the Dolomites in one long day, although most would choose to break their journey.

The French and Italian motorways are tolled, while use of Austrian motorways requires a 'vignette' sticker (valid for 10 days, 2 months or 1 year), which can be bought at border filling stations/shops or at tabacs if entering Austria by non-motorway routes (see www.vignette.at/oe for current prices). The main road into Italy, the Brenner pass, involves an additional fee and can be chaotic in high season. Both the fee and the crowds can be avoided by using the old SS12 road, but that is windy and slow, as is the final part of the journey on the mountain roads of the Dolomites.

Fast and reliable inter-city trains can be used to travel across Europe. However, as with flying, connecting travel into the mountains needs to be organised, which can eat into holiday schedules.

ACCOMMODATION

There is a wide range of options, from the basic, such as camping or mountain *rifugios*, to the height of luxury. Amongst the most popular choices are self-catering apartments and *meubles*. The latter are (usually smaller) hotels that do not provide evening meals, but which are good value for money if you are content with a modest meal in a nearby pizzeria. All major towns, and even most small villages, have tourist information offices which will help you find accommodation, although you will usually have to make your booking direct with the place you want to stay.

There is an extremely good network of *rifugios* throughout the Dolomites – some owned by the CAI and some privately owned. Most are well appointed and provide comfortable accommodation at reasonable prices, together with substantial meals of good quality. Sleeping arrangements usually involve dormitories, and whilst blankets are generally provided a sheet sleeping bag is required (although these can be hired at many of the larger *rifugios*). Washing facilities are provided, but these can be

quite basic and hot water should not be expected. Information about opening times can be obtained from local tourist offices or from the CAI's web site, much of which is now translated into English (see www.rifugio.it). Bivouac huts are common in the more remote mountain areas, although these are little more than emergency shelters, with facilities limited to a few bunks and blankets. Use is on an honesty basis, but anyone planning an overnight stay should carry all their needs, including food and water.

Italy has an excellent, albeit complicated, network of tourist information offices. The Italian State Tourist Board (ENIT) has offices in many capital cities, including London. The information they provide is often very attractive, but so general as to be of little practical help in planning your trip. It is better to contact the local tourist offices in the area you

Percorso Sass Brusai offers a good view of the normal descent path (BASAN 2)

plan to visit. Under the umbrella of ENIT, a hierarchy of tourist offices is maintained at regional level, provincial level, and in most towns and villages in holiday areas. These offices are known either as APT (Azienda di Promozione Turistica) or EPT (Ente Provinciale Turismo). Towns or villages not included in the ENIT network often maintain their own information offices, known as Assessorato al Turismo. Just to confuse even further, you will also see 'Ufficio Turistico' signs, which may be the APT office anyway! An approach to any of these offices generally elicits a wealth of detailed material about matters such as accommodation, public transport and lifts in the area. Whilst most of the staff in the larger offices speak good English, this is not necessarily the case with some of the smaller offices. So if you make your enquiries by phone, prepare yourself with a few Italian phrases.

The following addresses and web sites might prove useful.

- ENIT London office: Italian State Tourist Board, 1 Princess Street, London W1R 9AY, Tel. 0207 3551557/73551439 or web site: www.enit.it/uk
- Italian Tourist Web Guide: www.itwg.com.

These sites contain a huge amount of practical information, including links to local tourist offices, although not all the pages on the ENIT site are in English.

LOCAL TRANSPORT

Public transport in Italy is generally good and cheap, and many of the routes described in this book can be accessed by bus. There are a number of major operators, with well-integrated timetables, serving the area, including Atesina,

View north from eastern side of Passo Groste, the start of Sentiero Vidi and Sentiero Palete (BREN 10 and 12)

Dolomitibus and SAD. Get hold of a copy of their local timetables even if you have a car, as some routes involve extensive mountain traverses, which will deposit you some miles from where you started! You should note, however, that the services of all bus operators are reduced considerably on the middle weekend of September.

The Dolomites are well served by cable cars, which are often surprisingly cheap. Whilst a good many lifts are winter-only operations, those in the more popular areas operate throughout the summer months. As with bus services, the cable-car operators run reduced operations at the beginning and end of the summer, although this varies depending on the individual operating companies and unpredictable factors like the weather. As a general rule, however, most services operate from July through August, and remain in place into the beginning of September, with more popular routes continuing into October in some cases. Local tourist offices can usually advise on timetables, and it is wise to check the services in advance to enable you to plan your climbing timetable accordingly. Bus and cable-car timetables are referred to throughout this guide, since changes from one season to another have been very limited in recent years. It is, however, wise to check locally before finalising your itinerary for the day.

TELEPHONES

Telephoning Italy, or ringing home, is very simple. For calls both **to and within Italy** you need to dial the full telephone number, including the city code and leading zero (Italy's international access code is 0039). For **international calls** from Italy drop the leading zero of your home number (UK International access code is 0044). Some mobile phones now work across Europe, but you will need to check this with your operator before leaving home. Phone boxes in Italy generally use phone cards rather than cash. Full instructions are often found in English, but this does not include the need to break off the corner of your phone card before its use (otherwise it will not work!). Phone cards are available from newsagents, tabacs, bars or vending machines by the phone box.

Useful emergency numbers are: 113 (police); 115 (fire); 116 (ACI car rescue/repair); 118 (medical).

MAP AVAILABILITY AND PLACE NAMES

Visitors to the Dolomites are generally well served by mapmakers, and any good book shop should be able to offer you a range of products. The situation is not quite as good, however, in the more southerly areas covered in this volume, of which more later. For travelling around the region, it is hard to beat the series of road maps produced by the Italian Touring Club (TCI) at a scale of 1:200,000. Amongst British-produced rivals you might consider the AA road atlas at 1:250,000, the Michelin road atlas of Europe at 1:1,000,000, or even a computer product such as Microsoft AutoRoute Express.

There is also a choice of the more detailed maps needed in the mountains, with accurate and well-drawn maps available at a scale of both 1:50,000 and

1:25,000. While the 1:50,000 scale is perhaps most suitable for achieving an overview of the options available in an area, the complex nature of the terrain really requires a larger scale map out on the hills (although they are not available in some areas covered by this guide).

Also available locally (particularly in the Trentino area and the more southerly areas such as Bassano and Vicenza) are maps with strange scales such as 1:10,000, 1:20,000, 1:28,000, 1:30,000 and 1:40,000, which will test your map reading skills! Usually produced by local tourist organisations (occasionally in liaison with SAT), these are often available free from the local tourist office. Some are produced to a very high standard and with good detail, whilst others are little more than 'topos' of limited value.

The availability of maps in most of the areas covered by this volume is

Steep cables on Via Ferrata Giulio Segata (TRENT 7)

good, as most newsagents and gift shops, and many supermarkets, stock local maps, even in fairly small settlements. You may, however, have problems in Bassano and Vicenza, which are not geared up for mountain tourism, so the route descriptions identify specific problem areas and advise on the best map available.

Most people will want to get hold of the relevant maps beforehand, and the major UK-based map suppliers, such as Stanfords and the Map Shop in Upton on Severn, can usually provide what you need, often by return of post. Both these companies now maintain good web sites, which makes browsing and ordering easy (see Appendix 5 for details).

The two major publishers for the Dolomites are Tabacco and Kompass, with the latter having the wider coverage in the area covered by this volume. Each has its adherents (we favour Tabacco), but there is little to choose between them in terms of quality. Both are good quality products, which are easy to read, although neither can match the Ordnance Survey maps for detail and accuracy. The latest editions of the Tabacco and Kompass 1:25,000 series show grid references: GPS users should set datum to European 1950, Eur50, ED50 or Europ.

Other companies producing good 1:50,000 maps of the Dolomites are Lagir Alpina and Freytag & Berndt, while the Austrian Alpine Club's Alpenvereinskart maps are also available for the Brenta.

Magnetic variation: since magnetic variation in this part of Europe is limited (around 1 degree west) it is not generally referred to on maps. Nonetheless, whilst you might be accustomed to using your compass in featureless terrain in the UK, it is something you will rarely need to do in the Dolomites. Even if you do carry your compass, you are more likely to navigate by finding a path and following its red markers.

Finally, a word of warning about the use of place names on maps. In those areas which were historically Austrian, many settlements and natural features such as mountains have both an Italian and a German name. Both appear on maps and – depending on where you are and to whom you are speaking – Torri di Latemar might well be referred to as Latemarturme. This guide gives both the Italian and German names on first usage, but thereafter reverts to the Italian name only. You will also come across variations in the spelling of place names both on maps produced by different publishers and in different editions from the same publisher. This can be confusing, but it also means that whichever forms are used in this guide can easily be justified!

Grand scenery characterises the walk from Rif. Rosetta to Passo di Ball (S.MAR 3 and 4) (photo: Meg Fletcher)

WEATHER

As in all mountain areas, the weather in the Dolomites can be unpredictable, although a common pattern is a clear start, followed in the afternoon by increasing cloud and possibly a thunderstorm. Daily forecasts for the Dolomites are produced from the weather centre in Arabba (web site: www.arpa.veneto.it/csvdi, with a web cam at www.svm.it/webarpav). A localised Trentino forecast is available on www.provincia.tn.it/meteo). These

daily forecasts generally give a reliable indication of what to expect, even over a two- or three-day period, and are available from tourist offices and the local mountain guides offices. You will also find 'weather stations' outside shops and hotels in all mountain areas, with the barometer being a particularly useful guide to the weather patterns to expect.

It is essential to keep an eye on the forecasts. High-level mountain routes require a spell of settled weather, although for less serious routes an early start can pay dividends if bad weather threatens later in the day. Conversely, if the day starts badly, there are some shorter, more easily accessed routes that can be completed in the afternoon.

Although wet rock is not ideal, via ferratas, especially easier ones, can be climbed in the rain, but beware if temperatures are low, as icing can occur

23

throughout the summer and turn even the easiest route into a very serious undertaking.

Thunder and lightning is a totally different matter. Being attached to a metal cable in a high, exposed mountain situation is not where you want to be! So if storms threaten, avoid climbs which lack escape routes. If you are caught in a storm and are unable to escape from a route, there are some simple rules which should be followed to minimise the risk of being 'buzzed'.

- If a storm is approaching (warning signs include a build up of towering cumulo-nimbus cloud or the sound of distant thunder) evaluate possible escape routes as soon as possible.
- If possible, unclip from the cable and move a safe distance away. If an escape route is available, then use it. If you have no option but to sit it out, a wide ledge might provide an adequate safety zone on a cliff face. If on a ridge, however, try to get off it as soon as possible.
- In a storm, stay out in the open if this is possible – **do not** seek shelter under boulders or overhangs or go into caves, as these can be the natural spark points as lightning tries to find its way to earth.
- Keep as low as possible: sitting on your rucksack minimises both your profile and your contact with wet ground.
- Keep your core as dry as possible by putting on your waterproofs without delay.

This may all sound rather frightening; indeed it can be! However, remember that lightning strikes natural projec-

tions, such as mountain tops or rock pinnacles, so if you are unlucky enough to be caught in a storm, stay calm, make sound judgements, follow the good practice listed above, and the risks will be very small.

ROUTE GRADING

Grading is a subjective matter, not an exact science. The authors' starting point is the belief that any grading system should offer a view of the seriousness of a route as well as its difficulty. A route can be hard without being too serious, and vice versa.

Many people have experienced situations in which their confidence has proved to be misplaced, and have had to back off a route and leave it for another day. On a route which is not only hard but also serious, things might not be quite so straightforward! Big routes

Spectacular descent on Sentiero SOSAT (BREN 2)

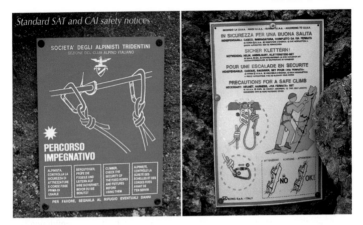

Standard SAT and CAI safety notices

on big mountains should be accorded a degree of respect, and factors like escape routes and even rescue access need to be considered. Bad weather and stone falls can also result in a carefree day on the hill turning into an epic.

The Dolomites abound with via ferratas which are technically easy, but in terrain which needs to be taken seriously. Consequently, it is important that the relatively inexperienced scrambler appreciates the degree of mountain commitment involved in the route he or she is planning to climb.

Each route in this guidebook is therefore **graded on a five-point scale of technical difficulty, with 1 the easiest and 5 the hardest grade**. Some of the ferratas in this volume are 'sport routes' which, like recently constructed routes in Provence and Austria, tend to be at the top end of the scale of difficulty.

The assessment of **seriousness** takes into account the mountain commitment involved, accessibility, potential escape routes, the level of fitness required and potential objective dangers. **Our three-point scale of seriousness is shown as A, B or C, where A is the least serious and C the most committing.**

Technical difficulty

1. Easy routes, with limited via ferrata climbing, entirely suitable for the young and inexperienced. Requires no more than a head for heights and sure-footedness.

2. Straightforward routes for the experienced mountain walker or scrambler with a head for heights.

3. Rather more difficult routes, not recommended for the completely novice via ferratist. At this level complete freedom from vertigo and sure-footedness are required, as is complete competence in the use of self-belay equipment.

4. Demanding routes, frequently involving steep rock faces and

25

The steep start of Via Attrezzata Rino Pisetta (RIVA 1)

requiring a fairly high standard of technical climbing ability. Definitely not for the novice or those unsure of their confidence in mountain situations.

5. Routes of the highest technical standard encountered in via ferrata climbing, suitable only for the most experienced via ferratist.

Seriousness

A. Straightforward outings in unthreatening mountain terrain. Routes will have easy access and/or escape opportunities, will be virtually risk free in the event of a change in the weather, and be relatively free from the risk of stone-fall.

B. Routes where a degree of mountain experience is required. Access might be more difficult, and opportunities to escape from the route will be limited, so minor mishaps could develop into quite serious situations. A change in the weather could potentially be more than merely inconvenient, and the climber needs to be aware of the risk of stone-fall.

C. Routes for only the experienced mountaineer. Such routes might lack any escape opportunities, be in remote areas, have passages of very exposed, unprotected terrain, or involve inaccessible situations where any mishap could have the most serious consequences. The threat of stone-fall might be a major consideration, or a change in the weather could add greatly to the problems posed by the route.

Route vital statistics

For each route an indication of the ascent, descent and length of via ferrata involved is given. Where a route involves extended traverses this can appear to give rather odd statistics where the length of the ferrata exceeds the ascent/descent figure (e.g. VICEN 2 Sentiero Alpinistico Angelo Pojesi).

Conditions in the mountains

The route descriptions and gradings in the guide assume, as they must, that conditions are good, that ice is not a problem and, in the case of some lower-level routes, that watercourses are not in spate. However, even in mid-summer the weather can be extremely variable. Sudden thunderstorms, snowfall, ice formation or flash flooding of watercourses can all occur unexpectedly in a Dolomite summer. So, when considering the given grading assessments, you should make appropriate allowances for additional difficulties resulting from adverse conditions.

EQUIPMENT

The basic equipment required to climb via ferratas safely is neither complicated nor expensive. The items below will suffice for all but the most demanding outings, but for the higher routes (and even lower ones early in the season) consideration needs to be given to additional gear such as ice axes and crampons.

Although some UK-based climbing shops do now stock via ferrata equipment, it can be bought readily in the Dolomites. As well as being cheaper in Italy, a wider variety of equipment is available.

Helmet: to UIAA (Union Internationale des Associations d'Alpinisme) standard; this is perhaps the single most important piece of equipment. To be effective it should be on your head, not in your sack, so put it on as soon as there is any risk of stone-fall. The approaches to some routes negotiate gullies which can be raked by stones falling from above, **so don't wait until you are about to start climbing before reaching for your helmet.**

Harness: many visitors to the Dolomites will already own a sit-harness, and whilst this will generally suffice for tackling via ferratas, do remember that you will probably be carrying a loaded rucksack, so if you were to take a fall you run the risk of being turned upside down. Consequently, a full body harness, much more popular in continental Europe, gives the best protection for climbing via ferratas. Alternatively you could supplement your sit-harness with a chest harness. *Whatever you choose to do, it is a personal decision and risk assessment.*

Via ferrata self-belay set: incorporating belay rope, KISA and karabiners. These have improved considerably in recent years to address the obvious problem with self-belaying on a vertical run of cable: a fall will only be arrested when the climber reaches the attaching peg below him. Thus, on a long cable run, a very high shock loading (anything up to 2 tonnes) will be generated. To help overcome this, a device called a Kinetic Impact Shock Absorber (KISA) has been developed. There are several different models in use, but they all function in the same way, acting as friction brakes which, in the event of a fall, absorb the energy generated, thus reducing the shock loading.

Full body harness showing Y-type self-belay system tie on

There are two different systems used to incorporate a KISA in the belay system, each containing the same components but configured differently, **which means that they must be used differently.**

Two different types of KISA

a) The most commonly used type employs a single rope, about 2 metres long, passing through the KISA and with a karabiner on each end. The KISA is attached to the harness with rope or tape. With this system, **only one** karabiner should be clipped into the cable, whilst the spare karabiner is clipped into

the harness or gear loop. In a fall, the loop of rope leading to the spare karabiner is pulled through the KISA under friction, thus absorbing much of the energy generated by the fall. On reaching a peg where the cable is attached to the rock, the spare karabiner is removed from the harness and clipped into the next cable run. The original karabiner is then unclipped and attached to the harness. **It is only at the moment of leapfrogging over the peg that both karabiners are clipped in to the cable, otherwise the KISA cannot function (see illustration).**

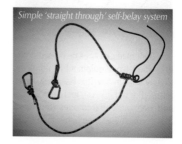

Simple 'straight through' self-belay system

b) In the alternative system, the karabiners are attached to two separate lengths of rope, joined by a knot or stitched to form a Y-shape. There are several permutations on the theme, particularly regarding the means of attachment to the harness, but the principle of how this type works is as follows. The single length of rope (the leg of the Y) is threaded through the KISA to leave a spare loop of rope which becomes part of the system incorporated in the tie-on, or is attached to the side of the harness or gear loop. The KISA is then attached to the harness with rope or tape. In a fall, it is the spare loop of rope which is pulled through the KISA under friction, thus absorbing the energy generated by the fall. With this method **both** karabiners can be clipped into the cable: at the end of a cable run, first one, then the other karabiner is leapfrogged over onto the next length of cable (see illustration).

Another roped variety of Y-type self-belay system

thus reducing the freedom of the climber to exploit the holds in the rock face.

A word of warning! DO NOT rely on a couple of slings in place of a proper self-belay system. Whilst these might give you a sense of security, they could well be useless if you were to take a significant fall.

Karabiners: if you buy a ready-made self-belay set, these will be included. However, there are several different models available, not all of which are equally suitable. Consequently, when buying your gear, pay close attention to the karabiners incorporated. Whichever type you have, they must always be the large D-type karabiners to clip over some of the thicker cables. Locking gates are, of course, much stronger. However, conventional screw gates are impractical for use on via ferratas, where you will be clipping and unclipping repeatedly. One suitable model has a spring-loaded gate, unlocked by simply pulling the gate-lock back with the index finger. Another type needs to be both pulled back and twisted through 90 degrees before the gate is unlocked; this becomes frustratingly fiddly after a couple of hours! Small clips are also

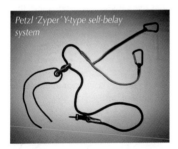

Petzl 'Zyper' Y-type self-belay system

Both methods are safe **if used properly**. The Y-type equipment is, arguably, slightly safer in that it is less likely to be misused! It is, however, more expensive, and one particular model (the Petzl Zyper, which uses tape rather than rope) has 'tails' which are somewhat short,

29

available to thread the rope through on the karabiner; these cost next to nothing but are extremely useful for holding the karabiner on the rope to stop it spinning round and potentially falling off. Best of all perhaps, but certainly the most expensive, is a model from Salewa, specially developed for via ferratas, where the rope is tied through a separately formed ring at the base of the karabiner, such that it cannot then spin round. On this type, the gate is released by pressure from the heel of the thumb, naturally applied as the karabiner is offered up to the cable, making for ease of use during a long day (see illustration for several commonly used types of karabiners).

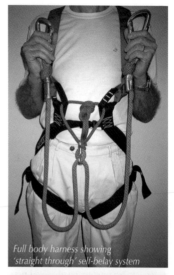

Full body harness showing 'straight through' self-belay system

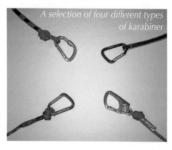

A selection of four different types of karabiner

Gloves: specially designed gloves for via ferratas are available. Whether you wear gloves is a matter of personal preference, although they do protect hands against frayed cables and can prove useful when the weather is cold and wet. They resemble cycling gloves, with padded palms and cut-off fingers, although a pair of gardening gloves may prove a cheaper alternative.

Refinements: An ice axe and crampons are suggested for several routes in this

Full body harness showing Petzl 'Zyper' self-belay system

guide. A rope is another important accessory if climbing with someone with limited experience and for some of the more demanding outings included in this guidebook. The authors favour carrying 20–30 metres of half-rope, a couple of tapes and a belay plate when climbing in such situations. A quick-draw is useful when taking photographs and to facilitate a rest, for example in 'traffic jams' or on unusually strenuous routes.

A useful source of information for the technically minded regarding safety equipment and shock loading is the Petzl web site at www.petzl.com.

CABLE ETIQUETTE

The ferrata cables and their use can be a real debating topic. Some prefer to regard via ferratas as rock climbs which happen to have permanently fixed protection. Others simply haul themselves up the cable by dint of brute strength! Most of us are happy to make our own compromises between these two extremes, climbing without use of the cable where we feel comfortable, but using it for a boost when required. Until you have found your own point of compromise, try climbing with one hand on the cable, with the karabiner(s) sitting on top of the clenched fist and being slid up by it, and using your other hand to exploit natural holds in the rock.

Popular routes can get very busy, and sooner or later you will find yourself being pressed from behind – this feels rather like being 'tailgated' on a motorway! The perpetrators are not only being discourteous, they are also putting both of you at risk since, should the upper climber fall, he will probably take the

lower climber with him. This would load the protection far beyond what it is designed to withstand. Therefore, observe this simple rule. Do not clip into a length of cable until the climber above you has progressed to the next cable length.

Climbers on ridge to Cima Capi with Lake Garda below (RIVA 8)

WHAT TO WEAR?

In making your choice of what to wear, you should take into account not only the anticipated weather, but also the situation of the route you are doing – whether a big, remote mountain day or a short, easily accessible route. Travelling light and carrying a small pack makes for a more enjoyable day on the hill when the weather is warm and settled. However, never lose sight of the fact that you are in a high mountain environment, with the potential for sudden and dramatic changes in the weather. A warm, sunny day, with a temperature of 20°C, can quickly drop by 10° or more, and hail or snow can be encountered down to 2500m, even in high summer. Do take this into consideration when selecting your gear for your via ferrata day.

ACCIDENTS AND MOUNTAIN RESCUE

As in most mountain regions the police have responsibility for organising mountain rescue. If you are unlucky enough to be involved in an accident the **emergency contact number for mountain rescue is 118** (see App.4).

SOME HISTORY

This section outlines the military campaigns of the First World War which helped shape the landscape of the southern Dolomites and contributed significant features now incorporated in via ferrata routes. (Volume one of this guide goes into greater detail on the history of Italy and the Dolomite region.)

When Italy entered the Great War in 1915 it overestimated the strength of its old adversary, Austria. Its advance was thus slow and cautious, giving the Austrians time to consolidate their defences. Consequently, a fairly stable front line developed, running from the Swiss/Italian/Austrian border (at Stelvio pass) in the west to the Italian/Slovenian border in the east. The front line ran through the Riva, Rovereto, Trento, Vicenza and Bassano areas covered in this book.

The western segment of the front, from the Stelvio pass to Lake Garda, was of little strategic importance, and had relatively small troop numbers. It was in the area east of Lake Garda, across the mountains and plateaux of

Wartime tunnels on Sentiero Galli (ROVER 2) (photo: Meg Fletcher)

the Piccole Dolomites, from Trento to Bassano, that most activity was seen (although the main battles were fought further to the east, along the present Slovenian/Italian border).

The relatively settled nature of the front line through the Piccole Dolomites was disturbed on two principal occasions. In May 1916, a major Austrian offensive was mounted, when their forces swept southwards over Val Sugana and temporarily occupied territory from Pasubio to Asiago and Monte Grappa. After a further period of relative stability, the Austrians launched an advance on the Asiago plateau, early in 1918, and crossed the Piave river. This failed, and proved to be the last significant Austrian offensive.

To learn more about the so-called mountain war, the internet site of the Great War Society (www.worldwar1.com/itafront/) is useful. Whilst there is a wealth of published material in Italian and German, English-language books are few in number. Perhaps the most accessible is *Battleground Europe (Italy): Asiago* by F. MacKay, in the Battleground Europe series. Museums can be found in several places, with those in San Michelle all'Adige, Trento, Rovereto and Fiera di Primiero being particularly worthwhile. Further details of museums in the area can be found in *Guide to the Museums and Collections in Trentino*, published by (and available free from) the APT, Trentino.

The Aftermath

Peace was cemented in 1919 by the treaty of San Germain, which established the national boundaries seen today. Territorially, Italy was a major beneficiary of the peace settlement. In addition to the whole of the Dolomite region, Italy also secured part of the Dalmation coast and the port of Trieste. Altogether, some 1.6 million new Italian citizens were acquired, many of whom could not speak Italian! Many families tell of older relatives who were born Austrian, but died Italian.

Despite their Italian nationality, the people of the northern Dolomites, including the Bolzano province, generally retain German as their first language, and demonstrate many expressions of their cultural traditions. Unsurprisingly, separatist sentiment can be found not far beneath the surface within the German-speaking community. To a degree these pressures were defused by the granting of special status to the Trentino–Alto Adige region. This has been reinforced by generous tax benefits and grant aid, cementing the position of the region as one of the richest in the country.

The ancient Ladin culture still survives in the northern Dolomites, and there are daily Ladin-language broadcasts from Bolzano (see volume 1 for more information). Interestingly some of the villages around Bolzano, west across to Paganella and the Brenta, speak their own variations of Ladin, unique to very small areas, such that you can encounter different spoken dialects even from village to village.

History of CAI and Rifugios

Prior to the First World War, mountain huts were built across the Alps, including the Sud Tyrol, by the then German

33

Route plaque memorabilia *Ferrata del Centenario SAT (RIVA 7)*

and Austrian Alpine Club. When the Sud-Tyrol was absorbed into Italy, following the treaty of San Germain, these huts were taken over by the CAI, becoming *rifugios*. Sadly, many were subsequently destroyed or used by Italian soldiers in their attempts to stop insurgency, and from 1922 to 1973 the Austro/Italian border was effectively closed to climbers. Happily, since 1973 many huts have been rebuilt or renovated, and now provide an excellent network of facilities throughout the region.

GEOLOGY

The name 'Dolomites' is derived from a French geologist, Deodat Guy Sylvain Tancre de Gratet de Dolomieu, a scholar who in 1789 was so fascinated by the carbonate rock that he sent samples to Switzerland for classification. When they were returned as of a previously unknown composition, they were named after him. In the 19th century it was mainly English mountaineers who applied the name 'Dolomia' to the area in recognition of the geological discovery.

Dolomite rock is made up of stratified calcium magnesium carbonate, with some areas of true limestone, some containing more stratified and folded rock than others depending on the area. Limestone has a reputation for loose rock, the Dolomites being no exception. Interestingly enough the colour of the rocks gives an indication of the firmness or friability. Generally, grey and black rocks are firm (though the black colour also indicates possible wetness), yellow-coloured rock is only reasonably firm, and red rock is the loosest.

FLORA

Flora – flowers, plants and trees – form a wonderful complement to the mountain environment! The Dolomite landscape is a result both of man's recent work and geological activity over millions of years. Scree and glacial debris carried down into the valleys was initially stony and barren, as can still be seen in vast areas. However, over time, the organic remains in the earth allowed vegetation to grow, and now an amazing array of flowers thrives in even the bleakest of landscapes.

Trees such as beech, fir and larch have become established in the valleys, with hardier pines on higher ground. Many varieties of fungi can be found, particularly in woodland, and their collection is an Italian obsession, albeit subject to strict controls.

Different plants live at different altitudes, with three principal growing zones identified. These are the sub-montane zone (below 1000m), the principally wooded montane zone (1000 to 2000m), and the high alpine zone (above 2000m), being that above the tree line. Alpine flora, usually abbreviated to alpines, is a generic term referring to plants which grow in this zone.

Factors such as temperature, light, soil, wind, rain, snow and ground slope combine to create complex environments. Plants adapt to different habitats by developing their own characteristics. Some grow in thick tufts to protect themselves against thermal fluctuations. Another common adaptation is to grow a protective covering of hair to act as a thermal cushion. Another device, where

soil is thin, such as in rock crevices, is the development of long root systems. Snow cover in the winter has a big impact on plant life, and it is truly amazing in spring or early summer to see flowers appearing even as the snow melts!

A wide variety of alpine flora exist in the Dolomites: edelweiss, soldanella, ranunculus (alpine buttercup), saxifrage, gentian, geranium, anemone, violet and primula, to name but a few. Some species are endangered and protected, but your general rule should always be – **do not pick flowers**, however abundant they may appear to be.

Although you will see flowers in all areas covered by this volume, there are two places of particular interest. One is the whole ridge of Monte Baldo rising above the eastern side of Lake Garda (routes ROVER 5, 6 and 7 are in this area). The other is the Alpine Garden at Viote on Monte Bondone, which boasts

Devil's Claw: a rare plant, but occasionally seen on ferrata routes

over 1000 species of alpine plants and is open to the public from June until September (see TRENT 7).

If you wish to pursue an interest in alpine flowers, then in addition to reading the excellent books which are available, you can contact the Alpine Garden Society in the UK (see Appendix 5).

WILDLIFE

Chamois, stambecco, deer and marmots are amongst the animals you are likely to see during your trip. The chamois, a type of goat, lives on the scant grass above the tree line, as does the less common long-haired stambecco. Roe deer are widespread at lower altitudes in, or close to, tree cover. Colonies of marmots, living in burrows above about 1600m, are more frequently heard than seen because of their high-pitched whistle. Whilst generally shy creatures, some colonies are becoming more used to human traffic, so you might well see one on look-out duty, erect on its hind legs.

Until the end of the 19th century, bears were common in the woods of the Dolomites, but hunting and deforestation led to many years of extinction. However, it is now thought that some may have migrated back towards the Dolomites from Slovenia – but are still a long way from the main areas for via ferratas!

Birds include eagles, buzzards, mountain choughs (swarms of which seem to arrive on every summit as soon as a sandwich is unwrapped!), woodland grouse or capercaille (at home in woods and undergrowth), white ptarmigan (which changes its plumage in summer to brown), crows, woodpeckers, owls, alpine tree creeper, jay, skylark and many species of finch.

Snakes are often encountered basking on paths on warm, sunny afternoons. Adders are common, easily recognised by their chevron patterning; tread carefully so as not to disturb, remembering that they are more frightened than you are!

Normally timid creatures, juvenile marmots can be very curious!

BOLZANO

Maps
see information for each route

Tourist Information Office
APT Bolzano, Piazza Walther, Bolzano, Italy
Tel: (0471) 307000
Fax: (0471) 980128
E-mail: info@bolzano.net
Internet: www.bolzano.net

Bolzano (Bozen) is the main town in the Adige valley and the capital of the Alto-Adige province. It is the heart of the German-speaking area and has a Tyrolean, rather than Italian, atmosphere. Bolzano has been chosen more as a starting point than as a place to stay, since the three routes in this section are rather dispersed, and there are many accommodation options available in the surrounding villages. This thriving commercial centre lies just off the Brennero *autostrada*, on the main rail link from Munich to Venice. It also has its own small airport with a few charter flights from the United Kingdom.

Bolzano is also a popular tourist destination, not least because of the excellent museum which has been constructed to house the 'Ice Man', nicknamed Otzi, as he was discovered in the Otztal Glacier. The forensic examination on his well-preserved 5000-year-old body was performed by Austrian scientists, and then he was returned to Bolzano (for political, rather than curatorial, reasons). A visit to the exhibition (where a recorded audio-guide can be hired in English) is a fascinating way to spend a day out from your climbing schedule, though, as many people consider it a bad weather option, queues are highly likely when it's wet.

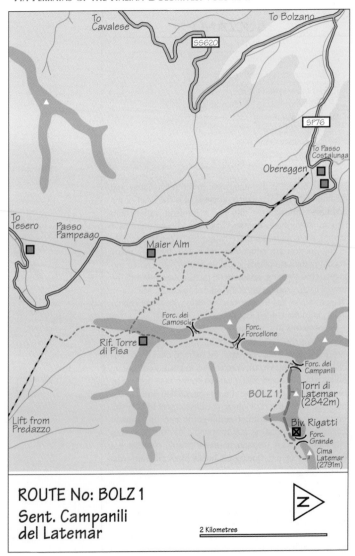

ROUTE No: BOLZ 1

Sent. Campanili del Latemar

2 Kilometres

N

BOLZ 1:
CAMPANILI DEL LATEMAR

Grade:	2
Seriousness:	C
Departure point:	Maier Alm, or Panorama Chairlift, Obereggen 2150m or Gardone Gondola Predazzo.
Ascent:	800m (from Maier Alm)
Descent:	800m
Via ferrata:	200m
Approximate time:	6–7 hours
Highest altitude:	2846m
Map:	Tabacco Carta Topographica 1:25,000 Sheet 014

The route runs along ledges and walking terrain through the Latemar towers, with grassy flanks to the south and stunning views down steep walls on the north. It is not as popular as the routes on Catinaccio (see *Via Ferratas of the Italian Dolomites*, volume 1, for details of routes in that area), and you will have a good chance of a quieter day out.

This route can be attacked from a variety of directions, your choice perhaps best dictated by where you are staying (Obereggen Tourist Information www.eggental.com, email obereggen@eggental.com, tel. 0471.615795, fax 0471. 615848; APT Val di Fiemme Cavalese from www.apt-fiemme.tn.it, email Info.fiemme@softcom.it, tel. 0462. 241111, fax 0462.241199).

From the west (Bolzano) or north (Passo Costalungo) you can not only drive to Obereggen, but take a chairlift (from the end of June to the end of September) up to Oberholz (2090m). It is also possible to drive up to Maier Alm, 2037m (which you will see on maps with a variety of different spellings), from the Obereggen side on a road which is surfaced, except for the final approach up to Maier Alm.

From the southern side you can drive from Cavalese up to Maier Alm via Pampeago and Passo Pampeago, though

This is a good mountain route with a superb panorama of the Dolomites, particularly the Catinaccio peaks immediately to the north of Passo Costalunga.

View of the Torri Di Latemar range from the south

the road is unsurfaced for the 2½km from Pampeago to the pass. Another approach from the south is to use the lift system from Predazzo (only operates from the end of June to the end of September) to Passo Feudo and walk in to Rifugi Torre di Pisa, 2671m, from there. The *rifugio* is in a wonderfully panoramic position.

The route is described here as a circuit from Maier Alm (large car park), climbing to Rif. Torre di Pisa. From there you descend into a vast scree-filled bowl (Conca Valsorda) and then to the start of the ferrata at Forcella dei Campanili. The ferrata is easy technically, and except for part of the final descent to Forcella Grande would only be Grade 1 not Grade 2. However, the route does have a lot of exposure, and a good head for heights and surefootedness are necessary on a number of unprotected sections on steep ground. Also, whichever approach you make, it is quite a long day requiring a good level of fitness – there is no slack in the timings. Try to do the route when the weather is stable and clear, as the views throughout the route make this a very satisfying mountain day out.

Follow the track up behind Maier Alm leading up a ski piste, and in 15 minutes, almost level with the top of a chairlift, there is a boulder field with waymarks for path 22 in both directions. Take the right fork which heads up through the boulders until, in about 10 minutes, you are above the chairlift. Path 22 continues ahead but the approach to Rifugio Torre di Pisa turns left, heading directly up to the steep scree above you. Waymarking at this junction point is not brilliant, though 22TV is painted faintly on a rock, and after about 5 minutes R.Pisa/Lat H is painted on a large rock (note that Rifugio Torre di Pisa is also known as the Latemar Hutte). The next 30 minutes or so are the hardest work of the day, as you climb arduously up the steep scree, gaining about 400m in the process, to arrive at a col with a large avalanche fence. From this col you can see 516 (the path to Rif. Torre di Pisa) painted in large numbers on a rock ahead. The path from here has been well engineered and in a further 30 minutes you arrive at the *rifugio*. It is a small, family-run *rifugio* (sleeps 20), open from the end of June to the beginning of October, tel. 0462.501564.

Path 516/18 climbs up behind the *rifugio* to a ridge where, on a clear day, fantastic views open up before you including Latemar (today's target), Piz Boe, Marmolada, Pelmo, Civetta and Pale San Martino. Waymarks are excellent now for the rest of the day, as you descend from the short ridge into a bowl which can hold snow early in the season; this (and other snow crossings mentioned later on) are on easy-angled ground. About 20 minutes from the *rifugio* you continue straight ahead passing the junction of the path on the left which leads up to Forcella dei Camosci. Path 516/18 continues for a further 20 minutes, with little height gain or loss, across the vast scree and rock bowl until you reach the well-signed junction of paths 511/18 and 516. Path 511 is indicated as Sentiero Attrezzata and Biv. Rigatti 1 hour 20 minutes; this is somewhat optimistic, as the climb up path 511 to Forcella dei Campanili takes about 20 minutes, and then a notice at the start of the ferrata informs you it will take 1½ hours! However the views from Forcella dei Campanili are quite stunning, looking down to Passo Costalunga and across to Roda di Vael and Punta Masare (see *Via Ferratas of the Italian Dolomites*, volume one). This viewpoint is the first of a number of amazing panoramas to the north.

Follow waymarks up from the route sign to the first cables in about 7 or 8 minutes. About 10 minutes of cabling (quite loosely tensioned and with long gaps between pegs)

The climb to the **Torre Diamantidi** summit is optional; it's about 100m (15 minutes) of additional uphill effort zigzagging up scree slopes and about 10 minutes for the descent.

leads up and along a series of ledges. From the end of the cable, about 5 minutes of walking (in places quite exposed) leads to a spectacular gully of brown eroding rock, where there may be early-season snow. Cables go across the gully and up onto a ledge on the other side. More exposed walking follows, with only one short cable protection, to reach another spectacular gully with large chock-stones in a further 10 minutes. Soon after crossing the gully there is an exposed move around a corner, and 10 minutes further on a large cairn indicates the path up to the highest peak of the Latemar group, Torre Diamantidi, 2842m (also known as Torri Di Latemar and Latemarturme). ◀

Offset ladder on descent at east end of BOLZ 1

If you choose to continue without the ascent of Torre Diamantidi, a good path continues ahead, passing the descent-path rejoin-point after only a few minutes. Following a very exposed unprotected down-climb, intermittent cabling leads in 10 minutes to an unusual vertical ladder with offset rungs; this is about 12m long and feels quite strange, with each step of down-climb having your feet at different heights. Some serious rock fall has occurred close to the ladder; it is not a place to hang around. Cross the gully (where the cable is quite high in the air) and climb up to a ledge where there is a view of Biv. M Rigati. Cables lead down from here to Forcella Grande and the bivuoac, 2620m, the ferrata thus taking about 1½ hours to complete. The bivouac is an open shelter with beds for nine people. ▶

It is possible to climb **Cima Latemar**, 2791m (also known as Schenon) from Forcella Grande. It is exposed in places, and ascent and descent would add at least an hour to the route timings for the day.

The return route is on path 18, which traverses back along the steep slopes of Torre Diamantidi around the 2600m contour. It is not well marked from the bivuoac, but follow a zigzag path down heading roughly south-east for a couple of minutes to a clear signpost. Path 18 heads east from this point to Passo Costalunga in 3 hours, and west (the direction for your return) back to Rif. Torre di Pisa in 2 hours. Simply follow the waymarks, with some exposed places, but nothing like those you have encountered on the ferrata, back to the junction of paths 18/516 and 511 below Forcella dei Campanili; this takes 35–40 minutes.

You can retrace the approach route back via the *rifugio*, but there is a different (and quite scenic) return to Maier Alm via Forcella dei Camosci. Either way, continue on path 18/516 back to Forcella la Forcellone, and if you are returning by the outward route follow the waymarks back to Rif. Torre di Pisa. However, we recommend following a good (though not waymarked) path which avoids further height loss and rises steadily from Forcella la Forcellone to Forcella dei Camosci in about 35 minutes.

From Forcella dei Camosci a short cable (easy handrail only) leads down a broken gully into a rock bowl (another place where there may be some snow early season). Follow waymarks, and in a few minutes see a warning triangle reading 'STOP' painted on a rock ahead. Path 18 turns 90 degrees right (heading generally north) here and goes through a spectacular narrow valley with towering peaks on either side. After 15–20 minutes the path exits the towering peaks to a steep zigzag descent on scree and broken ground. Keep an eye on the waymarks on the descent and simply follow path 18 down to the top of the Oberholz chair at about 2100m. Turn left to head south on fairly level ground on path 23 back to Maier Alm in about 20 minutes. Total descent time from Forcella Grande is 2¾–3 hours.

BOLZ 2:
VF ATTILIO SIEFF – PUNTA POLSE

Grade:	2
Seriousness:	A
Departure point:	Ziano di Fiemme
Ascent:	500m
Descent:	500m
Via ferrata:	100m
Approximate time:	3 hours
Highest altitude:	1450m
Map:	Tabacco Carta Topographica 1:25,000 Sheet 014

A short but pleasant route at a quite low altitude making it useful for a short day (even late afternoon) outing when weather may be unsuitable for climbing a higher-level route. Protection is good throughout, and although Punta Polse is not a high summit it has a very good view.

Ziano is in Val di Fiemme at the southern most end of Val di Fassa (see *Via Ferratas of the Italian Dolomites,* volume 1, for details of routes in that area). It is accessible by bus from Bolzano and Trento, and accommodation can be found at the ski resorts of Predazzo and Cavalese (information from www.aptfiemme.tn.it, email Info.fiemme@softcom.it, tel. 0462.241111).

In the village of Ziano parking is restricted, but there is a car park in the centre of the village close to the church and supermarket. From the main street take Via Zanon (opposite Zorri Max wine distributor). The approach to the ferrata is waymarked from the end of this road; it zigzags up through the trees for about an hour to the start of the route. You simply follow the ferrata to the summit of Punta Polse; it only takes about 30 minutes ascent and the same for the descent. Initially the ferrata follows a broad gully before moving up to the left on good rock with strategically placed

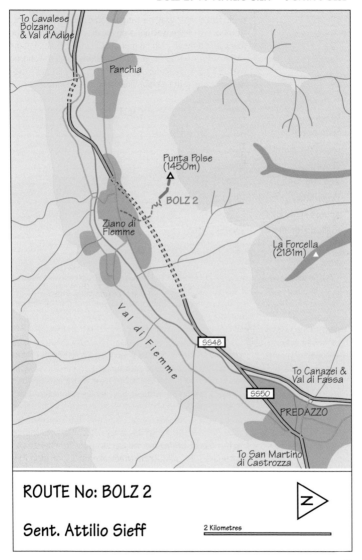

To Cavalese
Bolzano
& Val d'Adige

Panchia

Punta Polse
(1450m)

BOLZ 2

Ziano di
Fiemme

La Forcella
(2181m)

Val di Fiemme

SS48

To Canazei &
Val di Fassa

SS50

PREDAZZO

To San Martino
di Castrozza

ROUTE No: BOLZ 2

Sent. Attilio Sieff

N

2 Kilometres

pegs. Once you have enjoyed the view from the summit, climb down the route and retrace the approach path back down to Ziano.

BOLZ 3:
MONTE ROEN

Grade:	2
Seriousness:	A
Departure point:	Roen, Passo della Mendola
Ascent:	750m
Descent:	750m
Via ferrata:	100m
Approximate time:	4½–5 hours
Highest altitude:	2116m
Map:	Kompass Wanderkarte 1:50,000 Sheet 95

The ferrata is quite short, but with an excellent round walk on good paths; the wonderful views from the summit of Monte Roen make this route well worth doing if you are in the area, even though it is out on a limb in relation to other ferrata routes.

Passo della Mendola is 24km from Bolzano above the town of Caldaro; it has plenty of accommodation and is accessible by bus from Bolzano (information from the Val di Non Tourist Office, tel. 0463.830133, www.valdinon.cim.it, email aptvaldinon @cim.it).

From Passo della Mendola a good road (signed Roen 1.5km) leads south to a large car park by the Campo-Golf chairlift (not open in summer). The first of many waymarks for path 521 leads you up the wide ski piste by the side of the chairlift. At the top of the ski piste (about 30 minutes) follow signs leading right to Rif. Mezzavia 100m and 'Rif. Oltradige ore 1'. Go down to the side of Rif. Mezzavia and path 521 turns left. In a couple of minutes you ignore a CAI sign 'Bellavista, Monte Lira', and simply follow the waymarks for path 521 as it works its way up through woods for about 45 minutes to Rifugio Malga Roen, 1769m. It is a privately owned *rifugio* which has good food and nine beds (open end of May to end of October, tel. 0463.831642).

Rifugio Malga Roen is at the crossroads of a number of paths, the one leading to the ferrata being 560, heading south on a gravel road to reach CAI Rif. Oltradige, 1775m,

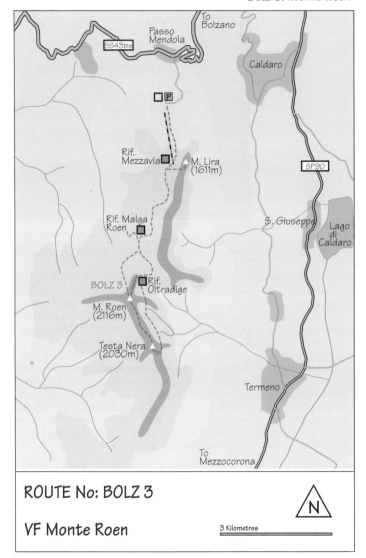

ROUTE No: BOLZ 3

VF Monte Roen

3 Kilometres

N

Monte Roen: waymarking here is difficult to see!

An **alternative descent**, which extends the day by about an hour, heads south on path 501/560 to the summit of Testa Nera (also known as Schwarzer Kopf), 2030m. Descend south-east from here on a protected path, 560 Sentiero dei Camosci (or Gemsensteig), back to Rif. Oltradige, from where you retrace your steps back to Rif. Malga Roen and to path 521 down to the start point.

in about 15–20 minutes. 'Cima Roen Ferrata 0.45, 523' is signposted behind the *rifugio*, and a path zigzags up to its start in 10–15 minutes.

The ferrata is well cabled as it makes its way up easy ledges for 15 minutes and then goes up an open gully on good rock with cables all the way to the top (another 15 minutes). From the top of the ferrata, path 523 leads through small pines to the summit of Monte Roen, 2116m, in a further 15 minutes (a total of 2 hours from the Campo-Golf car park). The views from the summit take in many major mountain ranges, to the west Adamello and Brenta, to the north Stubai and Zillertal, and to the east/north-east the peaks of the Dolomites.

The simplest descent is to follow path 521 north from the summit of Monte Roen back down to Rif. Malga Roen (30 minutes) and retrace path 521 back to the start point in a total time of about 2 hours. ◀

VALLE DI PRIMIERO AND
SAN MARTINO DI CASTROZZA

Map
(all routes) Tabacco Carta Topographica 1:25,000 Sheet 022

Tourist Information Office
APT Fiera di Primiero, Via Dante 6, 38054 Fiera di Primiero, Italy (TN)
Tel: 0439.62407
Fax: 0439.62992
E-mail: infoprimiero@sanmartino.com

Tourist Information Office
APT San Martino Di Castrozza, Via Passo Rolle 165, 38058 San Martino Di
Castrozza, Italy (TN)
Tel: 0439.768867
Fax: 0439.768814
E-mail: info@sanmartino.com
Internet (both offices): www.sanmartino.com

Pala di San Martino is a stunning group of mountains with a number of high-quality and serious via ferratas. There is an abundance of accommodation in the Primiero valley, with Fiera di Primiero at its southern end and San Martino di Castrozza to the north both providing a full range of facilities, including accommodation to suit all pockets. A two-stage lift system from S. Martino gives easy access to the north-western area of the group. There are large and helpful tourist offices in both resorts, as detailed above. Local mountain guides attend the S. Martino office each evening from 1730 to 1930hrs (or tel. 0439.768795, www.aquilesanmartino.com, Email info@aquilesanmartino.com). There are three campsites: Camping Sass Maor, Via Laghetto 48, San Martino, tel. 0439.68347, email sassmaor@freemail.it; Camping Castelpietra Val Canali, Transaqua, tel. 0439.62426, email info@castelpietra.it; Campeggio Calavise, Imer, tel. 0439.67468. Fiera di Primiero has a sports centre which includes an indoor swimming pool that opens at 1500hrs seven days a week throughout the summer.

The routes in the Pala resemble a giant game of snakes and ladders, with any number of permutations available

The soaring peaks of the southern Pala group, dominated by Sass Maor, seen from the west

for combining routes. In stable weather, the Pala mountains are superb for multi-day trips using *rifugios* to stay high up in the mountains and to link combinations of routes. Your choice is likely to depend on your transport arrangements; if you have a car, then you will probably select a circuit, whereas if you are using public transport, or are on a hutting tour, then you will perhaps choose a traverse.

For simplicity each ferrata in this section is described as a discrete entity, providing an explanation of how it can be linked with other routes. Where one route is generally used in ascent, and the other in descent, the most suitable way of completing the circuit is recommended. You can then choose your own combination of routes depending on fitness, weather and the time you have available.

Suggested Combinations of Routes

S.MAR 1 and 2 are complementary, but can be climbed separately.

S.MAR 3 – S.MAR 9 are in the central area of the Pala, between Rif. Rosetta and Val Canali. These seven routes offer numerous combinations: the best are as follows.

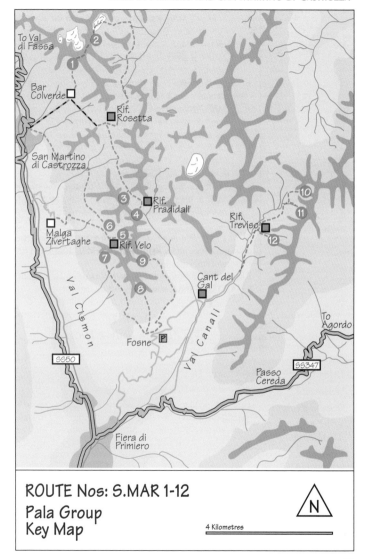

ROUTE Nos: S.MAR 1-12
Pala Group
Key Map

4 Kilometres

- Combine S.MAR 4 and 3 as a circuit from Rif. Rosetta, or climb either S.MAR 3 or S.MAR4 individually and then use S.MAR 6 as the descent route.
- S.MAR 5 is generally climbed with S.MAR 6 used as the descent route.
- S.MAR 6 is not often climbed, usually being used as a descent for the S.MAR 3, 4 or 5 routes.
- S.MAR 7 goes up to Rif. Velo and can easily be climbed up and down in the same day. Alternatively, use S.MAR 7 as a descent after climbing S.MAR 8 or S.MAR 9.
- S.MAR 8 is normally climbed in a clockwise circuit, using S.MAR 9 as the descent route (although S.MAR 7 could also be used as the descent).
- S.MAR 9 is normally used as the descent route from S.MAR 8, but it could be used as an ascent route, with S.MAR 7 (or even S.MAR 8) as the descent.

At the end of Val Canali, on its eastern side you will find the remaining three routes in this section, S.MAR 10, 11 and 12. They are climbed as follows.

S.MAR 10 is an ascent route with S.MAR 11 as descent.
S.MAR 12 is a short, stand-alone route.

S.MAR 1:
VIA FERRATA BOLVER LUGLI

Grade:	4
Seriousness:	C
Departure point:	Colverde gondola lift, San Martino di Castrozza to 1980m
Ascent:	1520m
Descent:	850m
Via ferrata:	500m
Approximate time:	7–7½ hours
Highest altitude:	3192m, Cima della Vezzana

These timings and height statistics include the ascent of Cima Vezzana and a return down Val dei Cantoni to the top of the Funivia Rosetta cable car.

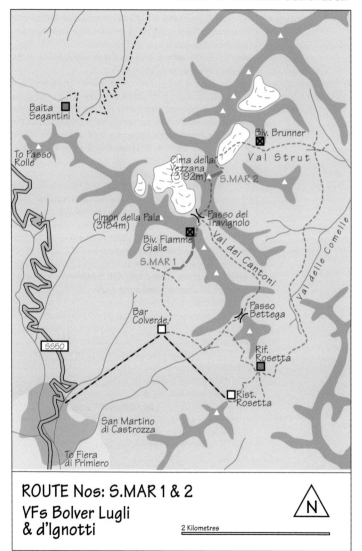

ROUTE Nos: S.MAR 1 & 2
VFs Bolver Lugli
& d'Ignotti

2 Kilometres

This route is one of the finest in the Dolomites. It is a serious expedition at a high altitude on a high-grade ferrata, and as such is not a route for beginners.

To complicate matters on this route you have a choice of length of day depending on experience, fitness levels, possible snow/ice conditions and the weather on the day. If attempting the route in a single day then try and be at the gondola when it opens at 0800hrs.

Access to the start of the route is made easy by using the gondola from San Martino di Castrozza to Colverde, 1970m; this operates in the summer from mid-June until the end of September and is open from 0800 to 1730hrs. (There are reductions for CAI, DAV and OeAV, as well as juniors and seniors.)

Ascend from the Colverde gondola station on path 712/706, which is clearly signed and well waymarked (although the sign does say the route should only be climbed with a guide 'Via Attrezzata B.Lugli Alla Spalla Del Cimon della Pala. Attenzione Percorribile Solo Con Guide Alpine'). The approach is on a good path rising up towards the red-coloured walls of Cimon della Pala. After 30–40 minutes' ascent the junction of paths 712 and 706 is reached, at about 2100m. Path 706 continues uphill and in a further 15 minutes reaches the route memorial plaque for Via Attrezzata Bolver Lugli, 9 August 1970. However, the start of the protected route is still 35–40 minutes away, and this unprotected scrambling will test your head for exposure and sets the tone for the seriousness of the route.

From the plaque follow red waymarks up a short rock scramble then zigzag up into a gully, and in about 5 minutes you reach a short section of cable at about 2400m. You can gear up here, but its not particularly worthwhile as you still have another 20 minutes of exposed uphill walking and unprotected scrambling before you reach the beginning of the cable protection at about 2580m; gear up here. Snow can lie here well into the season, and early in the summer may even obscure the cables.

Easy (but at least now protected!) climbing leads up a gully to a steep move on good rock. After a short break in the cable at about 2620m, followed by a few more minutes' scrambling, you arrive at the really good climbing. Cables lead up good rock trending rightwards then heading straight up. The situation here is superb with (if you are lucky enough to have clear weather) wonderful views, but if you were on

the first lift at 0800 hours then you will still be in shade. This section of the climb is as good as ferratas get, with good cables, good rock and great views. After about 30 minutes' climbing from the gear-up point (and about 2 hours from the top of the Colverde gondola) you reach a large flat ledge at about 2760m, which makes a very good break point.

Cima della Pala: VF Bolver Lugli ascends the middle wall to the right of the summit

You climb up quite steeply from the large resting ledge and you should then be getting into the sun at last! Next comes a steep chimney, at about 2820m, followed by a climb up a steep wall with some stemples to help you for footholds. The cables then lead left into another gully (15–20 minutes from the large ledge), and then round a corner and through a gap at about 2870m.

At about 2920m (25–30 minutes from the large ledge) climbing eases, and there is a large rock pinnacle on the right. The cables again lead left, and then Bivacco Fiamme Gialle comes in sight. The cable protection ends at about 2960m, and you now follow waymarks around an open bowl (probably snow early in the season) to walk to the bivacco. Your total time for ascent from the top of the gondola to here is about 3 hours.

One of the shortest ways to complete the Via Ferrata Bolver Lugli is to retrace your steps from Bivacco Fiamme Gialle and descend back down the ferrata to the top of the

Colverde gondola station for the return to San Martino di Castrozza. The descent of the ferrata to the memorial plaque takes about 2 hours, and then the descent to the gondola at Colverde 25–30 minutes. Total time for this option is 5½–6 hours.

However, depending on the weather and snow conditions (especially early in the season) you have the opportunity to climb Cima della Vezzana (the highest peak in the Pala group of mountains). Follow waymarks and descend to Passo Travignolo, 2925m, which is 80m and about 10 minutes below Bivacco Fiamme Gialle. (Note that the direct descent into Val dei Cantoni from the Bivacco is not recommended owing to its extra steepness.) If you are not climbing Cima Vezzana, see the continuation below for the descent from Passo Travignolo. If you are doing the climb, a steep zigzag path (waymarked but often snow covered, requiring ice axe and crampons, especially early in the season) leads from Passo Travignolo to the summit to Cima Vezzana, 3192m – an ascent of 270m, for which you should allow 50–60 minutes. It goes without saying that the panorama from this high peak is absolutely superb. ◀

Retrace your steps and descend from the summit Cima Vezzana by the ascent route to return to Passo Travignolo. To include time on the summit, allow about 2 hours for the return trip to the summit and back.

The descent from Passo Travignolo down into Val dei Cantoni is down a steep snow slope, which in most years will last throughout the season. An ice axe is therefore essential, as are crampons, depending on the snow (or ice) temperature. A rope is also recommended. At the end of the snowfield follow the waymarks of path 716 continuing down the south side (right hand looking down) of Val dei Cantoni to a low point at about 2540m (30 minutes or so from Passo Travignolo). The path, which was heading south-east, now turns south-west for a reascent of 130m up to Passo Bettega, 2667m, which takes about 20 minutes. From Passo Bettega descend, still on path 716, to a path junction below Cima Corona. A path continues down very steeply for another 600m to the Colverde gondola, but this is not recommended, unless of course you are too late for the last cable car and don't want to spend a night at Rif. Rosetta Pedrotti, 2581m (tel. 0439.68308, open 20 June – 20 September, 60 beds). However, to save your knees take the

Note: a very long and demanding 'Alpine' day can be had by continuing from the summit of Cima della Vezzana to descend by Ferrata Gabitta d'Ignotti instead of returning by your ascent route. This route is S.MAR 2 below; if you combine it with S.MAR 1 then you should allow 11–12 hours for the complete circuit.

left branch of path 716 (low point about 2550m) towards Rif. Rosetta (25–30 minutes from Passo Bettega). Continue past the *rifugio* and up to the cable car Funivia Rosetta in a further 10 minutes. Allow a total time for the descent from Cima Vezzana to the cable car of about 2½ hours (about 2 hours from Passo Travignolo). ▶

If you have the time (and energy) the peak of **La Rosetta**, 2743m, above the cable car, can be climbed in 15 minutes; it has good views to the south of the Pala group.

S.MAR 2:
VIA FERRATA GABITTA D'IGNOTTI

Grade:	4
Seriousness:	C
Departure point:	San Martino di Castrozza
Ascent:	1300m
Descent:	1300m
Via ferrata:	150m
Approximate time:	9 hours
Highest altitude:	3192m

These timings and height statistics are for a climb of Via Ferrata Gabitta d'Ignotti, the ascent of Cima Vezzana via Val Strut and a return down Val dei Cantoni to the top of the Funivia Rosetta, assuming the use of the cable car both up and down.

This route can be combined with route S.MAR 1 to make a really long but satisfying day out. Even to consider this excursion you must be fit, alpine experienced and lucky enough to be on the mountain in stable fine weather. Ice axes and crampons are usually essential, and a rope is recommended. An indication of the timings for this combined excursion is as follows:

- ascent of VF Bolver Lugli (S.MAR 1) to Cima Vezzana 4½–5½ hours
- descent VF Gabitta d'Ignotti to Bivacco Brunner, Valle delle Comelle to Rif. Pedrotti Rosetta about 5 hours.

Telecabina Colverde (still shown on some maps as a chairlift) opens at 0800hrs, but the cable car (Funivia Rosetta) doesn't start until 0830 (times may vary during the season, so check locally). The logistics of attempting this route in one day up

This route is a very remote high-altitude ferrata which is quite short but demanding in its location. It is a way of climbing Cima Vezzana on a long mountain day from Rif. Rosetta (details above in S.MAR 1).

and down from San Martino di Castrozza are extremely tight; you would need to be very fit and have optimum weather and mountain conditions. It is therefore better to stay overnight in Rif. Rosetta, making an early start to ensure you have enough time to catch the last cable car down (or perhaps use the first cable car and then stay at the *rifugio* after completing the climb). Also be aware that the last cable car down seems to vary depending on season (and even weather!); in high season it is 1700hrs but at other times it can be 1630 or even earlier, so make sure you confirm times before setting off.

The approach to the ferrata makes a fine day out in a remote mountain area simply for the walk alone. Descend from the Rosetta cable car to Rif. Rosetta (about 10 minutes). From Rif. Rosetta, 2581m, follow path 703/704 first east and

Descending to the Val Strut bivacco

then north north-east across the vast karsitic desert at the heart of the Pala mountains. Initially a laid path (almost like a road) leads down into Valle delle Comelle; it is well way-marked in red and cream paint. After about 40 minutes' descent you are down to about 2310m in Pian Dei Cantoni, where paths 703 and 704 part company. Path 704 continues down Valle delle Comelle/Gares, and path 703 is signed Passo Farangole/Rif. Mulaz.

Take path 703 as it climbs up to above 2400m and then traverses along a steep hillside. After 20–25 minutes some cables are encountered as you cross over Valle delle Galline; there are a couple of hundred metres of cables over a period of 15 minutes. The cables and bolts are in poor condition, and one could hardly call it a ferrata, simply handrails, though at times more of a hindrance than a help due to loose bolts. The path here is narrow on very steep ground, with some of the more exposed parts not cabled.

About an hour from Pian Dei Cantoni, path 703 bottoms out at about 2250m, with spectacular views down into Valle delle Comelle, a flat expanse of over 1km of dry streambed. After climbing for 10 minutes an emergency helipad is passed on the right just before arriving at the junction of path 703 and 716. Path 703 continues towards Rif. Mulaz and 716 heads left uphill into Val Strut, with 'Biv. Brunner' painted on a rock. The path heads quite steeply uphill, waymarked in red, passing large glacial erratic boulders, one of which has 'Bivacco Val Strut' painted on it in very large letters. Snow can lie in this valley for most, if not all, of the summer, and so some of the waymarks may be covered early in the season. Navigation is quite simple, as all you do is head uphill, reaching Biv. Brunner, 2667m, after 35–40 minutes' climbing from the path junction. The bivacco is well hidden from below, tucked right up against the rock walls of Cima delle Zirocole on the north side of Val Strut, and it is a surprise when you finally get there. An indication of how much snow lies here in the winter is given by the shovel secured high on the rock wall above the bivacco.

Continue climbing up Val Strut following red waymarks. If there is old snow then this makes things easier, otherwise it is a very tedious ascent up eroded glacial scree. Stay on the right (northern) side of the valley and then the right-hand side of the now quite small glacier to Passo dei Val Strut,

If you are just doing this as a high-level walking day without the ferrata then the timings for a **return descent from Passo dei Val Strut** are as follows: 30 minutes' descent from the pass to Bivacco Brunner; another 20 minutes down to path 703. 25 minutes on path 703 to the first cable, and 15 minutes for the cabled section. 20 minutes takes you back to the junction of paths 703/704 at about 2300m. A 40 minute climb takes you up to Rif. Rosetta, and it's a further 10 minutes to the cable car, making a total of about 3 hours.

mapped as 2870m, but 2888m according to a painted rock at the pass, 50–60 minutes from Bivacco Brunner. There is an exceptional view down to Passo Rolle from the Passo dei Val Strut. 'FV Strut' and 'Ferrata' are painted on a rock at the pass, and the start is less than 10 minutes away from here, south and then east, across the top of the glacier. To reach the cables scramble up rocks and follow the cables for approximately 150m up a rocky rib on the east ridge of Cima Vezzana. A further 10 minutes up rough scree leads to the summit, about 4 hours from the cable car. The whole of this ascent is subject to icing and stone fall; it is not a place to be in bad weather. ◀

The descent from the summit of Cima Vezzana is the same as detailed in S.MAR 1.

S.MAR 3:
SENTIERO ATTREZZATO NICO GUSELLA

Grade:	2
Seriousness:	B
Departure point:	Ristorante Rosetta (top station of Rosetta cable car) (about 2630m)
Ascent:	670m
Descent:	1780m (to cable car base station at S. Martino)
Via ferrata:	200m
Approximate time:	7½ hours
Highest altitude:	2791m, Cima di Val di Roda

This is a pleasant and undemanding route through some of the most dramatic scenery in the Pala. Since it sits at the heart of the group, the approach and walk-out can be quite lengthy, depending on your choice of route.

The following description assumes the use of the two-stage Col Verde Gondola and cable car from S. Martino, which is the least taxing option, but involves a long descent if you have to return to the town. Another option is to walk in from Val Canali to the south, whilst a stay in one of the three *rifugios* in the area (Rifs. Rosetta, Pradidali and Velo) opens up all sorts of possibilities for combining this route with others in the vicinity.

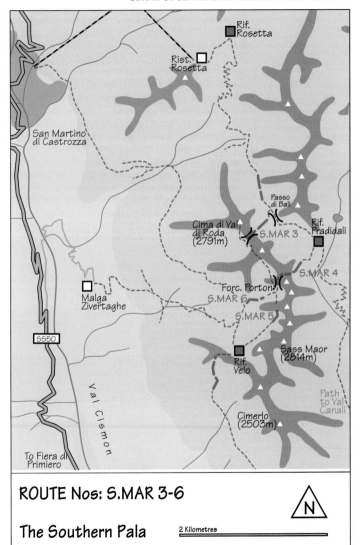

Rif.
Rosetta

Rist.
Rosetta

San Martino
di Castrozza

Passo
di Ball

Cima di Val
di Roda
(2791m)

S.MAR 3

Rif.
Pradidali

S.MAR 4

Forc. Porton
S.MAR 6

S.MAR 5

Malga
Zivertaghe

SS50

Sass Maor
(2814m)

Rif.
Velo

Path
to Val
Canali

V a l   C i s m o n

Cimerlo
(2503m)

To Fiera di
Primiero

ROUTE Nos: S.MAR 3-6

The Southern Pala

2 Kilometres

N

The lift from S. Martino (S.MAR 1 for details) whisks you up to about 2630m in a few minutes, ensuring that for much of the rest of the day you will be walking downhill! The landscape here is extraordinary, the more so because of the speed of transition from the smart resort and the lush valley. The mural outside the building claims an altitude of 2700m, which is clearly wrong (our altimeter read 2630m).

Rif. Rosetta (2581m) is about 10 minutes' to the northeast, reached by a good path across a real lunar landscape. From the *rifugio*, take path 702, signposted to Col delle Fede and Passo di Ball. This heads generally southwards, initially over fairly level ground, before starting the long descent towards Col delle Fede. The route takes the slope at an easy angle, zigzagging down endlessly, so it comes as a relief to reach a section of path (about 2265m) which is straight, as you turn in a south-easterly direction on a pleasant terrace, partly cut out of the rock face, and with an impressive drop below you to the right. A green area, full of wild flowers follows, in marked contrast to the terrain you have traversed so far. You can now pick out Passo di Ball to the south-east, a couple of hundred metres above you, whilst the walls of cliffs around the intervening bowl of mountains are quite stunning.

Climber on the lower part of Sentiero Gusella (S.MAR 3)

The path you have been following turns uphill towards the pass, at the junction where path 702 turns off to the right for S. Martino (at about 2285m). Your path, now numbered 715, continues straight ahead on a gently ascending traverse, soon passing an impressive perched boulder atop a pinnacle. As you approach the pass, the path climbs more steeply and (at about 2350m) reaches the start of a cable safeguarding an airy traverse. The first stretch has been cut out of the rock face, whilst the next safeguards a more gently angled area of slab. Whilst the cable is little more than a reassuring handrail, the slabs could well be iced up early in the season. You are now almost at Passo di Ball, 2443m, named after John Ball, the pioneer of many of the earliest ascents in the Dolomites.

As you approach the pass, you will notice an obvious gully, usually snow filled, a few hundred metres to its right (west). Your route is up the easily angled slabs between this gully and a second one, rather further to the right and not yet in view. Once at the pass, the path divides. Path 715 continues over the pass and heads east to Rif. Pradidali and Via Ferrata Porton (see S.MAR 4). Your path is waymarked 714 and signposted to Sentiero Nico Gusella and Cima di Val di Roda, and turns off to the right (west) just before you reach the crest of the pass. It takes about 1½ hours to reach here from the top station of the cable car.

You come to the start of the cable (at about 2545m) after about 15 minutes of easy climbing. The route climbs the easily angled rock a little to the left of a gloomy snow-filled gully. The rock is quite broken and well provided with holds, and you will make easy progress until you reach a steeper step equipped with a couple of stemples. Whilst this is straightforward, it frequently runs with water, so could be iced up early in the season. Above the step, the angle eases again as you approach the little forcella at the head of the gully on your right. A second step awaits you at the top of the area of slab: this bulges out slightly, but is easier than it looks, and takes you to the right-hand side of a smooth, easily angled slab.

There is a short break in the cable at this point, and the character of the rock changes abruptly as the sound, rounded limestone you have been climbing so far gives way to more friable rock. The cable takes you up a broken corner to the right, which is the last pitch of this, the main section of the ferrata. A few paces to your right is the floor of the upper gully, now at a more shallow angle. This might well hold some snow, but should give you no trouble in climbing up the easy angle amidst the boulders. (For climbers who are tackling the route in reverse, there is an important, but easily missed, way-mark to look out for. At the point where the route traverses into the floor of the gully, a red arrow is painted on the rock wall. It is on the right side, in descent, and about 30m below the forcella. It is vital that you spot this, or you will find your-self in difficulties if you descend into the steeper middle sec-tion of the gully.) The top of the gully, which you will reach about 45 minutes after starting the route, is Forcella Stephen (about 2690m), a grand spot to have lunch and enjoy the views. About 100m above are the twin summits of Cima di Val di Roda (2791m): the round-trip only takes about 15 minutes, but the views are stunning!

When you are ready to continue, take the waymarked path, signposted to Forcella Porton, down into the huge cirque below you. The gently descending traverse is over easily angled rock, nowhere at all difficult, but in a hugely impressive situation. It soon becomes apparent that you are heading for a small, but pronounced, notch in the ridge which forms the far edge of the cirque. As you near the notch, the route turns gently upwards again, traversing rather more airy terrain, safeguarded by three short lengths of cable. The last few metres are up a slightly dirty gully, and lead you into the notch, at about 2585m. From this vantage point, you now have splendid views into the huge bowl of Prati Ronz, at the head of which stands Rif. Velo. A pleasant, grassy area is now crossed, with a fairly steep descent towards the head of the shallow gully below you. As you descend, look up to your left, and you will be able to pick out Forcella Porton. This is the point where your route is rejoined by VF Porton (see S.MAR 4), after the two divided at Passo di Ball. Allow about 1½ hours from Forcella Stephen. Follow the waymarks down to the gully, and follow it down to the top of VF de la Vecchia (see S.MAR 6). Refer to the description of that route for details of the descent and for notes on the walk back to San Martino.

S.MAR 4:
VIA FERRATA PORTON

Grade:	3
Seriousness:	C
Departure point:	Ristorante Rosetta (top station of gondola from S. Martino) (about 2630m)
Ascent:	550m
Descent:	1650m (S.MAR 6 to cable car base at S. Martino)
Via ferrata:	1000m
Approximate time:	8 hours
Highest altitude:	2630m (starting point)

Whilst this route is quite intimidating on first sight, it involves very pleasant climbing, albeit with the standard of technical difficulty reduced because of the number of pegs and stemples which have been installed – in many cases unnecessarily, since natural holds abound. Whilst the rock on the route itself is mostly very sound, the last part of the walk-in and the first part of the walk-out involve some unpleasant scrambling in very dirty and unstable gullies. **It is not recommend to use the route in descent.**

This is a via ferrata for people who like exposure and the feel of stemples!

The approach is the same as for Sentiero Nico Gusella (S.MAR 3) as far as Passo di Ball (2443m). Once at the pass, the Gusella route turns right (south-west), whilst for VF Porton continue on over the pass, following the path way-marked 715. Descend easily to a flat area of scree at about 2385m, and then on down to Rif. Pradidali, which you will reach about 20 minutes after leaving the pass. Your onward path is waymarked 739, signposted to Rif. Velo and Ferrata Velo (there are real problems with route naming in this area: the first section of what this signpost refers to as Ferrata Velo is, in fact, VF Porton).

Within 5 minutes, you reach a rise with a signposted junction. To the right, waymarked 715, is a path back to Rif. Rosetta, whilst straight ahead is path 739, signposted to Rif. Velo. The path now drops into a dirty gully, and within 5

VF Porton: plenty of stemples, but still steep and exposed (S.MAR 4)

minutes you come to the red SAT sign, although at this stage there is no sign of a cable. The waymarks lead you down the gully, over easy but friable terrain, until (at about 2220m) you cross to the other side of the gully at a narrow point. There is normally old snow here, but crossing presents no problems. You are now standing on a small rock spur, with a smaller, subsidiary gully in front of you. Just ahead, about 30m away, you will spot a large red star painted on the rock, with a line of stemples climbing up the wall beyond. This first sight of the route can be somewhat intimidating in this gloomy corner. The black overhanging wall to the right is usually dripping water, whilst the stempled wall looks decidedly steep. Happily, it is easier than it looks, and the protection is positively industrial strength!

You arrive at the cable (at about 2200m) roughly 20 minutes after leaving the *rifugio*. Two flights of stemples take you about 35m up the first wall, which is steep, but not as steep as it first looked. An exposed leftward traverse follows, with several pegs to supplement the natural holds. Half a dozen stemples now take you to another exposed leftward traverse, again aided by a few pegs. A rising diagonal traverse leftwards now begins a lengthy passage of traversing, undulating across fairly easy and less exposed ground. After about 20 minutes or so of climbing, at an altitude of about 2260m, Ref. Pradidali starts to come into view over your right shoulder, along with the path down to Val Canali. You continue, with quite lengthy traverses interspersed with short vertical stemple pitches, for perhaps another 15 minutes, until at about 2290m you arrive at an arête, almost an à *cheval* stance.

The exposure is now considerable once more as the route looks down into a side gully, a subsidiary of the one you crossed in order to reach the foot of the cable. The steepest pitch so far follows, up a wall of some 20m, again equipped with stemples. A broken corner leads to yet more stemples, with a great deal of exposure, and then a corner (about 2335m), where the route begins to descend gently towards the subsidiary gully. The descent is initially very gradual, on an easy but airy path. However, another corner brings you to the top of a very steep pitch, with yet more stemples. The first few moves down are, in fact, slightly overhanging and at an awkward angle, and thus quite strenuous. However, the foot of that pitch (at about 2320m) represents the end of the difficulties, since all that remains is a gently descending traverse towards the floor of the gully, which has been rising up steeply to meet you. The cable ends at about 2310m in the floor of the gully. You should allow about an hour for the protected part of the route.

Waymarks lead up the right-hand side of the gully, which is extremely friable and dirty. Initially, it is simply a matter of choosing the least bad course, although the waymarks eventually take you over to the left-hand side to a poor path. As you approach the headwall of the gully, a left turn brings you to a final steep slope, with a battered ladder to aid the ascent of a friable corner, followed by a final length of cable. You now find yourself standing in Forcella Porton (about 2430m), with the huge bowl of Prati Ronz below you, whilst to your right is the red SAT sign marking the end of VF Porton. Allow about 20 minutes from the end of the cable to here. The path from Sentiero Gusella is about 10m or so below you, so it is now simply a matter of dropping down the slope to join it and continuing on down VF Vecchia (S.MAR 6) for the return to S. Martino.

S.MAR 5:
VIA FERRATA DEL VELO

Grade:	2
Seriousness:	A
Departure point:	Rif. Malga Zivertaghe (1375m)
Ascent:	1070m
Descent:	1070m (to Rif. Malga Zivertaghe)
Via ferrata:	100m
Approximate time:	4½ hours, plus descent (see text)
Highest altitude:	2410m (although some of the options for continuing your day involve more climbing)

This is a very pleasant little route, undemanding and perfectly protected, but in an impressive situation in the huge bowl of Prati Ronz formed by the walls of Cima di Ball, Sass Maor, Cima della Madonna and Cima della Stanga.

This perfectly illustrates how you can combine routes in this area in any number of permutations. It is commonly used as a descent route after completing VF Porton (S.MAR 4), as part of a splendid traverse, but it is also part of a popular circuit from Rif. Malga Zivertaghe combined with VF Vecchia (S.MAR 6). If this is your choice it is better to make an anti-clockwise circuit, tackling VF Velo first followed by a descent of VF Vecchia. The description below treats the route as a discrete entity, and you will need to make allowances for extra distances and climbing required in planning your day.

Rif. Malga Zivertaghe is reached from the S. Martino to Fiera road (SS50) by a good gravel track. From the *rifugio*, which is in fact simply a restaurant, take the track waymarked 713 and signposted to Rif. Velo della Madonna. This soon reverts to a path, which climbs pleasantly through the trees to cross over the good track waymarked 22/724 (at 1605m). Your path, which is still waymarked 713, continues straight ahead, more steeply now. In about 10 minutes, cross a major boulder slide which has swept away the original path and most of the surrounding trees. The tree cover soon thins and reverts to dwarf pines, and dramatic views open up of the bowl of cliffs ahead. A second lateral path is reached (at about 2085m), where a signpost indicates Ferrata de la Vecchia off to the left on path 739 bis. Ferrata

San Martino di Castrozza, seen from VF del Velo: the footpath below the rock wall is the best route back to the town

Velo, however, is beyond the *rifugio*, which sits atop the vertical wall ahead of you, so you need to turn right (south) on the path waymarked 713. This shortly traverses an area of slabs, safeguarded by cable, before turning steeply uphill to make the final approach to the *rifugio*. Allow about 3½ hours to here.

A signpost about 50m behind the *rifugio* indicates path 739 to Rif. Pradidali by Ferratas Velo and Porton (see S.MAR 4) off in a north-easterly direction. The ground is broken and the path not particularly clear, but waymarks take you, on a slightly descending course, to the start of the ferrata (at about 2320m) in about 10 minutes.

69

The route starts with a steep step of a couple of metres, which leads to a very easily angled slab. A second short, steep step follows, this slightly more strenuous than the first. Another area of easily angled slab follows, easy but quite exposed. A rocky shoulder then leads to a traverse above a ravine, and then on to a steep rock step of about 3m, equipped with stemples. An easy path, without cable, leads pleasantly above the ravine and below an area which holds old snow for much of the season. The head of the ravine is passed on a nice traverse, also equipped with stemples, which leads to the most sustained passage of the route. This is a very pleasant and easily angled wide groove, well supplied with natural holds, but still equipped with pegs, rings and some stemples. At the top of the groove, the angle falls back somewhat to a very easy traverse. A few paces further, the path crosses a small stream, and the route is almost finished. The cable ends at a path which traverses off in a generally northerly direction. You are now at about 2410m, and will have taken about 45 minutes to complete the climb.

There are two broad options for the rest of your day: either a descent by VF Vecchia (S.MAR 6) to complete a circuit or a traverse to Rif. Rosetta by Sentiero Gusella (S.MAR 3). Note that VF Porton (S.MAR 4) is not recommended as a descent route.

S.MAR 6:
VIA FERRATA DE LA VECCHIA

Grade:	2
Seriousness:	A
Departure point:	see text
Ascent:	not applicable (see text)
Descent:	1010m(to Rif. Zivertaghe) or 985m (to S. Martino)
Via ferrata:	100m
Approximate time:	3 hours, plus ascent of S.MAR 3, 4 or 5 (see text)
Highest altitude:	2385m (although each approach option on S.MAR 3, 4 or 5 involves a higher altitude)

The description starts at a point on path 739, a few hundred metres north of the end of Ferrata Velo. There is a distinct rise in the path at about 2390m, south of the broad, shallow gully below Forcella del Porton. A couple of paces down towards the gully, an inconspicuous path turns off downhill. This zigzags down a friable slope into the bottom of the gully, although it is apparent that many people coming down from Forcella del Porton simply walk down the gully as a shortcut. The path is not particularly clear and is way-marked in rather faded paint, but it takes a generally south-western course to the top of the wall of cliffs. You are now at about 2160m, and will have taken about 20 minutes to descend about 200m from path 739.

The route negotiates a section of the rock wall which is rather more broken, and thus less steep, than those on

This route is normally used as a means of descent, either as the conclusion of a traverse starting on the other side of Forcella del Porton (see S.MAR 3 and 4) or as the second half of a circuit which began with Ferrata del Velo (S.MAR 5). This description, therefore, is for a descent.

Via Ferrata de la Vecchia: this straightforward route is usually used in descent (S.MAR 6)

either side. The top pitch is a 5m flight of stemples leading to a good ledge, followed by a more easily angled wall, this time only partly equipped with stemples. An easy, leftward (facing the rock) descending traverse leads to another line of stemples, and then a rightward descending traverse, with the odd peg to help. After about 4m of vertical descent, the cable takes you on a final leftward descending traverse to the top of the steep wall which concludes the route. This is the steepest part of the descent, and involves two flights of stemples down smooth rock, broken by a broad ledge. The upper flight is steep but straightforward, although the top section of the lower flight passes through a bit of a squeeze, formed by an adjoining block which leans in towards you. This is the end of the route, as confirmed by the usual red SAT sign. You are at an altitude of about 2090m, and should have taken less than 30 minutes to complete the down-climb.

About 25m below you is the lateral path which traverses round the slope. Drop to this path, where you will find a signpost pointing back to the ferrata you have just descended. This is where you must decide how you are to return to the valley. If you take this path northwards, waymarked 721, it takes you to S. Martino in about 2½ hours. If you turn south, Rif. Velo is about ¾ hour away, whilst the path down to Rif. Malga Zivertaghe (waymarked 713, and described in S.MAR 5) takes about 1½ hours.

S.MAR 7:
SENTIERO ATTREZZATO CAMILLO DEPAOLI

Grade:	1
Seriousness:	A
Departure point:	parking area near Fosne (1326m)
Ascent:	1030m
Descent:	1030m (back to Fosne parking area)
Via ferrata:	100m
Approximate time:	5 hours
Highest altitude:	2358m, Rif. Velo della Madonna

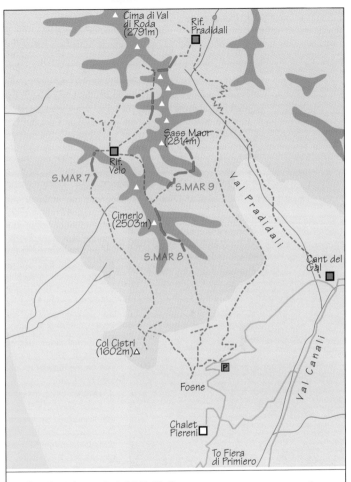

ROUTE Nos: S.MAR 7-9
Sent. Depaoli,
Buzzati & Cacciatore

2 Kilometres

This is an extremely straightforward outing, with only a few short lengths of cable to safeguard the final steep passages.

Sentiero Depaoli ends at a shoulder with a magnificent view of Sass Maor, with Rif. Velo at its foot

This quite delightful walk through grand terrain is a most pleasant way of reaching Rif. Velo della Madonna, one of the *rifugios* that you might consider using for a hut-touring trip into the Pala.

The route is approached from Val Canali, to the south. If you are dependent on public transport, there is a limited bus service (from the beginning of August until early September) which will take you to the restaurant at Cant del Gal (1180m). Depending on where you are staying, you can pick up the morning bus anywhere between Imer, its southern terminus, and Tonadico, at the entrance to Val Canali. Check times locally for variations (in summer 2002, the morning bus left Imer at 0820, whilst the afternoon return service left Val Canali at 1725). In planning your day, however, you would need to allow for the extra 150m of height gain and the 3km of extra walking involved to get to the highest point that can be reached by car, which is where this description starts. This is near Fosne, at the parking area by the road junction on the upper (north-west side) road in Val Canali, which is identified on the map by its altitude of 1326m.

Walk west up the gravel track waymarked 747 and signposted to Sentiero Dino Buzzati and Rif. Velo d'Madonna. Within 5 minutes you reach a junction of paths, where the Buzzati route is signposted up to the right on path 747. Your path is straight ahead, waymarked 731/734 and signposted to Col Cistri, where your waymarking then reverts to 734, and Sentiero Depaoli. After a steep walk up the line of a ridge, deep in trees, the path begins to contour near the top of the tree line. It eventually breaks cover and enters a more broken area with numerous rocky pinnacles. Shortly after passing beneath a huge overhanging boulder, the path turns steeply uphill and reaches the first length of cable. You are at about 2180m, and will have taken perhaps 2 hours to reach here.

The route takes a north-easterly course through a weakness in the wall of cliffs to the north-west of Cima Stanga. It is always well protected where necessary, and involves about 100m of very easy scrambling, less than half of which is cabled. It concludes at a beautiful grassy ridge (2263m), with outstanding views of the ring of peaks above Rif. Velo, which is an easy 15 minute stroll away. You can return by the same route or make other plans for the rest of your day, perhaps incorporating one of the more serious via ferratas described in this section.

S.MAR 8:
SENTIERO ATTREZZATO
DINO BUZZATI, CIMERLO

Grade:	2
Seriousness:	C
Departure point:	parking area near Fosne (1326m)
Ascent:	1220m
Descent:	1220m (back to Fosne parking area)
Via ferrata:	350m
Approximate time:	4½ hours, plus descent (see text)
Highest altitude:	2450m (2503m if summit of Cimerlo visited)

A long tape loop and spare karabiner will prove useful!

One obvious combination of routes here is an ascent by the Buzzati route and a descent by the Cacciatore route. The two provide a splendid traverse without making excessive

This is a route constructed by someone with a sense of humour! A squeeze through a narrow crack along the way means that it should not be attempted with a large, heavy rucksack!

technical demands of the climber, although the terrain is shattered, and there is the constant threat of stone fall, particularly after wet weather. The circuit could equally well be tackled in either direction, with a clockwise course providing a more sporting (and the authors' preferred) itinerary, whilst the anti-clockwise choice is considerably less strenuous. Needless to say, other descent options are available, and you should calculate the time required for the day on the basis of your choice. The approach to the route is described from the parking area near Fosne, identified on the map by its altitude of 1326m and described in S.MAR 7.

Walk west up the gravel track waymarked 747 and signposted to Sentiero Dino Buzzati and Rif. Velo d'Madonna. Within 5 minutes you reach a junction, where the waymarking takes you to the right (north) and up into thin tree cover. The path soon joins a gravel track coming up from the right and continues uphill, still waymarked to the Buzzati route. After about 5 minutes on the gravel track (at about 1445m), waymarking for path 747 takes you off to the right into the woods, climbing quite steeply. In less than 10 minutes, you reach a path running laterally across your line of ascent. Val Canali is indicated to the left, and the Buzzati route to the right, still waymarked 747. Follow this contouring path for a few minutes until path 747, signposted to the Buzzati route, turns off to the left (north) and resumes climbing steeply. At about 1785m you pass a large boulder on which a red arrow is painted, pointing up and to the left, and within 5 minutes reach the foot of a rock wall. The waymarking now takes you to the right and then turns uphill again, following an eroded slope between two large rock buttresses, at last out of the trees. The last few minutes of the approach take you through an area of large rocky pinnacles, over unpleasantly eroded ground, arriving eventually at the start of the cable (about 2100m) roughly 1¾ hours after setting out.

The climbing on this first pitch is the best of the route. About 45m of cable take you up an easily angled wall then, more steeply and slightly strenuously, up a broad crack line to the right. Most of the rest of the route is characterised by much easier scrambling, over extremely friable ground, where the intermittent cable is little more than a reassuring handrail. The waymarking takes you on a meandering course through this shattered area, gradually gaining height and crossing over a small wind gap to a point where you find yourself traversing above the intersection of two gullies, falling away to your right. In the gaps between cable lengths, waymarking indicates the route to follow, until at about 2205m care must be taken not to stray off course. A length of cable has taken you up a dirty and eroded gully, and at the top of the cable it is easy to continue scrambling straight on up. Instead, keep an eye out for rather inconspicuous waymarking traversing off to the right to another cable which safeguards a rising traverse over particularly broken ground.

The last section of cable now lies ahead. Intriguingly, the cable disappears into the depths of a narrow crack too narrow to walk into, other than by turning sideways. Shuffle in as best you can to reach a ladder up the back of the crack which leads into an upper chamber, even narrower than before. A second ladder leads up towards daylight, but it is all but impossible to climb it other than by hanging off its side until the crack widens sufficiently to enable you to swing round into a more conventional position. ▶

When you eventually emerge into daylight, follow the path uphill in easy zigzags for about 200m to a little grassy shoulder. This is the high point of the route, at about 2450m. The summit of Cimerlo is about 50m above you to the west, and can be reached in about 15 minutes or so, although the terrain is extremely friable, and you should take care if you decide to make the diversion.

The route continues over the grassy shoulder, beyond which a cable begins an easy descent on very broken rock. After a few minutes, you arrive at what looks dishearteningly like another constriction to negotiate, but this one is no more than a slightly tight squeeze between a couple of boulders. Continue on down a rather dirty gully and then right (in descent) over a little rocky shoulder, and on over still more shattered rock on a descending traverse line. When you pass in front of a shallow natural cave (on your left), you know you are nearing the end of the route. The cable finally ends in a dirty little forcella, beyond which you arrive at an undulating traverse on a fairly exposed grassy ridge. At its low point (about 2375m), the letters 'DB' are painted in red, marking

If you are wondering about your rucksack at this point, this is where that tape and karabiner come in handy. Before tackling the ladder, attach the tape to the haul loop of your sack and clip it to the ladder as high as you can. You should then be able to reach back down to drag it up behind you, although the chances are that it will snag on the underside of the ladder on the first few attempts!

the end of the route. Allow about 1½ hours for the ferrata, plus any time for exploration in the area of Cimerlo summit.

A few minutes further on, you arrive at a signposted junction (about 2385m): this is where you have to decide on your descent route. The path straight ahead, uphill, is signposted to Rif. Velo, which is about 45 minutes away. From there, you have a choice of several different routes back to the valley, depending on whether you need to retrieve your car or not. The path down to your right (east) is waymarked 742 and signposted Sentiero Cacciatore. This is the shortest option, and the route which sits most comfortably with Sentiero Buzzati to make a fulfilling tour of this area of the Pala. The route description for S.MAR 9 can be readily followed in reverse: you should allow about 2½ hours for the descent.

S.MAR 9:
SENTIERO DEL CACCIATORE

Grade:	2
Seriousness:	C
Departure point:	Parking area near Fosne (1326m)
Ascent:	1060m
Descent:	1060m (back to Fosne parking area)
Via ferrata:	250m
Approximate time:	3½ hours, plus descent (see text)
Highest altitude:	2385m (although descent by S.MAR 8 involves more climbing)

This is one of the easiest routes, technically, in the Pala group, with its grade being earned by one short pitch alone. The remainder of the route is little more than a protected walk, although it takes you through shattered terrain where there is the constant threat of rock fall, particularly after wet weather.

This route is most logically tackled in conjunction with Sentiero Dino Buzzati, a tour which provides a splendid traverse through this part of the Pala group. As the description of S.MAR 8 indicates, the circuit can be completed either in a clockwise or anti-clockwise direction, depending on whether you favour the sporting or the less strenuous option! For the sake of simplicity, the description which follows assumes an ascent, although it is a straightforward matter to follow the description in reverse.

The starting point is the same as for the previous two routes, so see S.MAR 7 for details of the approach and comments on access by bus. From the parking area (1326m), take track waymarked 742 (shown as 719 on the Tabacco map) and signposted Sentiero Attrezzato Cacciatore and Rif. Pradidali. This is a well-constructed logging road, and will take you round the south-eastern flank of Cimerlo, gaining height slowly and with minimal effort. After about 10 minutes of walking, at a left-hand hairpin take the track off to the right (north-east), which has vehicular access prevented by a barrier. The waymarking now changes to 709/719. After a further 20 minutes, pass a small path climbing into the woods on the left, with a sign painted on a boulder indicating 'Troi de Rodena', and continue steadily on to a drainage line where the track has been partly swept away.

The track now reverts to a lovely path, following a gently ascending traverse line as it penetrates deeper into Val Pradidali. About an hour after setting out, you pass a boulder to your left painted with redundant blue waymarking, but also with more recent lettering in red, 'RP': Rif. Pradidali. A few paces beyond that, you arrive at a signposted junction (1627m); your path is to the left, waymarked 742 and signposted to Rif. Velo and Sentiero Cacciatore.

The path becomes much rougher and climbs more steeply to an unpleasantly eroded scree slope, although you might be able to spot the line of the sentiero, picking its way up the broken shelves of the rock wall slightly to the left, to provide encouragement. You eventually arrive at the start of the cable, marked by the usual red SAT sign (at about 1845m), some 1¾ hours after setting out.

The first pitch is a leftward traverse along a good but exposed path, little more than a walk. Easy scrambling now takes you to a memorial plaque to Giancarlo Biasin, who died whilst climbing on Sass Maor in 1964. The cable resumes for an easy but pleasing ascending traverse to the

There are many dedications to the climber Giancarlo Biasin: this plaque is on Sentiero Cacciatore (S.MAR 9)

left following a series of ledges. The path now leads into much more broken and unstable terrain, protected where necessary, but still without difficulty. Pass along the foot of a steep rock wall, then through more shattered rock and on to a grassy knoll, where the path takes a sharp turn to the right.

Traverse along a good shelf (at about 2000m), exposed but protected, towards the back of a wild-looking ravine. This generally holds water, but is not a place to linger, as the extent of recent rock fall will indicate. Instead, hurry on past a cave on the right and a boulder with faded paint pointing up the path to Biv. Madonna. Easy scrambling now brings you to the only slightly difficult pitch of the climb, a wide 10m crack. The cable is not well tensioned, but good handholds help you to the top, which marks the end of the protected part of the route. Easy scrambling, albeit with a couple of slightly exposed moves, now takes you up into a fine cirque (about 2220m). Easy zigzags, still on very friable rock, now take you to the top of the steep slope above the cirque and up to a signposted junction. This is the end of the sentiero, at about 2385m, and is the point described in S.MAR 8 where choices need to be made about the means of descent. Allow about 1½ hours from starting out on the protected passage.

S.MAR 10:
VIA FERRATA DELLE
FIAMME GIALLE: CRODA GRANDA

Grade:	3
Seriousness:	C
Departure point:	Roadhead near Malga Canali, Val Canali (about 1300m)
Ascent:	1400m
Descent:	1400m
Via ferrata:	220m
Approximate time:	7¼ hours
Highest altitude:	2675m

(The optional ascent of Croda Granda (2849m) involves an additional ascent of some 320m, and requires a further 2 hours for the round-trip.)

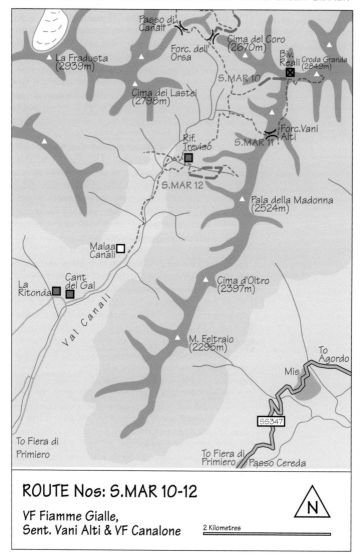

ROUTE Nos: S.MAR 10-12

VF Fiamme Gialle,
Sent. Vani Alti & VF Canalone

2 Kilometres

This is a relatively remote and quite serious route, although it is not particularly hard, technically. It is, however, an exhilarating climb, which takes you onto the barren plateau below Croda Granda.

The ascent to the Croda Granda summit is technically straightforward, although it adds significantly to what is already a fairly long, hard day. It should be stressed that the Pala group is notorious for the sudden formation of dense clouds, and that route-finding can be difficult, especially early in the season when much of the waymarking is covered by snow. Consequently, you should be sure of your experience and ability in difficult mountain terrain before embarking on a summit bid.

It is normal to combine the Fiamme Gialle route with Sentiero Vani Alti (S.MAR 11), ascending by the via ferrata and descending by the sentiero. However, the difficulties of the day are not over once you have completed the ferrata. The Vani Alti route, is, if anything, a more serious proposition, and is now completely unprotected.

The approach is up Val Canali, north-east of Fiera di Primiero. Whilst a good road penetrates into the upper reaches of the valley, those dependent on public transport will have to walk the last 2 or 3km, since the limited bus service (see S.MAR 7 for details) travels no further than Cant del Gal.

If you have a car available, drive to the roadhead near Malga Canali (about 1300m) and continue on the gravel track waymarked Rif. Treviso. The track reverts to a rougher path once it leaves the river and heads up into the woods, but it is a pleasant climb, with views of the towering rock walls which line the valley. Rif. Treviso is a pleasant stopping-off point for a coffee, where you might be able to watch from the terrace a climber on the VF Canalone (see S.MAR 12).

From the *rifugio*, continue up the valley on path 707/743, and within a few minutes pass a helicopter landing site. The path winds up pleasantly, and soon leaves the trees behind. At about 1950m, you pass a sign, painted on a boulder, indicating Sentiero Vani Alti up to the right. About 15 minutes later (about 2180m), you come to the point where you turn off up to the right, waymarked 743 and signposted to Bivacco Reali and 'Ferrata FFGG'.

The path steepens and enters a huge amphitheatre, out of which a series of smaller and often snow-filled gullies rise. A painted boulder (about 2190m) confirms you are en route for Biv. Reali. By now, depending on the time of year and the extent of spring snow fall, you may be picking your way up a tongue of debris between two long streaks of snow which will obscure much of the waymarking. The going steepens and becomes very unstable, but keep an eye out for an opportunity to head leftwards to an obvious platform at the foot of the rock wall. This is at about 2370m, so if you carry an altimeter make sure not to climb too high. The route starts a few metres to the side of the platform, which is a good place to gear up and have a snack. Allow about 3¼ hours to here.

From the outset, the cable (starting at about 2390m) is not particularly well tensioned, encouraging you to rely on the rock rather than the cable to make progress. The climb is, in any event, well provided with good holds, although some of the rock is suspect, and you should test your holds before relying on them.

Climbers on VF delle Fiamme Gialle (S.MAR 10)

You start by ascending diagonally up a series of easy ledges, before traversing into a shallow ravine and up on its right side. The best climbing follows, up a steep wall with good holds and, unusually, a well- tensioned cable to help if required. A rightward traverse leads to a break in the cable, where the route follows a gravely path on an exposed ridge for a few paces. The cable resumes to protect a traverse round the right side of a pinnacle which blocks progress along the ridge line, before crossing back over the ridge and into the bottom of the narrow gully on the left (at about 2540m). This is usually filled with snow and, depending on its condition, might need some care, particularly since the cable has been severed by rock fall (in summer 2002). The final pitch of the climb now lies ahead. This is a steep and very pleasant wall, quite exposed and with one or two strenuous moves. As you climb over the top you realise, with some surprise, that the ferrata section is over, and that you are standing in Forcella dei Marmor at 2570m. The climb will have taken you about 45 minutes to complete.

As already mentioned, this area is prone to dense cloud, so take care in following the waymarking off to the right (east), particularly early in the season when snow will still be obscuring much of the path. After about 10 minutes of gentle ascent, the path forks: Biv. Reali is signposted to the left, which is the way you should go if you wish to visit the summit of Croda Granda. The waymarking takes you past the bivacco, over Forcella Spirit (2530m) and to the summit by way of a circuitous route round the south-east side. You then return by the same route. Whilst technically straightforward, this is not an undertaking that should be embarked on lightly, and certainly not in poor weather.

To reach the descent route, take the right fork at the junction just referred to. A sign painted on a boulder indicates the way to Sentiero Vani Alti, as does a second painted boulder some 20m further on. The path now heads generally south, with waymarking which is less than ideal initially. You continue to climb gently to a high point of about 2675m, when the path begins a gentle descent and becomes easier to follow. The terrain is now extremely broken, with dramatic drops to your left, so this is not a place for carelessness. The path gradually veers to the right (west) and moves into less threatening terrain before arriving at an area of slabs scoured smooth by the action of ice. Painted signs on the rock, spread over several square metres rather than in a single spot, point back to Croda Granda and Biv. Reali, straight on to Forcella Mughe, and down to the right to Rif. Treviso. You are now standing in Forcella Vani Alti, at 2529m, about 45 minutes after finishing the ferrata. This is the point where you should refer to the description of the descent in S.MAR 11 below.

S.MAR 11:
SENTIERO VANI ALTI

Grade:	not applicable
Seriousness:	C
Departure point:	Forcella Vani Alti (2592m)
Ascent:	not applicable
Descent:	1230m
Via ferrata:	not applicable
Approximate time:	7¼ hours, when combined with S.MAR 10
Highest altitude:	2529m, Forcella Vani Alti

Sentiero Vani Alti is now described as a 'Percorso Alpinistico non Attrezzato', an unprotected climbing route. It is of considerable seriousness, particularly early in the season, when a good deal of snow will remain, so you should consider taking an ice axe and crampons with you.

As it is the normal descent route after completing Ferrata Fiamme Gialle, this is how it is described, although it would be an easy matter to reverse the description should you want to ascend by this route. The description begins at Forcella Vani Alti, which is where the previous route ended (see S.MAR 10).

From the painted waymarks in the forcella, walk steeply down towards a broken gully. The path is clear and the waymarks easy to follow, although both deteriorate as you descend. At about 2420m, you encounter the start of the bolts which previously secured the cable. Within a few metres, the path begins a descending traverse which zigzags across a steep wall. Nowhere is the scrambling difficult, but the rock is

Sentiero Vani Alti (sometimes referred to as VF Bagnin) is now completely unprotected, as the cable which previously safeguarded the exposed descent of the steep rock wall has been removed. Consequently, no grade is suggested, although the scrambling is not too difficult.

unreliable, and the exposure compels you to take great care. However, the pegs remain sound and would make useful belay points, and so a rope would be useful if you were climbing with an inexperienced partner. This passage takes you down some 75m, vertically, and ends with a slightly awkward move round a bulge, although the exposure is now limited. At the foot of the line of bolts, a memorial plaque to Renato Gobato, more commonly known as 'Bagnin', is located (hence the occasional reference to this route as VF Bagnin).

The route now continues down the gully, but you will almost certainly be encountering significant amounts of old, hard snow by now, and will be having problems spotting the waymarks. In fact, whilst the waymarks take a line down the left side (in descent) of the gully at this stage, it is important to ensure, as you get nearer the bottom of the gully, that you make your way over to the right, since this is where you will eventually pick up the beginning of the path which will take you down to easier terrain.

It is now simply a matter of following the path down to the main route up the valley, waymarked 707/743, rejoining it at the painted boulder at about 1950m which you noticed earlier. Retrace your steps to Rif. Treviso and back to the road, which you will reach about 2¼ hours after leaving Forcella Vani Alti.

S.MAR 12:
VIA FERRATA CANALONE

Grade:	4
Seriousness:	A
Departure point:	roadhead, near Malga Canali, Val Canali (about 1300m)
Ascent:	400m
Descent:	400m
Via ferrata:	180m
Approximate time:	3 hours
Highest altitude:	1700m

Given that this route can be climbed in about 30 minutes, including the descent, it is unlikely to be your choice for a whole day's expedition. Consequently, you might wish to consider treating it as an aperitif, before dinner at Rif. Treviso, en route for a day in the bigger routes (see S.MAR 9 & 10) further up the valley.

The approach is up Val Canali, from the roadhead near Malga Canali, as described in S.MAR 9. The route can be seen clearly from the terrace of Rif. Treviso, and is less than 10 minutes' easy walk away on the signposted footpath. The bottom of the cable is marked with the usual red SAT signpost, whilst the descent route, also cabled, is a few metres to the left up the slope from the starting point. ▶

The cable takes a zigzag course up the wall just to the right of the arête. Although the climbing is steep and sometimes delicate, it is never too strenuous, and the rock is sound and generally well provided with holds. The two short sections which would otherwise prove rather 'thin' are equipped with several metal pegs and a few stemples. The climbing is most enjoyable, but over all too soon. The high point of the route, about 60m vertically above the start, is marked by a slightly unusual arrangement of cables. The main cable joins a noticeably thinner cable, which heads off both to the left and right. The right-hand course takes you up to the dwarf- pine-covered slope above the arete, and meanders uphill towards the main ridge. Your route is to the left, and takes a steeply descending traverse line. You are now attached to three strands of the thin cable, crudely woven together.

An interesting traverse follows: the woven cables are supplemented by a less than new log, which is balanced on three pegs and is a substitute for footholds. Normality returns just round the corner on the left, where you join a new length of cable heading easily down the broken rock of the gully. After a few metres the cable traverses off to the left (looking outwards as you descend) across a steep wall. Whilst this length of cable was installed as recently as 2002, it has already been seriously damaged by stonefall, so care is needed. Continue round a corner, still on steep rock, and join a much more easily angled crack which takes you back to a point very close to where you started. You might even be tempted to do it again!

This is a grand little climb, following an attractive line up an exposed arête. It is consistently steep and requires a degree of boldness for a couple of moves, although the difficulties are less than they appear.

Rif. Treviso was closed for refurbishment in 2004, the work also requiring the diversion of the footpath approach. Progress appears slow, and it seems unlikely to be completed for the 2005 season.

AGORDINO

Maps
Tabacco Carta Topografica 1:25,000 Sheet 015 (Routes 1–4) and 022
(Routes 5–8)

Tourist Information Office
APT Agordo or Alleghe, Italy
Tel: Agordo (0437) 62105; Fax (0437) 65205
Tel: Alleghe (0437) 523333; Fax (0437) 723881
E-mail: info@dolomiti.it
Internet: www.agordo.bl.it or www.dolomiti.com/localita/agordo/agordo

Agordo is the 'capital' of the Agordino area. It is a town rich
with history, culture and architectural curiosities, as well as
once being a well-known mining area. Agordo also has a
strong mountaineering tradition: the first section of the CAI
in the Eastern Alps was founded here in 1868. The busy little village of Alleghe, with its attractive lakeside setting, sits
under the great Civetta massif.

The Cordevole valley is well provided with facilities,
particularly in the four main villages of Agordo,
Cencenighe, Alleghe and Caprile. There is also a large
campsite just south of Alleghe, Camping Alleghe Località
Masarè 32022 Alleghe (BL), tel. 0437.72.37.37, fax
0437.72.38.74, www.camping.dolomiti.com/alleghe/,
e-mail alleghecamp@dolomites.com.

The valley has good road access to other nearby centres, including Arabba and Cortina (see volume 1 for more
details), which would be equally suitable as jumping-off
points, particularly for routes in this section which involve
overnight *rifugio* stays.

Civetta is the main mountain group of the Agordino
area, with two really big routes that go to the summit of
Monte Civetta, so ice axe and crampons are recommended
early in the season. Both are best done from an overnight
base in a *rifugio*: Via Ferrata degli Alleghesi (AGORD 1) from
Rif. Coldai, and VF Attilio Tissi (AGORD 2) from Rif.
Vazzoler. The other two routes in the Civetta group are also
of high grading and good quality and are both accessible
from the Cordevole valley.

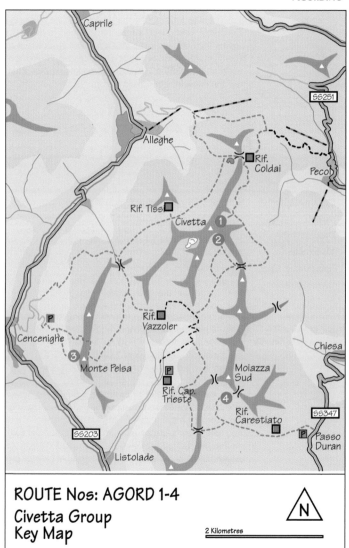

ROUTE Nos: AGORD 1-4
Civetta Group
Key Map

N

2 Kilometres

The other four routes in this section lie to the west of the Cordevole valley, with a real classic round in the Stella Alpina and Canalone routes (AGORD 5 and 6), for which an overnight stay in Rif. Scarpa is recommended. The remaining routes, whilst less difficult, nevertheless provide splendid and committing mountain days.

AGORD 1:
VF degli Alleghesi – Civetta

Grade:	4
Seriousness:	C
Departure point:	Col dei Baldi (or overnight in Rif. Coldai)
Ascent:	1650m
Descent:	1650m
Via ferrata:	900m
Approximate time:	10–12 hours
Highest altitude:	3220m, Civetta

This is a big mountain route, requiring a high degree of fitness.

This route demands a very committing, long day and should only be planned during periods of really settled weather as there are no easy escapes from the ferrata. The route could be combined with Via Ferrata Tissi to complete a splendid, though very long, traverse of Civetta (see AGORD 2).

The usual starting point for this route is Rif. Coldai, with a return trip to the summit taking about 8½ hours. If choosing this approach a start from Rif. Coldai at 0700hrs should give you time to complete the route and return to Col dei Baldi in time for the last lift down to Alleghe at 1700hrs. The Alleghe gondola and chair run from the end of June to early September.

An alternative approach to Rif. Coldai can be made from the eastern side but it cannot be recommended. It was previously possible to drive as far as Forcella di Alleghe, but this is now closed to traffic, so walking is the only option. From Rif. Coldai follow the waymarked path 557 (Sentiero Tivan). The path traverses the east side of Civetta,

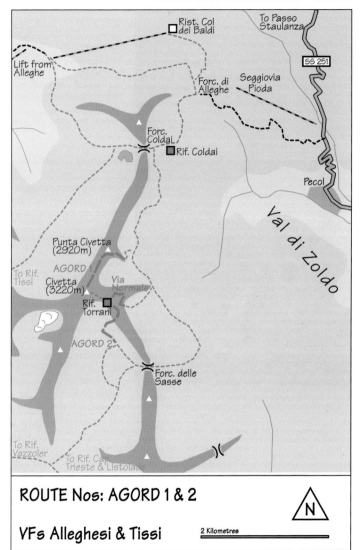

ROUTE Nos: AGORD 1 & 2

VFs Alleghesi & Tissi

2 Kilometres

Climbers on VF degli Alleghesi, Monte Civetta (AGORD 1)

undulating along the way. About 20 minutes from the *rifugio* there is a short section of cable which acts as a handrail; it does not really require gearing up. About 1 hour and 20 minutes from the *rifugio*, after passing through a col with a rock buttress on the left, waymarks indicate the start of the route a little way up a rock spur on the right. There is a disappearing glacier in a rock amphitheatre ahead to the right, and already you have stunning views down to Val di Zoldo on the left (east).

There is little that needs to be said about the detail of the ferrata route except that it is never overly technically difficult, but there are many unprotected passages where a head for heights and an ability to climb up to UIAA Grade II in exposed positions is essential. Also, the majority of the route is on the east/north-east side of the Civetta massif, and due to its altitude can be subject to snow and ice at any time of the year (especially towards the summit). On the protected sections of the top half of the climb there are some unusual metal tubes on some of the wires which may be useful to hold onto, though they impede the movement of your karabiners along the wire.

The route starts with a short wire, then a walk up to the left; this is followed by a stemple pitch and a short ladder. About an hour into the ferrata there is a steep chimney with some interesting, well-protected moves up a series of stemples. Wires and (on un-wired sections) waymarks lead up a series of gullies, rock faces and traverses, arriving at a gap below Punta Civetta after about 2½ hours of climbing. Waymarks continue from the gap, with some very exposed moves along an unprotected ledge leading around to the right to the narrow ridge connecting Punta Civetta to Punta Tissi. From here there is one of the most spectacular vertical views you will see on any ferrata all the way down to Alleghe, 2000m below on the west side with Val di Zoldo down to the east. About 30 minutes from the gap a sign indicates an escape route (the only one apart from reversing the ferrata) traversing off to the left to Rifugio Torrani in case of 'Brutto tempo' (severe weather!). Cima Civetta is also signed one hour to the summit from this point, with more unprotected than protected scrambling ahead before you arrive at the summit in about 4½ hours from Rif. Coldai.

Your descent follows waymarks down the Via Normale on steep, friable rock, generally without any ferrata protection, to Rif. Torrani. You continue down Via Normale to join the Sentiero Tivan at 2217m and a return north to Rif. Coldai in about 4 hours. Though it is well waymarked throughout, 'via normale' is somewhat of a misnomer as almost every kind of scree, loose rock, unprotected downclimbing and wired ferrata is encountered on its 1000m descent! ▶

Overall this is a very demanding day; it is long, has considerable exposure, is committing with limited escape potential and it climbs to 3220m. At this altitude it goes without saying that the route is subject to snow and icing in cold weather at any time of the summer and is not recommended in those conditions. **The Alleghesi route should only be undertaken by experienced climbers who have a good level of fitness.**

AGORD 2:
VIA FERRATA ATTILIO TISSI – CIVETTA

Grade:	4
Seriousness:	C
Departure point:	Rifugio Vazzoler, 1714m
To Rif. Torrani:	
Ascent:	1400m
Descent:	1980m
Via ferrata:	400m
To Civetta summit:	
Ascent:	1640m
Descent:	2220m
Via ferrata:	400m
Approximate timings:	4–5 hours Ascent from Rif. Vazzoler to Rif. Torrani, Civetta summit 1½ hours up and down. Descent from Rif. Torrani to Cap. Trieste 4 hours.
Highest altitude:	2984m, Rif. Torrani (or Civetta summit, 3220m)

VF Tissi is a classic high-mountain route: it is a serious undertaking requiring a good level of fitness and stable weather conditions.

This route can be climbed and down-climbed on its own in a single day from Rif. Vazzoler. Alternatively VF Tissi could be combined with VF Alleghesi (AGORD 1) and an ascent of Monte Civetta. Of course VF Tissi could be climbed from Capanna Trieste, but this would make even the ascent to Rif. Toranni, 1850m, a pretty big day! It is best therefore to do the height gain from Capanna Trieste (580m) to Rif. Vazzoler the day before and stay at the *rifugio* overnight.

Early in the season it is highly likely that there will be snow in both the lower and upper parts of the route, and even in the middle of summer there may be some icing in cold weather. Because the original line of the route had become dangerous, a new route was constructed. However, there are still parts of the new route which climb through sections where rock fall is a danger, and concentration, good judgement and a helmet are imperative.

To approach Rif. Vazzoler, turn off the Agordo to Caprile road in Listolade almost opposite Albergo Monte Civetta; there is actually a sign for Rif. Vazzoler. Follow the narrow road which runs through the village of Listolade and continue up to Rif. Capanna Trieste, 1135m (private *rifugio*, bar, restaurant and some accommodation tel. 0437.660122). The road is single track for most of the 4km, but there are fairly regular passing places and it is metalled all the way to Capanna Trieste (the end of the publicly driveable road), where there is ample parking.

The ascent from Rif. Capanna Treiste to Rif. Vazzoler is on a gravel road (path 555); it is a steady climb, as the road is used to supply the *rifugio*, and takes

The start of VF Tissi (AGORD 2)

1¼–1½ hours. After about 1–1¼ hours (and about 15 minutes from Rif. Vazzoler) you pass the point where path 558 goes off to the start of VF Tissi, signed 'Rif. Torranni 4.00 hours'. Rif. Vazzoler, 1714m, is a large *rifugio*, but it is a focal point for some major Civetta climbing routes and can be busy at weekends and in high season (tel. 0437.660008). ▶

From Rif. Vazzoler go back down the approach road to the sign you passed on the way up (less than 15 minutes away): 'Path 558 Van Delle Sasse, Innesto Ferrata Tissi, Innesto Sentiero 557, Rif. M.V. Toranni Ore 4.00'. Follow the path as it climbs up through small pines before levelling out and descending a little as it passes around the steep walls of Torre Trieste. The path now crosses an enormous gully and 5 minutes further on comes to a junction of paths. Van Delle Nevere is signed straight ahead; this leads up to Biv. Ghedini Moiaza and Moiazza Sud (the subject of route AGORD 4,

For information, the signed times from Rif. Vazzoler to other *rifugios* around Monte Civetta are as follows: Rif. Tissi 2 hours; Rif. Coldai 3½ hours, tel. 0437.5234373; Rif. Carestiato 3½ hours (see approach to AGORD 4 below); and the return down to Listolade 2 hours.

95

VF Costantini). For VF Tissi follow the path to the right, which is signed Van delle Sasse.

There is little respite for the next 1½ hours as the path zigzags relentlessly uphill with views back down to Listolade, Rif. Vazzoler and peaks towering all around, with Torre Trieste, on the left, perhaps being the most impressive. After about 45 minutes of climbing the path flattens out in the first of a succession of glacial bowls as it passes to the left (west) of the peak Col Dei Camorz. It is a good path throughout, but so far (except for an occasional green paint mark) has been hardly waymarked at all, and so care is needed in mist, especially when returning downhill. However the path works its way cleverly up a series of scoured vertical walls, with occasional cairns, until at about 2300m things improve with regular orange waymarking.

Continue climbing until, at about 2400m, you arrive in the amazing glacial bowl which is Van delle Sasse. It's easy walking now around and across vast limestone slabs surrounded by peaks, with views which include Cima Di Tome (the location of VF Tissi) and Piccola Civetta (which is above Rif. Toranni). Waymarks lead quite quickly to the well-signed junction of path 558, Forcella delle Sasse, to the right and Ferrata Tissi/Rif. M.V. Toranni, 1hour 30 minutes to the left. Altitude at this point is about 2410m.

Follow a good path as it traverses around the large scree bowl at the head of Van delle Sasse where, as you pass the broken gully where the old route used to go, you appreciate why it was rerouted! VF Tissi now starts under Cima Di Tome at about 2630m; it is indicated with a large red waymark visible from a good distance away. The time from Rif. Vazzoler to the start of the ferrata is 3–3½ hours.

The ferrata has new cabling, but even so some of the bolts are broken, apparently due to rock fall, so be alert all the time, even if there are no other climbers on the route. After a short cable an exposed walk leads to the next cable (possible old snow early season). Good cables now lead left-wards up a wide ramp on good rock but with some water seepage. In cold weather this can be icy, but there are some strategically placed foot-pegs on the ramp for assistance. A short, steep climb up, then right, then up again leads to a ledge after about 30 minutes' climbing. After rain, or if there is still snow melt, be prepared for a shower as you make a rising traverse leftwards for about 5 minutes to another steep wall, climbed with the help of two stemples at about 2750m.

Things are easier now, with another 30–35 minutes' climbing leading to the end of the ferrata. This involves repeat sequences of climbing up and trending left along ledges (passing another potential water course). Ten minutes from the end of the route, after a noticeably airy step, there is a break in the cable, and as you go around the next corner you can see the service lift for Rif. Toranni. After another two short cabled sections the route, which takes 1–1½ hours to climb, ends at about 2900m. If you are only climbing VF Tissi then you

The potentially slippery ramp on VF Tissi (AGORD 2)

may choose to turn around here and head back down to retrace your steps.

From the end of the ferrata Rif. Toranni, 2984m, is a 15–20 minute walk away; this will probably involve a snow crossing well into July. In fact this *rifugio* is only wardened from the middle of July to the end of August. ▶

You have a choice of descents; if you are doing the round-trip from Rif. Vazzoler and back to Capanna Trieste then the reversal of VF Tissi is the best option. From Rif. Toranni to the bottom of the ferrata takes about 1½ hours (less if you did not go all the way up to Rif. Toranni). The return from the bottom of the ferrata to the path junction 558 takes about 30 minutes, and a further hour gets you to the path junction for Van del Nevere and Van delle Sasse. Continuing down, another 15–20 minutes leads to the Rif. Vazzoler approach road junction, and another 45 minutes

Civetta summit
involves another 236m of height gain from Rif. Toranni following waymarks over steep and (in places) quite friable ground. If you are including the summit allow about 1½ hours for the return ascent and descent from Rif. Toranni.

Another **descent option** is to follow the Via Normale from Rif. Torrani (as described in AGORD 1); this will take about an hour longer than reversing the ferrata. Via Normale descends to join the Sentiero Tivan at 2217m, and then to return to Rif. Vazzoler you head south on path 557 before climbing back up to Forcella delle Sasse, 2476m, into Van delle Sasse and back to Rif. Vazzoler, or Capanna Trieste, retracing your ascent route. If you descend the Via Normale route to Sentiero Tivan you could then to go to Rif. Coldai; this takes about 4 hours.

This is an excellent ferrata, but it is a long and sustained climb with a height gain and loss of 1400m (the best climbing is at the top of the route, where the 'variante difficile' justifies a Grade 4; the rest of the route is only Grade 3).

takes you down to Cap. Trieste. Total descent time is at least 4 hours. ◀

Whichever descent option you choose will depend on your fitness, the weather and how many days you want to spend exploring Monte Civetta. From the summit of Civetta you could descend Via Ferrata Alleghesi down to Rif. Coldai, but this would be an incredibly long day, and if combining these two routes it is much better to do it the other way around – ascend Alleghesi first then descend Tissi.

AGORD 3:
VF FIAMME GIALLE – MONTE PELSA

Grade:	4
Seriousness:	B
Departure point:	Bastiani, 971m
Ascent:	1400m
Descent:	1400m
Via ferrata:	500m
Approximate time:	6–8 hours (using direct descent, add 1 hour for alternative descent)
Highest altitude:	2255m, La Palaza Alta

Approach this route by taking a narrow mountain road from Cencenighe to the hamlet of Bastiani at 971m. There are only seven parking spaces in Bastiani, and this limits the number of people on the route.

The via ferrata and path 562 are well waymarked, initially following a dirt road and then on a good path which works its way unremittingly uphill through a beech forest that gives some welcome shade. It continues up steeply through an area of small pine shrubs until reaching some open ground in 50–60 minutes of ascent where 'ferrata' is painted on a large rock. From here there is a narrow path which traverses south along the hillside (descending slightly) to

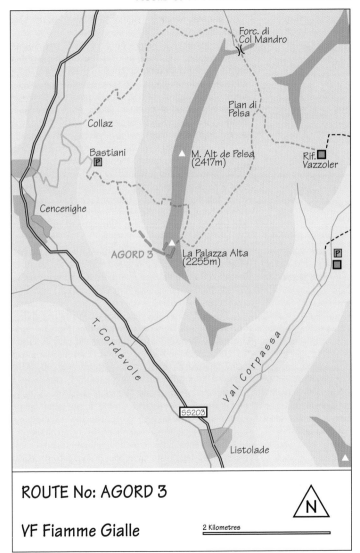

ROUTE No: AGORD 3

VF Fiamme Gialle

N

2 Kilometres

the start of the ferrata in a further 15–20 minutes; this path is quite airy in places and has occasional protection.

The first real section of ferrata is quite easy, taking 20–30 minutes, and this is followed by a further series of ledges. These ledges continue upwards (well waymarked at all times), with occasional short sections of ferrata, and an unpleasant stretch of walking through small pine shrubs in the middle section of the route. (**Note:** a sign is passed at about 1550m, 'Variante facile per discesa'; this is the only escape point, other than route reversal, before the summit.)

The top 300m or so of the route are quite outstanding, with views directly down to the valley 1400m below. The climbing is steep and sustained on solid rock in excellent situations. About 100m from the top the route goes round to the left through a rocky amphitheatre, then a walk up steep ground leads to the final 75m of ferrata. There are two versions of the final climb, one clearly marked 'facile' and the other, further left, 'difficile'. Unless the weather has turned bad or you are very tired, then the *difficile* option is outstanding and not to be missed. On arrival at the summit of La Palazza Alta there is a superb view of Civetta. Total climbing time from Bastiani to the summit is a sustained 4–5 hours.

The direct descent is very steep with some scrambling, but on fairly solid rock; it takes 2–3 hours. From the summit, follow waymarks north through small pine shrubs for 15–20 minutes until open ground is reached at a gap below Mont Alt de Pelsa. The descent down the gully to the left (west) is clearly marked on a large rock, along with a 562 waymark in the gully. The route descends the gully then traverses (even ascends a little at one point) before continuing down another gully with more scrambling down. There is some real exposure here and no protection, so full concentration is required at all times, and for less experienced ferratists a short rope would provide useful insurance. Eventually you return back down to the start of the original starting traverse path and then descend back through the forest on path 562 to Bastiani. Your total descent by this route is about 2–3 hours. ◀

There is an **alternative descent** (longer but easier) which can be made by descending path 562 to the right for about 5 minutes from the summit towards Rif. Vazzoler. At Pian di Pelsa, 1914m, fork left on path 560, then left again on path 567 to Folcella Col Mandro. Continue down on path 567 to the hamlet of Collaz and then on a path back to Bastiani. This route is over an hour longer than the main descent route, taking about 3½–4 hours.

AGORD 4:
VF GIANNI COSTANTINI –
CRESTA DELLE MASENADE

Grade:	5
Seriousness:	C
Departure point:	Passo Duran, 1598m
Ascent:	1530m
Descent:	1530m
Via ferrata:	1500m
Approximate time:	9½–11 hours
Highest altitude:	2878m, Cima Moiazza

This route is serious and committing, needing a high level of fitness and stamina as well as good climbing skills, and (importantly) stable weather conditions. For the complete round-trip from Passo Duran you should allow at least 9½ hours, including an hour to the start of the ferrata, then 5–5½ hours for the ferrata ascent and about 3½ hours for the descent.

From Passo Duran, above Agordo, it's a 45 minute walk to Rif. Carestiato, 1834m, where you could stay overnight and shorten your ascent day (tel. 0437.62949, 38 beds, open mid-June to end September). The start of the ferrata is clearly signposted and is about 15 minutes from the *rifugio* (about 1 hour from Passo Duran). The ferrata starts with a traverse, crossing a narrow bridge and continuing on a rising traverse before heading upwards. ▶ Rock quality here is excellent, and although there are some footholds, the strength and technique requirements of the route immediately let you know that this is top grade! After about an hour of good climbing there is a break in the protection and some uphill walking, with the opportunity to take a break. More good quality climbing leads up, in a further 40 minutes, to a massive U-shaped rock portal, and the route emerges into a large scree bowl with a red-and-white notice indicating that you are at 'Pala del Belia 2295m'.

VF Gianni Costantini is a top-quality and top-grade via ferrata.

Recabling of the start of the route has resulted in the bridge being removed.

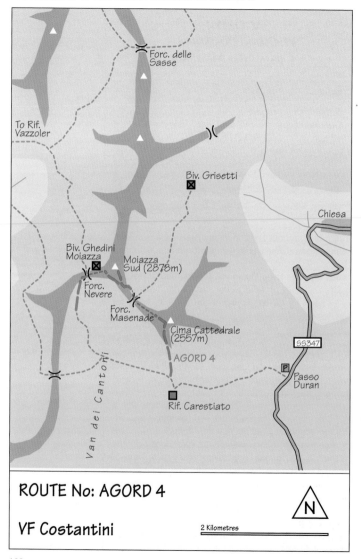

ROUTE No: AGORD 4

VF Costantini

N

2 Kilometres

'Discessa Al Rif. Carestiato' is painted on the rock to the left, although this is hardly a suitable escape route from the ferrata. ▶

This is a popular descent route for climbers after completing routes on the adjoining rock walls.

The ferrata continues up a large open gully on the right (with some loose rock at this point), and in a further 30 minutes leads onto open scree ledges with some exposure and non-continuous protection on this part of the climb. A sign indicates 'Cima Cattedrale 2557m', and waymarks define the route where there are no wires. About 3½ hours' climbing from the start of the ferrata, the summit of Cresta delle Masenade (2704m) is reached.

The route goes along the ridge to Forcella Masenade; it is obvious and waymarked, but there is very little protection, and some very exposed scrambling is required on the ridge's narrowest points. At Forcella delle Masenade (2650m) a path leads down into the scree bowl on the right (north-east) side; this is a potential escape route (back in the direction of Passo Duran) and is signposted to 'Biv. Grisetti 40 minutes'. The traverse of the ridge takes about 30 minutes.

Now follow waymarks on a rising (then level) traverse all the way across a wide sloping slab until, at its end, a path leads down to the right and wire protection (new and very good) begins again. After a short down-sloping ledge to the right a steep, strenuous climb leads out onto open ground, where again the way forward is a waymarked path zigzagging its way up hill. About 30 minutes from Forcella Masenade there is a path junction where a steep rock wall ahead, with wires to the right, leads to the summit of Cima Moiazza. At this point waymarks on the left lead round a corner on the traverse to Forcella delle Nevere; this is the return point after visiting the summit. The final route to the summit is partly wired and partly free scrambling, taking you to the summit of Cima Moiazza after at least 5 hours of fairly sustained climbing from the start of the ferrata. ▶

The round trip to the summit takes about 45 minutes and involves and additional 100m of climbing.

Reverse the final summit section back to the path junction for Forcella delle Nevere and follow the waymarks (on the right coming down) round the corner and along a narrow ledge, passing a sign, onto the Cengia Angelini section of the route. After an initial exposed, unprotected section, the traverse is well protected as it continues on a rising rock ledge. However, protection again is intermittent before the route descends to the left on steep scree, and then traverses further left to arrive at Forcella Nevere (2601m) and the excellent small bivouac hut Ghedini Moiazza (four beds). The descent from the summit of Cima Moiazza to here takes about 1 hour.

From Forcella Nevere the route goes down towards Van Dei Cantoi to the left (south), although it is also possible to follow a path through the scree bowl to the north (this leads to Rif. Vazzoler). Initially the Van Dei Cantoi descent has good wire protection on the right-hand side (looking down) of the valley. As downward progress is made some unprotected scrambling is again required on sloping slabs (with interesting flutings) and scree-covered ledges; this can be quite difficult in places if the rock is wet. Follow cables and waymarks down to a junction with path 554 at about 1780m (for the descent from Forcella Nevere to this junction allow about 1½ hours, with a further 30 minutes on a good path back to Rif. Carestiato). A further 30 minutes leads back down to the road at Passo Duran.

AGORD 5:
VIA FERRATA STELLA ALPINA
(VF EDELWEISS), MONTE AGNER (2872m)

Grade:	5
Seriousness:	C
Departure point:	Rif. Scarpa (1748m), near Frassene
Ascent:	1230m
Descent:	1230m
Via ferrata:	320m (plus 120m on ascent to summit)
Approximate time:	8½ hours (including descent by either VF Canalone, AGORD 6 or Via Normale)
Highest altitude:	2872m, Monte Agner

Via Ferrata Stella Alpina has a richly deserved reputation as one of the real classics, and is amongst the hardest via ferratas.

Although the rock on this route itself is generally very sound, the ascent to the summit of Monte Agner negotiates a great deal of extremely friable rock, much of which is exposed and unprotected, and has poor waymarking. It is, therefore, an excursion to be taken seriously, and should not be undertaken unless the weather is settled. It is best to descend by

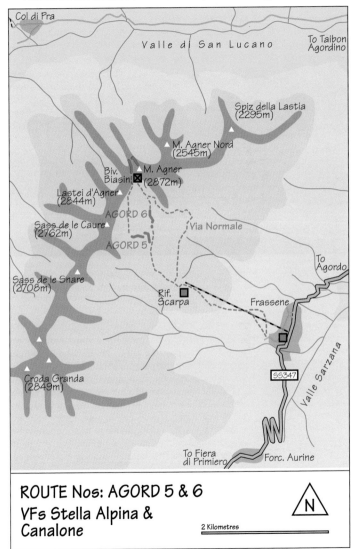

Col di Pra

Valle di San Lucano

To Taibon
Agordino

Spiz della Lastia
(2295m)

M. Agner Nord
(2545m)

Biv.
Biasin
M. Agner
(2872m)

Lastei d'Agner
(2844m)

AGORD 6

Sass de le Caure
(2762m)

Via Normale

AGORD 5

Sass de le Snare
(2708m)

Rif.
Scarpa

Frassene

To
Agordo

Croda Granda
(2849m)

Valle Sarzana

SS347

To Fiera
di Primiero

Forc. Aurine

ROUTE Nos: AGORD 5 & 6
VFs Stella Alpina &
Canalone

N

2 Kilometres

Early morning light on VF Stella Alpina (AGORD 5): the summit of M. Agner is to its right, in the centre of the photo

VF Canalone (see AGORD 6), although you have the option of returning to the *rifugio* by the rather more circuitous Via Normale if the weather is deteriorating.

The approach is from the little village of Frassene, on the road from Agordo to Fiera di Primiero. If you are dependent on public transport, the rather limited bus service from Agordo enables you to reach the village, where you can find accommodation at the hospitable Albergo Belvedere. ◀

Whilst there is a chairlift from Frassene to Rif. Scarpa, which saves nearly 700m of climbing, this is only likely to be running during August, and even this cannot be relied upon, so you will probably decide to stay overnight at the *rifugio* to reduce the amount of walking in a day to an acceptable amount. If you plan to leave your car in the village, note that most of the parking in the main street is time limited, so you should use the car park on the lower road, reached by turning south off the main street at the church.

Rif. Scarpa and Albergo Belvedere are signposted up the same lane from the village. Walk up past the *albergo* through a scatter of new houses for about 400m to a point where the road makes a double hairpin. Don't try to interpret your map

Since summer 2003 the lift has been operating for a more extended season, with promotions which include an all-in price for the lift, a stay in the *rifugio*, and dinner. It would be wise, however, to check that this has continued. Contact the Tourist Office: tel. 0348/4935967 or see website http://web.infinito.it/utenti/s/seggioviafrassene/

too literally here, since the detail has been overtaken by new development, but the path to the *rifugio* begins to the left on the second hairpin, waymarked 771. After a few hundred metres you arrive at a junction, where the *rifugio* is signposted off to the left (the main path continues straight ahead, and also goes to the *rifugio*, but by a slightly more circuitous route which is becoming quite badly eroded in places). Allow about 1½ hours from the village to the *rifugio*, which occupies a pleasant sunny position, with an excellent view of Monte Agner and the ferrata. ▶

From the *rifugio* (1748m), take the signposted path for Ferrata Stella Alpina, north-west towards the wall of rocks below Lastei d'Agner and Sass de le Caure. After about 15 minutes, fork left onto a minor track by a very large boulder on the left. ▶

The path now traverses along the foot of the wall, passing a large cave a little before a signpost directs you to the left. Mustard-yellow waymarks now take you to the start of the cable, which you reach about 45 minutes from leaving the *rifugio*. Whilst the cable starts here (about 1955m), this is fairly recently installed and safeguards previously unprotected scrambling leading to the start of the route proper. This initial scrambling is very easy, and you will be in no doubt when you reach the start of the route itself, within 5 or 10 minutes (at about 2060m), as it tackles near vertical rock from the outset.

The route begins with a short traverse before going up a 5m wall, well supplied with holds, but vertical and strenuous. The angle falls back briefly for an ascending right-hand traverse in a shallow cleft. You then reach a short chimney, which can be awkward unless you move out onto its lip to use the peg on the adjoining wall. A short, easily angled rake now leads to a steep crack and then onto an airy leftward traverse (at about 2130m), which then turns up into a steep ascending traverse again in a very airy position, but proving to be rather easier than it looks from below. The leftward traverse continues for another few metres, now undulating somewhat, before the next vertical passage. The angle then falls back slightly for a sustained passage of extremely pleasant climbing up a very exposed groove, always on good holds.

This brings you (at about 2235m) to the foot of the final demanding passage, another very steep wall, this time of

Before you set out to make your climb, take the advice of the signpost a few metres from the *rifugio*, and register your plan for the day with the warden, who takes care to ensure that everyone is safely back from the mountain.

Note that, in addition to a sign for Ferrata Stella Alpina, there is a painted sign on the boulder for **Ferrata Edelweiss** – the German form of the name is as commonly used in northern Italy as the Italian form.

about 40m. From a few metres below, this wall looks vertical and very hard, although when you confront it the angle is less severe than first appeared, and good holds are evident throughout its length, as are three pegs to boost you up an awkwardly bulging section near the top. It is, however, fairly strenuous, so gather your strength before embarking on the initial broad crack. A good-sized ledge provides you with the chance of a breather just below the half-way point, and a final burst of energy takes you over the bulge and on to more easily angled rock, which marks the end of the technical difficulties. You reach the end of the route (at about 2275m) some 1¾ hours after starting to climb, although you still have a long way to go to the summit of Monte Agner, including quite a lot more cable climbing.

*Climber on
VF Stella Alpina
(AGORD 5)*

You are now on the broad and quite well-vegetated slabs of the eastern flank of Sass de le Caure and Lastei d'Agner. The route takes a generally northern course across the gently sloping slabs, waymarked with mustard-yellow paint. The first few minutes of easy scrambling are quite airy and on rather friable rock: indeed, you soon pass a painted sign reading 'Guardate e non toccate' (roughly 'Beware of the loose rock'). Biv. Giancarlo Biasin (2650m) soon comes into sight, albeit briefly, although pay close attention to the waymarking, since it would be easy to stray off course in this area. A small forcella, at about 2500m, is one of the few notable features in this landscape, beyond which you continue to climb gradually over the easy, slabby rock towards Forcella del Pizzon and the bivacco.

You reach the forcella (2623m) about 1½ hours after finishing the ferrata. ▶ Biv. Giancarlo Biasin (2650m) is now a short scramble above you, but take care, since the position is exposed and the rock is very friable.

From the bivacco (2650m), the path for the summit follows a circuitous and gently angled course round to the north. The first stretch of cable is encountered almost immediately, although this is little more than a reassuring handrail for a rather airy scramble, and then a lengthy traverse. The cable continues intermittently, although some particularly exposed sections remain unprotected and potentially hazardous, given the amount of loose material overlaying smooth, slabby rock. The waymarking also needs close attention, particularly at a shoulder at about 2750m, where a line of cairns marches off invitingly towards a snowfield straight ahead. The route, cabled for a time, turns up to the right here and is easily missed.

You eventually reach the summit of Monte Agner, at 2872m, about an hour after leaving the bivacco. The view is stunning, with many of the major mountain groups on display. Interestingly, the cross which you will have spotted from the *rifugio* is several hundred metres away, and some 50m below you, and should be visited for the view down into the valley. ▶

From the forcella the view to the north is dramatic, and you may well find yourself keeping company with a group of *camosci* (chamois) which are often to be seen here. They are an unusually bold family, some wearing collars with small radio transmitters to enable their movements to be tracked.

For the route back to the valley, see AGORD 6, below.

AGORD 6:
VIA FERRATA CANALONE

Grade:	2
Seriousness:	C
Departure point:	summit of Monte Agner (2872m)
Ascent:	not applicable
Descent:	1120m
Via ferrata:	270m
Approximate time:	3½ hours (plus time taken to ascend to summit)
Highest altitude:	2872m, Monte Agner

This route was formerly known as Via del Nevaio, a name you might come across on some older maps.

Since this route is normally used in descent from the summit of Monte Agner, after climbing VF Stella Alpina (see AGORD 5), this is how it is described. It is, however, an entirely feasible ascent route for climbers of rather less ambition or experience who would like to visit a fine summit.

The descent from Monte Agner to Bivacco Giancarlo Biasin, which takes about 45 minutes, involves reversing the ascent route (described in AGORD 5), and requires just as much care. Once back down to the bivacco, rather than continuing to the forcella, follow the waymarked descent route beginning just by the doorway of the building, on its south side. This takes you down over easy but friable rock, with a great deal of loose material, which requires care. About 40 minutes after leaving the bivacco (at about 2450m), the Via Normale and the path to VF Canalone part company. This is quite easy to miss, particularly in poor visibility, so look out for the sign painted on the rocks when you think you are getting close. The Via Normale heads off to the south-east, towards slightly easier terrain, but involves a circuitous trip back to the *rifugio*, taking about 30 minutes longer than VF Canalone. It is a suitable alternative if the weather is deteriorating or if you are tired of cables.

The more exciting option is to continue down the broken rocks, following the waymarks as they lead closer to the gully opening up to your right (in descent). It is, nonetheless, a full 45 minutes from the junction before the start of the cable (at about 2170m). The only difficult passage is encountered fairly quickly and involves a rather tight chimney, about 7m in height. The route, intermittently protected, then traverses to the right (facing out), then to the left, as it gradually drops towards the gully floor. Whilst the climbing is never too difficult, the terrain is very shattered in places, and the route frequently involves exposed, unprotected scrambling on loose material, so this is no place to become careless. A fairly lengthy, unbroken stretch of cable now leads down over scree covered terraces and a broken buttress to the floor of the gully (about 2000m). Those ascending the route should watch out for a wooden sign here, reading 'Variante Attrezzata'.

You might encounter some old snow here, but the angle is easy and you only have a narrow tongue to cross to reach the grassy slope on the other side. Follow the path running south along the foot of the great rock ramparts of Lastei d'Agner. You soon encounter a further sign, painted on a boulder, which reads 'ADS Variante Attrezzata' to confirm the route if you are ascending. It is now a straightforward walk back to the *rifugio*, which you should reach about 45 minutes after finishing the ferrata descent.

AGORD 7:
Sentiero del Dottor, Forcella dell'Orsa

Grade:	2
Seriousness:	C
Departure point:	Col di Pra, Valle di San Lucano
Ascent:	1800m
Descent:	1800m
Via ferrata:	800m
Approximate time:	8 hours
Highest altitude:	2520m, Forcella del Miel

Whilst this is not a particularly hard via ferrata, it is a long, tiring and committing itinerary. Although it is generally well way-marked, route-finding is difficult in poor weather, so it should only be tackled in settled weather conditions.

The upper parts of the route, particularly between Passo di Canali and Forcella del Miel, can hold snow quite late in the season, which can obscure waymarking. Consequently, if you arrive at the start of the cabled section and find more than relatively small cones of old snow, you should think seriously about proceeding, since there will be much more snow 1000m higher up! Having said that, it is a super day out in grand and lonely mountain terrain, so if the conditions are right, it is well worth including in your climbing programme.

The route is approached up Valle di San Lucano, which runs westwards from the main Cordevole valley from Taibon Agordino. ▶

A car is essential for this route, since the limited bus service terminates at Villanova, about 6km down the valley. Drive to the hamlet of Col di Pra (843m), where there is ample parking (although avoid the area reserved for customers of the bar). The via ferrata is signposted in front of the

The name of one of its subsidiary settlements, Villanova, is revealing. It was built as a replacement for the original settlement which was totally destroyed by a landslide in 1908. You will notice a fountain at the roadside, bearing the insignia of the CAI, who erected it to commemorate the 33 people who died.

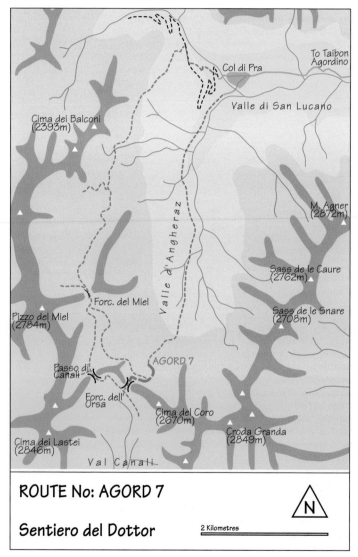

To Taibon
Agordino

Col di Pra

Valle di San Lucano

Cima dei Balconi
(2393m)

M. Agner
(2872m)

Valle d'Angheraz

Sass de le Caure
(2762m)

Forc. del Miel

Pizzo del Miel
(2784m)

Sass de le Snare
(2708m)

AGORD 7

Passo di
Canali

Forc. dell'
Orsa

Cima del Coro
(2670m)

Cima dei Lastei
(2846m)

Croda Granda
(2849m)

Val Canali

ROUTE No: AGORD 7

Sentiero del Dottor

N

2 Kilometres

bar, up the gravel track way-marked 767. The track is initially good, but the surface gradually deteriorates to a rougher path as you climb above the river on your left. The waymarking includes splashes of mustard-yellow paint as well as the normal red and white; this becomes significant higher up, where two routes separate (see below). You are climbing through trees at this stage, and after crossing a dry streambed (about 1290m) you pass through a particularly pleasant area of beech woodland. In another 5 minutes you reach a further, much wider dry riverbed on the left.

The path takes a sharp right turn here, so don't be misled by the waymarking which appears to direct you across to the other side. In the course of the next 20 minutes or so you cross and re-cross yet another dry stream bed, and then eventually find yourself following waymarks up its right-hand side. At about 1380m, you reach a large boulder in the riverbed, with old painted lettering reading 'FER'. You can now see the headwall of the valley, with a path zigzagging up to an obvious diagonal crack: this is the line of Sentiero del Dottor. The waymarking continues up the dried-up stream, then up the steep, eroded slope to the start of the first cable, at about 1545m, some 2 hours after setting out.

Approaching Forc. dell'Orsa, on Sentiero del Dottor (AGORD 7)

The cable takes you up the slabby wall to the right of the crack you spotted from below. The rock is generally good and well supplied with holds, so the climbing is never too demanding. You reach the first short ladder after about 30m of climbing. This leads to more straightforward climbing up the side of the crack, and then to a good ledge. The angle of the wall eases for a few metres until, after a rising traverse to the left, you come to a steeper passage. This contains three further short ladders, although the wall is still well provided with good holds. As the angle falls back again, a rightward ascending traverse leads onto much easier rock; the technical difficulties, such as they are, are now behind you, and you can enjoy easy scrambling up the broken face. The exposure, however, is still quite considerable, so the protective cable continues for a further 50m or so. The climb to this point will take you about 30 minutes. Further cabled passages occur higher up, although these are little more than reassuring handrails. You should, however, keep your gear on and take advantage of the protection, since this is an area where stone fall is always possible.

It is a further 600m of pleasant walking, interspersed with easy scrambling, intermittently protected, to reach Forcella dell'Orsa. Follow the waymarking carefully through the dramatic rock scenery, crossing and recrossing the gully. About 45 minutes after finishing the main climbing passage, you arrive at the foot of a rock wall with the altitude '1920' painted on it in red. Another 20 minutes of scrambling brings you to the first of two large boulders with painted waymarking (the first occurs at about 2060m, the second at about 2085m). Each indicates both Forcella dell'Orsa and Forcella del Miel off to the right. It is easier to ignore the first boulder, but follow the waymarking on the second, because you will probably encounter snow in this location, and you might be able to traverse across the slope above it.

You should also note that Forcella dell'Orsa is painted in red, whilst Forcella del Miel is in the same mustard yellow that you encountered several hours earlier. The reason for the colour scheme becomes apparent about 10 minutes further on. Just beyond a slope which will be carpeted with wild flowers, if you are lucky with your timing, you enter a shallow gully. Here, the mustard yellow markings go to the right (west), whilst the red-and-white waymarks, which you should follow, take a route somewhat to the left on a south-westerly course. A further 30 minutes of easy scrambling brings you to the last of the cable (about 2290m), which leads up to Forcella dell'Orsa (2330m, about 4 hours since you set out). There are superb views back down the way you have climbed, but now also to the south into Val Canali. Don't be confused by the altitude figure of 2672m painted on the rock at your side: this relates to the height of Cima del Coro (though maps show 2670m), to the south-east.

Whilst you can safely pack your ferrata gear away now, you still have a good deal of climbing before you finally start your descent. Start down the unpleasantly eroded slope towards Val Canali. You need to drop about 50m before you can turn right (west) at the foot of a rock wall to escape the gully. You can now see your path, below and to your right, so cross over the slope to join it and head for Passo di Canali, following waymarkings for path 707 up to this next forcella in about 20 minutes. Maps record the height as 2469m, but this is higher than the authors' reading, so it is perhaps not a good place to re-calibrate your altimeter.

Follow the signposts to Forcella del Miel, Col di Pra and Taibon, waymarked 707/705. The path takes you down into a large, oval-shaped depression, and then on to a low point of about 2325m before you start to climb once more. About 25 minutes after leaving Passo di Canali, you reach a large boulder (about 2410m) with red, green and mustard-yellow writing, most of it too faded to read. This is where the paths, which separated earlier, rejoin, the mustard course having missed out your last two forcellas. Forcella del Miel is now only 10 minutes away and, at a claimed altitude of 2520m, is the highest point of your itinerary (although, again, our reading suggested this to be generous). Whatever the figure, it will have taken you about 1½ hours since leaving Forcella dell'Orsa, but you can now finally say you are starting your descent.

Follow the path signposted to Col di Pra, waymarked 705, down into a huge expanse of limestone pavement, quite broken and tilted at an angle of some 20 degrees. The waymarking twists and turns to follow the easiest course, so keep your eyes open or you could find yourself backtracking to rejoin the route. This section takes about 40 minutes and brings you to a large, grassy bowl (Casera, 1866m), beyond which you can see the start of the trees below. Once in the trees, the path initially descends in an easily angled traverse before steepening markedly for the final few hundred metres of descent. You reach a gravel road (spot height 1098m), where you turn right (south-east) for a couple of hundred metres before taking a path to the left into the trees to cut off a hairpin bend in the road. Your path crosses the road once more before you finally reach the outskirts of Col di Pra, about 2½ hours after leaving Forcella del Miel. Have a well-deserved drink at the village bar and relive what will have been a memorable mountain day!

AGORD 8:
SENTIERO GIANNI MIOLA

Grade:	not applicable (see text)
Seriousness:	C
Departure point:	Valle di San Lucano, near Taibon Agordino
Ascent:	1750m
Descent:	1670m
Via ferrata:	see text
Approximate time:	8½ hours
Highest altitude:	2210m, Bivacco Bedin

This is the second route in this area which has caused tensions between local hunting interests and the climbing fraternity. The nearby Via Ferrata Miola was dismantled several years ago, and now this protected *sentiero* has also become unusable as a result of the removal of signposting and equipment. The current (2004) advice of the local section of CAI is not to attempt the route at the moment, but it is worth making local enquiries in the future to see if the issues have been resolved, since it is a fine itinerary in splendid mountain terrain. If and when the route is reopened, it will be a serious undertaking. It is a very long and committing itinerary, and very little used. In no circumstances should it be attempted in uncertain weather.

The route is best tackled from south to north, starting from Valle di San Lucano, just west of the pleasant little village of Taibon Agordino. The transport logistics need considering, since the route finishes about 10km further north, at Pradimezzo, near Cencenighe. If a second car is available,

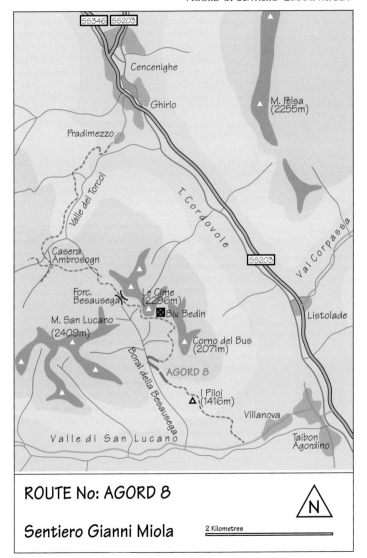

ROUTE No: AGORD 8

Sentiero Gianni Miola

2 Kilometres

this could be left at Pradimezzo to be collected later; there are a few car spaces at the entrance to the hamlet. A better alternative would be to use the local bus services. A conveniently early bus leaves Agordo at 0742, passes through Taibon, and terminates at Villanova, a few hundred metres short of the starting point. For the return journey to Agordo, there are buses from Ghirlo (on the main road, about 400m south of the junction for Pradimezzo) at 1725 and 1830. Check times locally for any variation from season to season.

The day begins most inauspiciously. Path 765, to Bivacco Bedin and Casera Ambrosogn, heads into an old quarry, now the town's rubbish tip! This turns sharp left behind a small office building on the left, goes on through one of several rubbish storage areas, and continues up to the right. The way is soon barred by a steel gate, although it is easy to walk round it if it is locked. A faint waymark at the foot of the left-hand gatepost confirms that you are on the right route. Continue up the track for another few minutes until a small path strikes off to the left into the woods (about 770m).

The route is frequently quite difficult to follow, but goes generally north-westwards, and eventually into the floor of Boral della Besausega, an impressive gully cutting deep into the Pale di San Lucano mountains. This is where the protected passage was located.

The route now continues to the west of, and below, Corno del Bus, and onto the lonely plateau, through impressive rocky scenery, to Bivacco Bedin (2210m, and about 4½ hours after setting out), which is suitable for emergency accommodation only. The views of the surrounding mountain groups are quite stunning along these higher sections of the route. A gentle descent now takes you to Forcella Besausega (2131m), which marks the end of the more serious part of the itinerary. An initially fairly steep descent leads to a descending traverse across the tree-covered slopes above Valle del Torcol, near the head of which you pick up path 764, which meanders pleasantly along the north-west side of the valley down to Pradimezzo, where you might have been able to leave a second car. Allow about 3½ hours for the descent to here from Biv. Bedin. If you are relying on the bus to take you back, continue on down to the main road, turn right towards Agordo, and walk for about 400m to the nearest bus stop, just before you enter Ghirlo.

BELLUNO

Map
(all routes) Tabacco Carta Topographica 1:25,000 Sheet 024

Tourist Information Office
APT Belluno, Piazza Duomo, 2, 32100 Belluno
Tel: 0437.94300
Fax: 0437.94350
E-mail: info@dolomiti.it
Internet: http://www.dolomiti.it/eng and select Belluno

Belluno is a thriving town at the head of the 'Prealps'. It is close to the motorway from Venice and is a major centre for bus and rail connections. To the north-west are the Schiara mountains, where you will find the five routes in this section.

Belluno is a major commercial centre, and its outlying areas sport the usual collection of ugly out-of-town retail outlets. The historic centre is, however, of considerable interest and great beauty, with many public buildings displaying the lion of St Mark, demonstrating the town's links

Sunset on the Schiara, seen from Rif. Scarpa, above Frassene

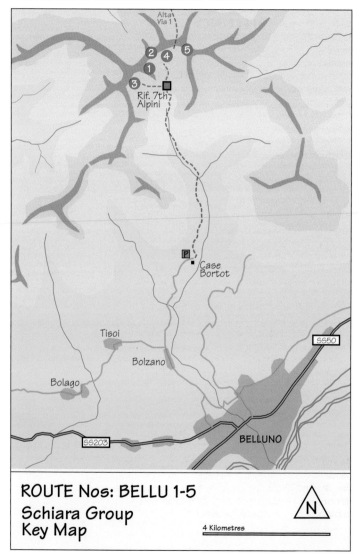

ROUTE Nos: BELLU 1-5
Schiara Group
Key Map

4 Kilometres

N

with the Venetian Republic. There is a Tourist Information Office in the centre, and a good range of shops, banks and restaurants, although the town functions mainly as a commercial centre for the region, rather than as a focus for tourism. Consequently, hotel facilities are fairly limited and quite expensive. If you do want a base in the valley, then perhaps the best option is the Albergo Mirella, in the northern suburbs, which is well located to approach the Schiara group (Via Don Minzoni 6, tel. 0437-942039). The nearest campsite is Camping Sarathei, 32016 Farra D Alpago (BL), tel/fax 0437.46996, 19km to the east of Belluno.

Most climbers base themselves at Rif. 7th (pronounced 'settimo') Alpini, which is about 2½ hours' walk from the roadhead at Case Bortot. A large parking area is to be found 20m further on at the start of the track up to the *rifugio* (incidentally, whilst maps still indicate the existence of a bar and restaurant here, this closed some time ago).

Since all these routes involve an ascent to either a summit or a high forcella, it is customary to combine them, one with another, in any number of permutations. As most climbers want to complete as many routes as possible during their time in the mountains, this guidebook includes two different itineraries, which enable all five routes to be climbed in just two days. Needless to say, there is much scope for improvisation if you want to work out a different itinerary for your trip through these beautiful mountains.

It is worth adding that the Schiara, the point where the Dolomites begin to drop to the plain to the south, are prone to afternoon storms accompanied by torrential rain. Consequently, an early start is advisable.

Itinerary 1 (Bellu 1, 2 & 3)

Ascend VF Zacchi to Biv. Bernardina, climb to the summit of Monte Schiara by ascending, and then reversing, VF Berti, then descend VF Sperti. Allow up to 9 hours for the whole itinerary, but see details of the individual routes if you wish to combine them in different permutations.

BELLU 1:
VIA FERRATA ZACCHI

Grade:	3
Seriousness:	B
Departure point:	Rif. 7th Alpini (1498m)
Ascent:	820m (from *rifugio* to Biv. Bernardina)
Descent:	dependent on choice of route
Via ferrata:	700m (of which 75% is protected)
Approximate time:	2½ hours (from *rifugio* to Biv. Bernardina, plus allowance for choice of descent route)
Highest altitude:	2320m, Biv. Bernardina

Whilst this was the first via ferrata to be constructed in the Schiara group as long ago as 1952, it sets a standard, in terms of interest, that more recent routes have been unable to match.

Of the three ferratas which ascend to the ridge, this one offers the most sustained climbing. Consequently, you should ensure that you use this route as the means of ascent to the ridge, and one of the other routes to return to the *rifugio*.

The path from the *rifugio*, which is clearly signed and way-marked 503, takes about 45 minutes. As you approach the rock wall, you will notice a large tunnel-shaped recess, blackened by running water. This is Il Porton (about 1770m), which marks the start of the route. Interestingly, in the back of the recess is a mural, now quite badly damaged by water, but apparently extolling the virtues of Faith, Hope and Charity.

The cable, which starts just to the right of Il Porton, was renewed in the summer of 2001 and offers faultless protection throughout the route. The first 10m or so involve an ascending right-hand traverse over quite broken rock, well supplied with good holds. As you round the corner you enter a gully, about 4m high, which is ascended with the aid of a couple of short ladders. This can be rather wet after rain. You are now in a ravine, out of which the cable traverses left on a small shelf. A steep little wall follows, also equipped with ladders, leading into a groove and then a deeper cleft. This is initially ascended on the right wall, then the left wall, both quite steep and slightly strenuous (at about 1830m). A break in the cable follows, whilst you zigzag easily up a

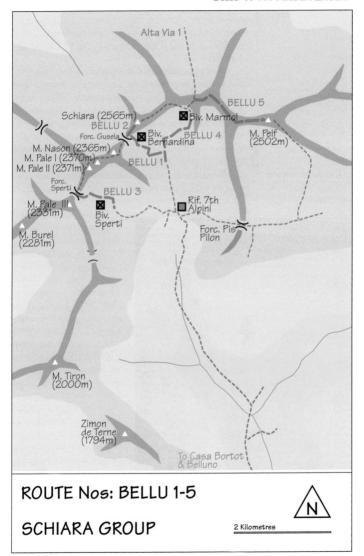

ROUTE Nos: BELLU 1-5

SCHIARA GROUP

2 Kilometres

N

gravel path to a junction (about 1860m). This is the point where VF Marmol turns off to the right (north-east), and is described in BELLU 4 (see Itinerary 2), but VF Zacchi continues to the left.

A few more minutes of easy walking follow before the cable resumes to protect some airy climbing above a deep ravine to the right. A short but steep chimney follows (about 1920m), which marks the end of the cable for a few minutes. The protection resumes at about 1990m, although the climbing is again straightforward, but occasionally airy. The imposing pinnacle of Gusela del Vescova comes into view during this passage of climbing, after which some airy walking follows. The next section of cable safeguards a steep groove, also equipped with several stemples. You are now on the upper wall and reaching the most interesting parts of the route.

The Gusela pinnacle marks the end of VF Zacchi (BELLU 1)

A very exposed rightward traverse follows (at about 2170m), which involves laying back off a metal handrail. This takes you to the foot of the 'Diagonale', a steep rib of about 60m, leaning off to the right. Whilst this is very exposed, it is not unduly difficult and is equipped with ladders in its steeper sections. A left-hand traverse follows, along Cengia Zacchi (Zacchi Ledge, at about 2300m), a distinctive feature of the rock wall which can be readily picked out from below, since it traverses straight to the foot of the Gusela pinnacle. The traverse is initially no more than a stroll, but soon becomes very airy. However, Biv. Bernardina (2320m) is now in view, marking the end of the route. Like the other two bivaccos in the Schiara, this is well equipped and provides excellent shelter in the event that you are caught out in one of the frequent afternoon storms which afflict the area. ▶

BELLU 2:
VIA FERRATA BERTI

Grade:	3
Seriousness:	C
Departure point:	Biv. Bernardina
Ascent:	245m
Descent:	dependent on choice of route
Via ferrata:	300m (of which less than 50% is protected)
Approximate time:	1 hour (from bivacco to Monte Schiara, plus allowance for choice of descent route. Allow 45 minutes to reverse route back to bivacco)
Highest altitude:	2565m, Monte Schiara

Having climbed to the bivacco by VF Zacchi, you now have the opportunity of an ascent to the high point of the Schiara. The trip to and from the summit by this ferrata takes less than 2 hours, but is a fairly serious undertaking, given the extent of exposed and unprotected scrambling on distinctly friable rock.

Follow the painted waymarking to 'Cima' and 'Schiara' just by the bivacco. The waymarking is quite good throughout, but care is needed, since it would be easy to stray off course. Less than half of the climb is equipped with a protective cable, since the angle is generally quite gentle and the scrambling easy. The steeper passages, which are protected, are sometimes equipped with ladders, which make for a straightforward ascent, with the exception of the first one you reach. This is the passage of the climb which earns the

Note: a few metres short of the bivacco, painted waymarking points up to the right, indicating 'Cima' and 'Schiara'. This marks the start of VF Berti, the continuation of this itinerary (see below). Two other routes begin here also: to the left (south-west) is VF Sperti, which we will come to shortly, whilst to the north-west path 503 heads down to Rif. Bianchet, near the head of Val Vescova.

There are only limited difficulties on this route, and with care and good luck with the weather you will enjoy superb views through 180 degrees.

route its grade. A short but steep ladder leads to an awkward move up to the right, which tends to throw you out of balance and requires a bit of muscle to pull out over the top. Needless to say, this is rather more awkward in descent. The route does not entirely follow the ridge line, avoiding the minor eminence of Cresta Ovest on its south side.

The summit is a grand spot, but you still have about 5 hours to go if you are following the suggested itinerary. There is, however, a fine alternative which you might wish to consider. From the summit, an easy path follows the ridge northeast down to Forcella Marmol. This would be the route to take if you were descending by VF Marmol (see BELLU 4) or wanting to make the traverse over to Monte Pelf by the Guardiano route (BELLU 5). It would also enable a connection to be made to Alta Via 1, if you were making for points north. The itinerary below, however, assumes that you will now reverse the route you followed in ascent and continue on VF Sperti.

BELLU 3:
VIA FERRATA SPERTI

Grade:	3
Seriousness:	B
Departure point:	Biv. Bernardina
Ascent:	100m
Descent:	920m (from Biv. Bernardina to Rif. 7th Alpini)
Via ferrata:	1400m (of which about 50% is protected)
Approximate time:	4¾ hours (plus allowance for choice of ascent to Biv. Bernardina)
Highest altitude:	on Pale del Balcon, about 2370m

VF Sperti is here described in descent.

Whilst this itinerary assumes that you are following this route from east to west along the Pale del Balcon and then descending to Rif. 7th Alpini, you might care to devise your own plans, in which case it is a simple matter to follow these notes in reverse. However, you should add about an hour to the estimated timing given above, since this assumes the speedier progress possible in descent.

The cable begins just to the side of the bivacco and leads down towards the forcella, on the other side of which is the Gusela del Vescova pinnacle. Like VF Berti, this is a route with few significant difficulties, much of which is unprotected walking or scrambling. It is, however, quite a lengthy undertaking, with the traverse of Pale del Balcon undulating endlessly from one forcella to the next. The waymarking is generally good, although it would be easy to wander off line if you were too engrossed in the spectacular scenery. Whilst you initially follow a line on the south side of the ridge, around the minor peak of Nason, the rest of the route sticks to the north side, which also offers better views.

About 1¼ hours after leaving Biv. Bernardina, during which only the steeper passages have been protected, you arrive at the start of an obviously sustained descent. This is Forcella Sperti, at 2250m, and the point where the route begins the long descent to the *rifugio*. The first 130m or so follow the line of a great cleft, involving several quite steep sections, some of which are equipped with ladders. You then arrive at the start of a long traverse to the east (left, looking out in descent), which starts as an innocuous terrace but soon becomes a very airy ledge. This winds its way, at about 2100m, across the face of the Torre Bianchet, the great buttress running down from the summit of Pala II. The traverse is about 400m in length before the descent resumes, now over easy ground, much of which requires no protection.

A little over an hour after leaving Forcella Sperti you arrive at Biv. Sperti, on a grassy shoulder at 2000m. Whilst this is not the end of the route, all the main difficulties are now behind you. The protection is once again intermittent, although the rock is now much more friable, as the route winds its way through a maze of little pinnacles and gullies, always at a very easy angle. A distinctive feature, at about 1935m, is a 'pair of eyes' through the rock on your right as you pass through a shallow gully. You now know that you are nearing the end of the route, with the last length of cable occurring at about 1850m, some 4 hours after leaving Biv. Bernardina. Whilst you now have no more than a pleasant walk on path 504 back to the *rifugio*, you might want to keep your gear on for another 20 minutes or so, since you will encounter an isolated wire safeguarding the descent into, and then out of, a steep stream bed at about 1620m. Allow about ¾ hour back to the *rifugio*.

Itinerary 2 (Bellu 4 & 5)

Ascend VF Marmol to Forcella Marmol, then climb Monte Pelf by Sentiero Attrezzato Guardiano. Return to Rif. 7th Alpini by Sentieri 511 and 505 over Forcella Pis Pilon. Allow up to 8 hours for this whole itinerary, but see details of the individual routes if you wish to combine them in different permutations.

BELLU 4:
VIA FERRATA MARMOL

Grade:	3
Seriousness:	B
Departure point:	Rif. 7th Alpini
Ascent:	850m (from Rif. 7th Alpini to Forcella Marmol)
Descent:	90m (plus allowance for choice of descent route)
Via ferrata:	600m (of which 75% is protected)
Approximate time:	2½ hours (plus allowance for choice of descent route)
Highest altitude:	about 2350m, above Forcella Marmol

This itinerary combines two routes of very different character, the most recent to be constructed in the Schiara, which combine to make an unforgettable traverse.

The Marmol route is generally quite straightforward (and indeed, is designated as a section of Alta Via 1), whilst Sentiero Guardiano (BELLU 5) is a much stiffer prospect. Both have fairly long sections of unprotected walking.

VF Marmol was completed in 1967, and follows a line from a point some 90m up VF Zacchi to Forcella. Marmol. Consequently, for the approach from the *rifugio* and the first 25 minutes or so of climbing, refer to BELLU 1.

From the junction (1860m), follow the signpost and waymarks off to the right (north) for Ferrata Marmol. The ledge you are following leads across the back of a ravine. This is clearly no place to linger after heavy rain, since the recently replaced protection is already damaged by stone fall. An easily angled broad rib now takes you up to a broken slab, the upper part of which is equipped with a ladder on the right. This brings you to what is probably the hardest passage of the climb (at about 1935m), an awkward and

exposed move round a cor-
ner to the right, followed by
an equally exposed and quite
long traverse, on which you
need to lay back off metal
handrails. The traverse takes
you into the flat bottom of a
broad gully.

You have been climbing
for perhaps an hour, and are
now at the first place where
you might miss the route. The
gully leads up to your left,
very broken and at an easy
angle, and is an attractive
point of weakness in the rock
here. However, the route
takes a less obvious line
opposite you, so look out for
the waymarks up the start of
the easy angled diagonal
crack, where the cable
resumes shortly. The angle
drops back still further, and
the cable becomes intermittent until you reach steeper
and more sustained climbing
for a time, although still with no real difficulties.

*On the extended
traverse of VF Marmol
(BELLU 4)*

The route reverts to little more than occasionally protected walking now, with no passages of particular note, save for
the distinctive rectangular cave up to your left, at about
2120m. About 25m higher, you come to another distinctive
point, a small forcella with striking views. A cable leads up
easy rock on your left, and you begin a passage of particularly pleasant and easy climbing up very good rock, although
some parts run with water, and could be icy early in the season. Biv. Marmol (2260m) comes into view about now, mostly an easy walk away, but with protection to safeguard a section of smooth slabs just before the building. This occupies a
pleasant grassy shoulder and, like the other bivaccos in the
Schiara, is well equipped for an impromptu stop. A longer,
planned stop might be a problem, however, since there is no

obvious source of water near here, and you cannot rely on finding patches of snow nearby.

The **continuation** of the itinerary, by Sentiero Attrezzato Marino Guardiano, is immediately in front of you on the other side of the forcella (refer to BELLU 5 below).

Whilst you are close to the level of Forcella Marmol, the route has to overcome a steep, rounded spur to reach it. Consequently, you are taken up, partly protected, to a high point of about 2350m, where you reach a signposted junction, where the path comes down from Monte Schiara.

The ferrata now starts the diagonal descent to the forcella over easily angled slabs, but slightly exposed and also running with water, so care is needed. You finally reach the forcella (2262m) some 4 hours after leaving Rif. 7th Alpini. ◀

BELLU 5:
SENTIERO ATTREZZATO MARINO GUARDIANO (MONTE PELF, 2506m)

Grade:	4
Seriousness:	B
Departure point:	Forcella Marmol
Ascent:	250m
Descent:	1000m (from Monte Pelf to Rif. 7th Alpini, via Forcella Pis Pilon)
Via ferrata:	250m (of which about 50% is protected)
Approximate time:	4 hours (from Forcella Marmol to Rif. 7th Alpini, plus allowance for choice of ascent route)
Highest altitude:	2506m, Monte Pelf subsidiary summit

The protected passages of this route are fairly short, but include some steep and strenuous climbing. The airy, unprotected passages require care, as they frequently involve negotiating very friable rock.

On the approach to Forcella Marmol, you were perhaps struck by the disconcertingly steep angle of the rock facing you, particularly after several hours of fairly easy, relaxed climbing. Once in the forcella, you are confronted by a slightly confusing array of waymarks, one of which appears to be directing you to the right (south-east). The route, however, is to the left, and you will spot the cable, beginning easily enough, just a few metres away. Whilst the protection has been very recently upgraded, it uses an unusually narrow diameter cable, which adds to the difficulties.

The first few metres are relatively easy, but the route soon rears up steeply and becomes more exposed and quite strenuous. It takes a line climbing somewhat diagonally leftwards, uncompromising in its course and avoiding no difficulties for some 50m. Then, after about 25 minutes of climbing, the angle falls back markedly and the climbing becomes much easier. You reach the top of the cable (about 2345m) about 35 minutes after starting to climb, finding yourself on a pleasant grassy plateau, with areas of volcanic rock outcropping all around. Whilst the remainder of the route, to the twin summits of Monte Pelf, is largely a lovely unprotected ridge traverse, there are several sections of cable to safeguard the airier passages, of which there are many! The higher of the two summits (2506m) is reached first, but it is the second, slightly lower, one (2502m) which is marked by a cairn, a couple of memorial tablets and the route book. Expect to reach here about 1¼ hours after leaving Forcella Marmol, and about 5½ hours after setting out from the *rifugio*.

If the weather is still clear, you will have an outstanding view, including back to the cross on Monte Schiara and over sections of the routes you have been climbing over the last couple of days. However, it is a long way down and torrential afternoon rain is common here, so keep an eye on the time. When you move on, follow the only viable route off the ridge, to the south-east and waymarked 511 on the map. The descent is immediately steep, exposed and over very friable rock, so care is needed. As you lose height, the terrain becomes more lush and you will see many varieties of wild flowers, including more edelweiss than you are ever likely to have seen in one location. The path, however, is fairly faint, particularly below about 1900m.

About 1½ hours after leaving the summit, you arrive at the junction (about 1780m) with path 505, where you turn right (west) for Rif. 7th Alpini. A second junction follows about 25 minutes later (about 1725m), where the signpost indicates that this is Forcella Pis Pilon. The forcella is, in fact, a few minutes' walk further on, and if you are returning to the *rifugio* for the night you have a further 30 minutes' walking. ▶

An **alternative** is available if you plan to return to Case Bortot and the valley, your climbing now complete. That is to turn south, on path 511, which is a delight! Lovely views, wild flowers and insects galore, and relaxing green meadows mark a dramatic contrast to the harsh rock environment you have inhabited for the last few days. Be warned, however, the walk adds 2½ hours to the timing for the day, making a total descent of about 2100m.

BASSANO DEL GRAPPA

Maps
BASAN 1 & 2 Valle di S. Liberale: Carta dei Sentieri Percorsi Attrezzati sul
Massicio del Grappa. MEL, Paderno, 1:15,000
BASAN 3 Kompass Wanderkarte 1:50,000 Number 76 or 1:25,000 626

Tourist Information Office
Ufficio Informazioni Turistiche, Largo Corona d'Italia, 35, 36061 Bassano del
Grappa, Italy
Tel: 0424.524351
Fax: 0424.525301
E-mail: infobassano@libero.it
Internet: www.vicenzae.org and select 'Information Offices'

The three routes in this section are centred on Bassano del
Grappa, but are quite remote, with two on Monte Grappa
and one (some way to the north) on Cima d'Asta.

With the exception of its historic core, much of the
character of Bassano has been lost under 20th-century
development, although it is easy to forgive this, given the
town's reputation for its grappa distilleries and other culi-
nary delicacies. There is a reasonable range of shops, restaurants and hotels in the town, although the most convenient
overnight accommodation for BASAN 1 & 2 is found about
10km to the north-east on the southern outskirts of Fietta,
near Crespano del Grappa (Albergo da Romano, 31010
Paderno del Grappa, Via Piave 1, tel: 0423-930329).
Accommodation is also available at Rifugio Bassano (contact Coletto F.lli S.A.S. di Coletto G&C, Via Madonna del
Covolo, 161 – 31017 Crespano del Grappa (TV) Italy,
tel/fax: (0423) 531010). Although the *rifugio* is open all year
round it only has six beds.

The area is not a major holiday destination, and outside
Bassano facilities for tourists are limited. The majority of visitors to nearby Monte Grappa are Italians on weekend outings to the War Museum, memorials and ossario (mausoleum) on the summit. The availability of maps suitable for
use in the mountains is a problem here. The most useful one
(at 1:15,000) is published by a co-operative of local tourist-
related businesses, and is fairly widely available in local

shops and cafes. Whilst this won't find its way into the Cartographers' Hall of Fame, it is serviceable, and shows the location and numbers of footpaths.

BASAN 3 is in the Lagorai group of mountains, and offers the chance of climbing the highest peak in that group, Cima d'Asta, 2847m. The route it is a long way from any other you may wish to climb, and is described below by two different approaches. If you appreciate quiet, but nonetheless spectacular days in the mountains, do not be put off either by the remoteness or shortness of the via ferrata; it is a grand day out.

BASAN 1:
PERCORSO ATTREZZATO
CARLO GUZZELLA, MONTE GRAPPA

Grade:	3
Seriousness:	B
Departure point:	San Liberale, 625m
Ascent:	1150m
Descent:	1150m
Via ferrata:	250m
Approximate time:	6 hours
Highest altitude:	1775m, Monte Grappa

Three great battles were fought here, spanning 1917 and 1918, as the Austro-Hungarian forces, supported by German troops, tried to dislodge the Italians. The fighting left nearly 25,000 dead, the remains of whom are interred in the great ossario (mausoleum) on the summit.

Each of these two routes makes a full mountain day, and each visits a summit to provide a suitable climax. They can, however, be combined into a single itinerary, although you will probably have to sacrifice one or both of the summits. Should you wish to tackle both routes in a single day, then it is perhaps best to ascend by BASAN 1 and descend by BASAN 2, although an anti-clockwise circuit would also be

Both this and BASAN 2 are very good climbs in extremely attractive mountain terrain with considerable historic resonance, having been a major Italian fortified position during the First World War.

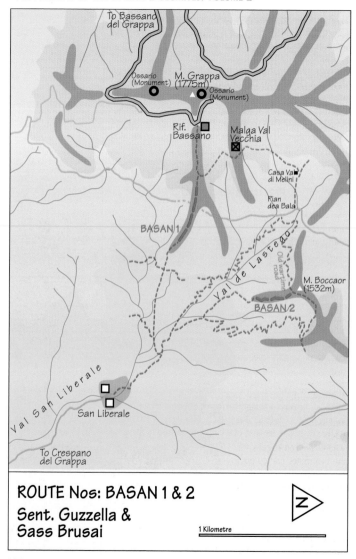

To Bassano
del Grappa

Ossario
(Monument)

M. Grappa
(1775m)

Ossario
(Monument)

Rif.
Bassano

Malga Val
Vecchia

Casa Val
di Melini

Rian
dea Bala

BASAN 1

Val de Lastego

Old wartime
road

M. Boccaor
(1532m)

BASAN 2

Val San Liberale

San Liberale

To Crespano
del Grappa

ROUTE Nos: BASAN 1 & 2

Sent. Guzzella &
Sass Brusai

1 Kilometre

N

very satisfying. The descriptions which follow presume that each route is climbed as a separate itinerary, but there is also information on the best way to make the connection between the two.

The starting point is San Liberale, with a couple of cafes (but no overnight accommodation) – a peaceful spot during the week, it is transformed at summer weekends, with live music and hundreds of visitors from the nearby towns. The nearest accommodation is about 15 minutes drive away in Fietta, near Crespano del Grappa. The local road system can be confusing, so take the road up by the side of Albergo da Romano, passing the church, to a little square with a bar and alimentari (shop); take the road up to the left of the bar, signposted Val San Liberale, and continue to the next fork in the road. Take the left fork, which is Via Sant' Andrea, drive up

Percorso Guzzella follows the line of this splendid ridge, which is only intermittently protected (BASAN 1)

past the taverna, and continue straight up the road until you reach San Liberale (625m), where there is ample parking. If you have not managed to find a map of the area already, both cafes usually have stocks available.

Walk up the metalled road to the left of Restaurant San Liberale, go over the stream, past signposts referring to several paths (and both ferratas), through a scatter of houses, and on to a fork in the track. This is the point where the approaches for the two routes part company. Take the left fork, signposted San Liberale (why, is unclear, since you've already passed it!) and Sentiero Carlo Guzzella. Pass a large shrine, and in a further few minutes come to a path leading up to the right, into the trees, signposted to Cima Grappa and Sentiero Carlo Guzzella (about 700m). The path is initially fairly steep, but the gradient eases as it climbs up through mixed woodland, taking the slope in easy zigzags heading generally westwards. At about 995m the path crosses over a more clearly defined path, waymarked 102; your path is signposted straight ahead up the slope. You eventually reach the cabled route at about 1170m, about 1½ hours after setting out. A couple of metres above the start of the cable is a plaque dedicating the route to Carlo Guzzella.

The route follows one of several ridges on the eastern slopes of Monte Grappa. It has quite a number of steep passages to negotiate, interspersed with sections of airy walking on the occasionally knife-edged grassy ridge. Consequently protection is intermittent, but always there when needed and completely sound. The rock is generally good, but with some slightly friable areas. However, the route is in full sun, so make sure you carry plenty of water. From the starting point to about 1400m the scrambling is fairly undemanding, but frequently delightful, as the cable takes you up steep buttresses, well supplied with holds. You then arrive at a point where the route passes within a few paces of the tarmac road which traverses the hillside from north to south, just at the point where it enters a series of tunnels; indeed, the tunnel passes underneath the next stage of the climb. ◄

The continuation of the route is straight up the rock step ahead, with its painted signs. This is the most testing part of the climb, as the route goes up and round the slightly bulging corner. More straightforward climbing follows to a strange arrangement of cables, fashioned to provide a ladder up a wide crack, otherwise devoid of decent holds. A nice, sustained passage of climbing up a fairly steep buttress follows. This is airy and well provided with holds, although inclined to be slightly friable. More intermittent protection follows, as the angle eases somewhat until, at about 1525m, you reach the top of the cable and the end of the route. A yellow plastic tube contains what used to be a route book; in summer 2002 the tube had sprung a leak, and the book was pulp!

You now have a lovely walk up the grassy ridge, initially through dwarf pines, but soon into the open. All around is evidence of wartime dugouts, and above you stands the

The road provides a suitable **escape point** should you need one: bear in mind that the grading of this route is earned by what is still to come, rather than what you have just negotiated. If you do decide to leave the route, walk north along the road to Pian dea Bala and return to the valley (in about 1½ hours) on path 151, down Val de Lastego.

vast ossario, constructed in 1935 during the Fascist period, as the architecture readily demonstrates.

The summit of Monte Grappa is a straightforward 200m climb from here and is well worth a visit, despite the uniformly awful architecture on display and the crowds you can sometimes encounter. Should you decide to do so, the best route to return to the valley is to partly retrace your steps, and then follow path 151 from Rif. Bassano down to Malga Val Vecchia (a largely unused collection of buildings, although containing an emergency bivouac), and then down to the metalled road referred to above. Take the road northwards over Pian dea Bala, and then pick up path 151 down Val de Lastego to the valley and San Liberale.

If, instead of the summit, you favour more via ferrata action, make your way over to the top of Sentiero Sass Brusai and use that route in descent. The best way of making the link is to walk up the ridge from the top of Sentiero Carlo Guzzella to the grassy shoulder at about 1600m, where a path goes off to the right (north), signposted 151bis. This takes you across the slope, in a descending traverse, to Malga Val Vecchia, referred to in the previous paragraph. From here take the track down past the ruins of Casa Val di Melini and on to Pian dea Bala at the metalled road which traverses the hillside (1381m). From the junction, walk along the road to the large timber crucifix, a couple of hundred metres to the north. At this point, just below you on your right (east), a gravel path can be seen. Make your way down to the path at the point where it executes a hairpin and, if you imagine this as a fork, take the fork to the left.

You now find yourself on a super little wartime road (waymarked 152), which heads generally eastwards on a shelf cut into the rock face. There are dramatic drops down to your right, but no real exposure, since metal cables have been installed as handrails at critical points. Climb gently for about 30 minutes (to about 1460m) to a left-hand corner, with painted waymarking on the rock wall to your left indicating path 152 in each direction. On your right, there is a memorial plaque to one Grando Armando. Since this is tucked away on the rock face to your right, it is easily missed, so keep looking over your right shoulder when you think you are getting close. This marks the top of the ferrata. It is a straightforward matter to follow the description for Sentiero Sass Brusai in reverse.

BASAN 2:
PERCORSO ATTREZZATO
SASS BRUSAI, MONTE BOCCAOR

Grade:	3
Seriousness:	A
Departure point:	San Liberale (625m)
Ascent:	900m
Descent:	900m
Via ferrata:	225m
Approximate time:	5 hours
Highest altitude:	1532m, Monte Boccaor

A pleasant route in a lovely situation.

The description of BASAN 1 includes details of how to reach San Liberale, the starting point for these two routes, and offers guidance on the routes and how they could be combined, with Sentiero Sass Brusai being used as the descent. The description which follows, however, assumes this route is climbed in its own right, a worthy option in itself.

From San Liberale, follow the metalled track to the left of the restaurant, as described above, as far as the fork referred to as the point where the approaches to the two routes part company. Sentiero Sass Brusai is waymarked up the right fork. Pass a scatter of houses, continue past the point where the metalled road reverts to gravel, and on to the next fork. You are now at about 750m and have been walking for about 15 minutes. Path 151/102 continue straight ahead, whilst to the right your path is signposted 153 to Sass Brusai. Another 10 minutes of steady climbing brings you to yet another fork (at about 840m), where the main path swings to the right, whilst your path, still waymarked Sass Brusai, continues straight ahead and becomes narrower. The path winds uphill, becoming gradually steeper, until you break out of the cover of the trees on a pleasant grassy ridge at about 1135m. You are now only about 5 minutes from the start of the route, at about 1180m (allow about 1½ hours from setting out).

The first pitch is perhaps the most pleasing of the route – a steep crack, on excellent rock, with an abundance of good holds. It is also in the shade, whilst the rest of the route is in full sun, which can sap your energy. Above this first pitch, the route initially appears somewhat directionless as it meanders up through thin tree cover, apparently searching out climbable outcrops. It soon becomes apparent, however, that you are following the line of a rocky spine running down from Monte Boccaor, a minor subsidiary of Monte Grappa. The climbing and the cable are intermittent, but pleasant, until a more sustained passage up a steep 40m buttress (at about 1280m).

Another 30m or so of intermittent climbing brings you to Sella del Candidato, which is marked by a Madonna, an old climbing helmet and a memorial plaque. Whatever the explanation for the helmet, this is a place to pause in the shade before resuming the climb. You will now have a good view of your descent route as it zigzags down through the outcrops off to your right. At about 1455m you reach a point where a path turns off to the right, waymarked 152. Sentiero Sass Brusai is indicated to the left, but you are nearing its end now. A few minutes of easy scrambling brings you to the lovely little military road referred to in BASAN 1, waymarked 152 in each direction, which marks the end of the climb (at about 1460m, having taken some 1½ hours).

The summit of Monte Boccaor is about 100m above you, and can be reached in about 20 minutes by turning right and climbing up through the trees. To return to the valley, follow the old military road generally eastwards to the junction with path 153, which you will have spotted during your climb. This is a well-constructed descent, and brings you down to the valley in about 2 hours.

BASAN 3:
FERRATA GIULIO GABRIELLI, CIMA D'ASTA

Grade:	2
Seriousness:	C
Departure point:	Malga Sorgazza, 1450m (via Pieve Tesino, 871m, and Val Tolva)

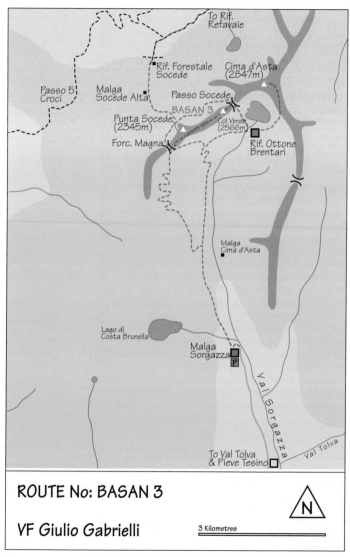

ROUTE No: BASAN 3

VF Giulio Gabrielli

3 Kilometres

Ascent:	1400m
Descent:	1400m
Via ferrata:	120m (includes Cima d'Asta ascent)
Approximate time:	9–10 hours
Highest altitude:	2847m, Cima d'Asta
Map:	Kompass 1:50,000 Number 76 or 1:25,000 626

This route makes a superb (though long) mountain day out. For a good two-day excursion make an overnight stay at the Rif. O. Brentari, 2473m (open from 20 June to 20 September); it has 56 beds and is in a wonderful location at the foot of the south wall of Cima d'Asta.

From Pieve Tesino follow the road for Val Malene for 11km to Malga Sorgazza. At the end of Val Malene (1129m) where the road forks into Val Sorgazza and Val Tolva, 7km from Pieve Tesino, there is a bar ristorante, shop and camp site, Info Family Nervo, tel. 0461.594214.

Follow path 326/327 to climb past Malga Cima d'Asta towards Forcella Magna. The track divides in about 3km (an hour), with the right fork continuing towards Rif. Ottone Brentari (this is the return route). Follow path 326, which is the left fork; this heads south-west before turning north-west, climbing steadily at first before zigzagging more steeply to Forcella Magna, 2117m (about 2 hours from Malga Sorgazza). There is some evidence of the importance of Forcella Magna in the First World War, with rusty barbed wire, grown-over trenches and some caves (see note at end of route description).

Path 326/375 (signed VF G. Gabrielli Col Verde 2.00) zigzags uphill, going east from the forcella and onto an old wartime mule track. In about 15 minutes path 326 continues ahead, with path 375 (signed Rif. Cima d'Asta and Sentiero Attrezzata G. Gabrielli) following the wartime track as it zigzags uphill to the left. Follow the waymarks for path 375 to continue climbing for about 20 minutes, with views of Cima d'Asta and Rif. Otone Brentari (also known as Rif. Cima d'Asta) opening up to the north-east. The path goes downhill for a few minutes along a grassy hillside to pass

Although a very short ferrata (there are only two protected sections of about 60m each), the route does take you into the heart of the Lagorai group of mountains with the chance to climb the highest peak in that group, Cima d'Asta, 2847m.

through Forcella Tellina and reach the start of the ferrata about 35 minutes from Forcella Magna.

The first cabled section is indicated with a large asterisk painted in red and white on a rock. (Please note that if you go past this and up into a gully you will quickly arrive at a rusty old ladder. If this happens you have gone too far and must return down the scree to locate the start.) About 10 minutes' climbing on good rock for 50–60m leads to a walk across a wide gully with some loose rock. Follow waymarks, past 'Punta Socede' painted on a rock, through a gap and then descend in and around some rock pinnacles to reach the second protected part of the route about 10 minutes'

The stempled section of Ferrata Guilio Gabrielli (BASAN 3)

walk from the first cable. It is a well-protected climb (again of about 50–60m) up a series of four walls and ledges on very firm stemples; this is the end of the ferrata protection. From here follow a good waymarked path as it climbs up to the high point of Cresta di Socede, Col Verde, 2566m, in a further 35 minutes. From the summit of Col Verde it is 10 minutes descent to Passo Socede, 2518m, with Rifugio Ottone Brentari only 15 minutes away to the east, sitting above a sweep of glacial slabs overlooking Lago di Cima d'Asta.

Having completed the ferrata, you could return directly back to Malga Sorgazza, but by doing this you miss out on a wonderful remote mountain summit with very good views. To ascend Cima d'Asta from the *rifugio* takes about 2 hours' climbing on path 364 to Forzelletta, 2680m, and then up the eastern slope to the summit. Start by descending north-east from the *rifugio* to pass around the east side of Lago di Cima d'Asta (2451m) before climbing steadily to the summit of Cima d'Asta, 2847m, where there was an important First World War observatory. Depending on how long you lingered at the *rifugio* your ascent to the summit of Cima d'Asta from Malga Sorgazza is likely to have taken a total of 6–7 hours.

Your descent retraces the ascent route back to Rif. Ottone Brentari (about an hour) and then follows path 327 back down to the starting point at Malga Sorgazza; this will take a further 2 hours (a total descent of about 3 hours). ▶

Note: On 24 May 1915 Italy declared war on the Austro-Hungarian Empire. As early as 4 June 1915 Italians were patrolling at Forcella Magna, and at Cima Socede by 31 July. Italian forces held Forcella Magna until mid-November 1917, when they retreated from the Cima d'Asta massif towards Monte Grappa (see BASAN 1 & 2). After the war, the Italians returned into Val delle Vanoi in November 1918 (see BASAN 3A).

BASAN 3A:
FERRATA GIULIO GABRIELLI

Grade:	2
Seriousness:	C
Departure point:	Rif. Refavaie, 1116m
Ascent:	1400m
Descent:	1400m
Via ferrata:	120m
Approximate time:	9–10 hours (add at least 3 hours for ascent of Cima d'Asta)
Highest altitude:	2566m (without the ascent of Cima d'Asta)

This route provides an alternative approach to Ferrata Giulio Gabrielli from the north, and makes a superb (but long) mountain day.

If you are staying in the Primiero valley (San Martino, Fiera, etc.) it is possible to reduce driving time, and instead of approaching from Pieve Tesino to complete a circuit from Rif. Refavaie. The downside of the northern approach is that it is a longer walk-in and involves an additional 330m of ascent, as Rif. Refavaie is at 1116m, whereas Malga Sorgazza is at 1450m. However, this is more than compensated by the remoteness and mountain situation of the climb up to Forcella Magna. As with the southern approach, you could include an overnight stay in Rif. O Brentari and an ascent of Cima d'Asta.

Drive from Primiero via the SP79 from Imer to Passo Gobbera, and then the SP56 through Canal San Bovo and Caoria to the end of the public road at Rif. Refavaie, 1116m. There are a number of mountain walks from here and a small amount of accommodation is available (tel. 0439.710009 or see www.rifugiorefavaie.com, email: refavaie@wappi.com).

From Rif. Refavaie follow path 380 all the way to Forcella Magna; this takes at least 3 hours, with the first half of the climb on a forestry road which gains height at a steady gradient. Some 25 minutes from Rif. Refavaie the track forks and you take the left fork, signed Rif. Socede/Passo 5 Croci. It is another 50 minutes to the next fork in the track, where there is a cross dated year 2000. The right fork here is to Passo Cinque Croci, but continue on the left fork (still path 380) signed to 'Forcella Magna – Sorgazza and 380 bis Rif. Cima d'Asta, occidentale Passo Socede'. Ten minutes further on there is a crossroads; follow the track leftwards and in 100m arrive at Rif. Forestale Socede, 1537m.

The track ends here and becomes a path which is not signed, but goes uphill just before the *rifugio* and is well waymarked with red and white paint on trees at regular intervals as it leads up through the woods. In a little over 30 minutes the woods open out, firstly into beech shrubs and small pines and then across Malga Socede Alta, 1730m, which is tussocky and in places wet underfoot. The path (indistinct in places now, but waymarked at regular intervals) stays on the left side of the stream, passing a ruined shepherds' hut on the right, and then starts to climb more steeply, heading generally south-east. After 20 minutes or so of the steeper climbing you arrive at the split of paths 380 and 380 bis (about 1980m); this is a well-waymarked spot, with large signs painted on a both a rock face and a large boulder. Path 380 bis is the return path, but follow path 380, heading roughly south, on a steadily rising path to Forcella Magna in about 30 minutes from the junction. From Forcella Magna follow the route as described in BASAN 3 above from here to Passo Socede, 2518m.

To descend back to Rif. Refavaie takes 3–3½ hours from Passo Socede, following path 380 bis back to the junction with path 380 and then retracing your steps. Again there are good waymarks, but it is not always a good path, and early in the season there may be snow lying around the pass. The descent is steep in places and makes its way quite cunningly down glacial slabs, stony sections and grassy slopes; keep an eye out for the waymarks, especially if visibility is not so good. In 35 minutes you reach an unusual split rock 'Al Seole del Sasso Spacca, M2203', and a further 20 minutes takes you back to the junction with path 380. Retrace your steps from here, and in about 2½ hours you will be back down to Rif. Refavaie and some well-earned refreshment!

VICENZA

Maps
(all routes) Vicentine Section of CAI map 'Sentieri Pasubio Carega' 1:20,000 or
Kompass Wanderkarte 1:50,000 Sheet 101

Tourist Information Office
Ufficio Informazioni Turistiche, Piazza Matteotti, 12, 36100 Vicenza
Tel: 0444.320854
Fax: 0444 327072
E-mail: iat.matteotti@libero.it
Internet: www.vicenzae.org and select 'Information Offices' or
E-mail: aptvicenza@ascom.vi.it
Internet: www.ascom.vi.it/aptvicenza

*The little village of
Giazza, in Val d'Illassi,
is a good base to
tackle the routes in
the Vicenza section*

Vicenza has been identified more as a starting point than as
the ideal base from which to tackle these five routes
(indeed, these mountains are known as the Alpi Vicentine).
The routes are, however, quite remote if you do decide to
base yourself down on the plain in Vicenza or Verona.
Consequently, you may wish to stay in one or more of the

rifugios up in the mountains. If you prefer to look for accommodation somewhere along the approach valleys, a good choice is the Albergo Belvedere at Giazza, in Val d'Illasi, about 25km up the SP10, north of the A4/SS11 (37030 Giazza, tel. 0457.847020, fax 0457.847908).

The cultural treasures of Vicenza and Verona need no elaboration, but the adjoining mountain areas are less well known. They are in one of Italy's Regional Parks, Parco Regionale della Lessinia, and are attractive and varied in character, although not much visited by tourists. It is, however, a very popular weekend destination for residents of the nearby big towns. Consequently, whilst the routes can be busy at weekends, you can often have the mountain to yourself during midweek.

Of the five routes in this section, four are approached up Val d'Illasi. Its relative isolation has enabled the survival of an old dialect, which is celebrated in a small museum in Giazza – or Ljetsan, as it is called in this ancient tongue. This is as far as the bus service from Verona penetrates, still the best part of 10km from the routes described in this section, so a car is essential to explore this area.

Each of these *rifugios*, all open from mid-June to late September, makes an excellent base for your explorations.

- Rif. Alpino Revolto, Val d'Illasi, 25 beds, tel. 045.7847039
- Rif. Pertica, Passo Pertica, 15 beds, tel. 045.7847011 (also open weekends in winter)
- Rif. Scalorbi, Passo della Pelagatta, 14 beds, tel. 045.7847029
- Rif. Fraccaroli, Cima Carega, 22 beds, tel. 045.7050033
- Rif. C. Battisti (alternative approach from Recoaro Terme to the east), 50 beds, tel. 044.575235 (also open weekends in winter).
- Rif Boschetto di Cappelletti Leonella, Via Revolto, tel. 045 7847005 (open May to October, winter weekends only – half and full pension available)
- Rif Campogrosso, tel. 0445 363333 (open all year)

VICEN 5, however, is approached up a different valley, as explained in the route description.

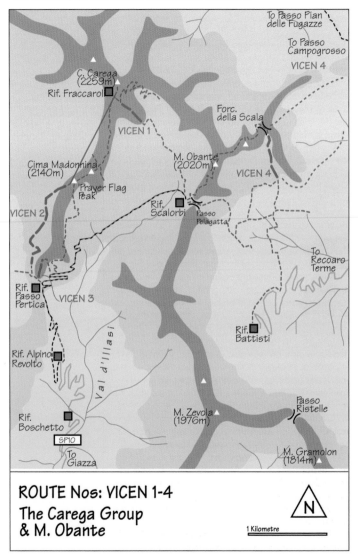

ROUTE Nos: VICEN 1-4
The Carega Group
& M. Obante

1 Kilometre

N

VICEN 1:
VIA FERRATA CARLO CAMPALANI, CIMA CAREGA

Grade:	3
Seriousness:	B
Departure point:	Rifugio Alpino Revolto, 1336m
Ascent:	1000m
Descent:	1000m
Via ferrata:	130m
Approximate time:	6 hours
Highest altitude:	2259m, Cima Carega

When undertaken separately this route climbs to the summit of Cima Carega, 2259m, returning to Rif. Revolto by a section of the Costa Media, a beautiful ridge, before you return to your car. Alternatively (and the authors' recommendation), it can be combined with VICEN 2 to complete a very satisfying traverse of Cima Carega and the Costa Media. Should this be your choice, it is preferable to ascend by this route and descend VICEN 2, Sentiero Angelo Pojesi. This makes for a relatively long day, however, so each route is described in isolation.

This is a particularly pleasing route which can be climbed on its own or combined with VICEN 2.

The public road climbs to Rif. Alpino Revolto, where there is ample verge parking available, but be warned that parking is not allowed on the road itself. Beyond Rif. Revolto the road reverts to a gravel track, a former military road, which then continues via Rif. Passo Pertica (1522m) to Rif. Scalorbi (1767m). It is easy walking and traverses the attractive upper reaches of Val d'Illasi. A few hundred metres short of Rif. Scalorbi, you reach a path off to the left (north), waymarked 109 and E5, to Rif. Fraccaroli. (The E5 is the long-distance path from Lake Constance to the Adriatic Sea at Venice.) Follow this path for about 20 minutes, making sure you stick to the main route rather than drifting off onto one of the many little paths which wander off in various directions, until you reach a junction.

The main path continues straight ahead as the E5, whilst your track is that on the left signed simply 'Ferrata'. You are heading for the obvious south-east ridge running down from Cima Carega, although the path takes a rather circuitous course. It becomes somewhat indistinct in areas of minor landslips, but heads a little to the east of the spur forming the end of the ridge before traversing back south-west to the starting point of the route (about 2030m). Allow about 2½ hours to here.

Three plaques adjoin the first length of cable, including one dedicating the route to Carlo Campalani. The climb is immediately quite strenuous, with the first move being up a slightly overhanging crack, although a metal peg and stemple help. The angle eases for a few metres before a rightward traverse across a broken wall. This leads to a chimney, which is rather tight if you pick a line within its rather gloomy confines; better to bridge up the outer edge, which is well provided with holds. About 20m of easier climbing follows, although there are several steeper steps to negotiate, none of which present any real problems. An airy, rightward traverse follows, taking a line along a broken ledge. About half-way across, a metal box containing the route book is attached to the wall. Like others in this area, it is a quality production, properly bound and printed up with the route's title. Take care not to drop it whilst making your entry, since the position does not lend itself to writing! An area of slightly more friable rock follows, on an ascending traverse line, about the only section of the route not on good, clean rock. The next, fairly steep, pitch in a corner leads to a further ascending rightward traverse. You have now reached the last pitch of the climb, another fairly steep groove, which brings you to the top of the cable, unmarked, but the point where you can safely remove your gear (about 2120m). The ascent of the ferrata takes about 1 hour.

The way ahead is not waymarked, but follow the narrow, and rather exposed, crest of the ridge, taking care because the rock is quite friable. Pass over the high point of the ridge and drop to the main track on a sharp bend. Follow this up to Rif. Fraccaroli (2238m), which stands a few metres above the little col you reach on the track. From here, it is an easy 5 minute climb up to the summit of Cima Carega (2259m), overlooking the *rifugio* (allow about 30 minutes from the top of the ferrata).

The next stage of the itinerary follows path 108 south-west along the Costa Media ridge. The path takes a slightly lazy course which avoids a couple of the minor peaks along the way, but it is still lovely ridge walking. After about 20 minutes you reach a small col (about 2085m), where minor paths drop off to left and right. Continue on to the next significant peak on the ridge, Cima Madonnina (2140m). As the name suggests, this is adorned by a Madonna, and attached to the statue's plinth is a route book for you to sign. Continue along the ridge towards its next high point, distinguished by strings of Tibetan prayer flags, which symbolize the local section of the CAI's support for the Free Tibet campaign.

This is also the point (at about 2090m) where you must decide whether to head for home or to tackle Sentiero Angelo Pojesi. If you have an appetite for more cables, then take the path down to the right (south-west), which leads in easy zigzags over a little shoulder (about 1975m), and down to the top of the route (at about 1930m). It is then a straightforward matter to follow, in reverse, the description in VICEN 2 (below). To return directly to your car, however, take the path, waymarked 108, down to the left (south) past a ruined wartime building to join the old military road a few hundred metres short of Rif. Pertica, and then continue on to Rif. Revolto. Allow about 2 hours for the return trip from the top of Cima Carega to your car.

VICEN 2:
SENTIERO ALPINISTICO ANGELO POJESI

Grade:	2
Seriousness:	B
Departure point:	Rif. Alpino Revolto, 1336m
Ascent:	850m
Descent:	850m
Via ferrata:	1000m, of which about 500m is cabled
Approximate time:	5 hours
Highest altitude:	2090m (unnamed summit)

This route offers easy climbing in grand situations.

Many climbers choose to combine this route with VICEN 1, in which case the Pojesi route is the best one to use for your descent. If the two routes are combined into a single circuit, this makes for a relatively long day, so the description below assumes that this sentiero, which is a worthy outing in itself, is tackled in isolation.

The route begins at Rif. Passo Pertica, the approach to which is described in VICEN 1. The sentiero is signposted at the *rifu-gio*, along the path waymarked 109 to Ronchi. Within about 100m, a smaller path goes off to the right, signposted to the sentiero. You arrive at the start of the route within a further 100m, some 45 minutes after leaving your car. A commemorative plaque, erected by the Cesare Battisti Group of the Veronesi Section of the CAI, dedicates the route to Angelo Pojesi (it was formerly known as Sentiero Cesare Battisti).

Whilst the cable is somewhat old (in summer 2002) it is, nonetheless, sound. The first stretch, about 400m in length, protects a good, but friable, ledge on a gently ascending traverse line. The path then rounds a corner to the right (east) to enter a large bowl; the route can be seen running along the foot of the rock wall, at about 1600m, around the whole of this bowl. Protection on this stretch of the route is limited to several metal gangways and a few lengths of cable, although there are several friable sections which are unprotected and where care is needed. As you leave the bowl, round a corner to the right, you enter an area of dwarf conifers. Further intermittent protection leads up to a path which zigzags up through the vegetation, where you need to keep an eye on the waymarking. A 3m wall, climbed by a crack up its centre, leads to more gentle scrambling, again with only intermittent protection, to arrive at a crest (about 1805m). The route then drops some 40m, partly in a short, cabled gully. A traverse leads to the foot of a broad, broken gully, which provides easy scrambling. At about 1790m a line of stemples surmounts a 6m wall, beyond which the route book is located.

The route continues up the gully, protected where necessary, and with a couple more short flights of stemples. By now, the cable has deserted the gully's centre in favour of a line up a crack to the left. This is the most sustained climbing on the route, and enjoys continuous protection until the

end of the route, at about 1930m. Allow about 2½ hours after embarking on the sentiero to this point. A further 30 minutes following the path up the more easily angled slope to a small shoulder, and then in easy zigzags (and with one final length of cable), leads to the little un-named summit (at about 2090m) with the Tibetan prayer flags described in VICEN 1. Whilst the direct way back (less than 2 hours) is by path 108 returning by Rif. Pertica, also described in VICEN 1, there is ample opportunity to extend your day with some excellent ridge walking, now that you have spent so much energy getting here.

Climber on Sentiero Pojesi (VICEN 2)

VICEN 3:
VIA FERRATA GIANCARLO BIASIN

Grade:	5
Seriousness:	A
Departure point:	Rifugio Alpino Revolto, 1336m
Ascent:	350m

Descent:	350m
Via ferrata:	100m
Approximate time:	2½ hours
Highest altitude:	1743m (top of via ferrata)

The route is just 5 minutes' walk from Rif. Pertica. Indeed, visitors to the rifugio have a ringside seat, so make sure you climb with as much style and confidence as you can muster!

Whilst this is a very short route, taking no more than about 30 minutes, it is a super little climb, right at the top of the scale in terms of the standard of technical climbing ability required for via ferratas. It is unremittingly steep, at least until the final few metres, and negotiates several bulges, which require good standards of fitness and a degree of boldness. It is not a route on which you should carry a large rucksack.

The approach to Rif. Passo Pertica is described in VICEN 1. Scramble up the steep gravel slope behind the memorial at the front of the *rifugio*, heading for the unmistakable crack running vertically up the wall ahead. The memorial plaque at the start of the cable dedicates the route to Giancarlo Biasin, who died whilst climbing in the Pala Group in 1964. Climb steeply up broken rock in the narrow gully at the foot of the crack to the first cable, attached to the right-hand wall. This immediately switches to the left wall, and reaches the first line of the stemples, which are such a feature of this ferrata. The wall now bulges outwards, whilst the stemples take you diagonally leftwards, so maintaining balance is somewhat awkward. Indeed, throughout the climb, it is necessary to utilise natural holds to supplement the stemples in order to remain in balance.

At the top of the stemples, step across the crack to a ledge on the right, the first of several good resting places where you can inspect the route ahead. The crack now splits, and the right fork, which the rest of the route follows, becomes a rather tight and damp-looking chimney a little way ahead. The next flight of stemples takes a line adjoining the right-hand crack, and is another steep pitch requiring a bit of muscle. The cable now takes you into the chimney, which is indeed as damp as it looked from below, so your foot placement needs to take account of the slippery rock. The chimney is tight, and some of the moves are quite awkward to execute in such a confined space, but you are now within sight of the final passage of the route, which is a much more easily angled wall. The climbing is now much easier, but the rock is somewhat friable, so be sure of your holds before you rely on them.

At the top of the cable, waymarking takes you to the right into the vegetation, where a choice of routes opens up. To the left is a path waymarked to the Via delle Greste, which leads to the Costa Media ridge described in VICEN 1 above. To the right is the quick way back to the *rifugio*, which has a couple of short lengths of cable to safeguard slightly precarious passages. The path winds down through the conifers until it joins path 108 coming down from Cima Carega, which then reaches the old military road at about 1560m, some 10 minutes' walk above Rif. Pertica.

VICEN 4:
Sentiero Alpinistico del Vaio Scuro, Monte Obante

Grade:	3
Seriousness:	C
Departure point:	Rifugio Alpino Revolto (1336m)
Ascent:	1400m
Descent:	1400m
Via ferrata:	300m
Approximate time:	8–9 hours
Highest altitude:	2020m, Monte Obante

Much of this terrain is very friable, and most of the itinerary is unprotected. Way-marking is frequently poor, and route finding not always easy. Consequently, it is a route to be taken seriously.

Inspection of maps of the area suggests that the most appropriate approach is from the north. However, both roads from Passo Pian delle Fugazze to Rif. Campogrosso are now closed to general traffic. The most appropriate approach, therefore, is from the south, from Val d'Illasi (see VICEN 1 for details). The less demanding round described later, from Rif.

This is a long, hard day for a route in these relatively modest mountains, perhaps the reason why it is so infrequently tackled.

Guglie del Fumante: the impressive ridge approach to Vaio Scuro (VICEN 4)

Campogrosso, involves a much longer drive from Recoaro Terme.

From Rif. Revolto (1336m) walk up, via Rif. Passo Pertica, to Rif. Scalorbi (1767m). Allow about 1½ hours for the approach.

The route is a circuit from Rif. Scalorbi and, as such, can be tackled in either direction. However, a clockwise course is recommended (even though this involves a descent of the protected section), since the traverse of Guglie del Fumante involves terrain best undertaken when you are fresh and your concentration is sharp.

From Rif. Scalorbi, climb the friable slope to the north-east, passing several wartime tunnels. The path is way-marked 6 and has faded paint splashes, mainly in red and white, but occasionally green. ◀

Note that the Kompass maps have the correct path number, whilst the CAI map (otherwise to be greatly preferred) shows this as path 109 and G05, neither of which appears on the ground!

The high point of M. Obante (2020m) is reached in about 50 minutes. Whilst this is an undistinguished spot, the ridge off to the north-east, Guglie del Fumante, is a wild and exciting prospect. The path is now waymarked 'Alpinistico Campogrosso 6' in rather faded paint. An exposed and fri-able terrace takes you to a corner, round which you get a good view of the route ahead, as it picks its way between the twisted pinnacles of the crest of the ridge. After zigzagging down a steep, eroded slope, swing to the right on another exposed terrace, scramble up a 2m block, and then drop to the crest of a grassy ridge below.

About 30 minutes after the summit, at about 1915m, you reach a short cable safeguarding an exposed section above a gully falling away to your right. This is followed immediately by a tight squeeze between two large boulders. In a further 15 minutes, you will be nearing the impressive little peak, surmounted by a metal cross, which you have been glimpsing along the way. The ground here is particularly broken, although there are several bolts for belay points on the scramble up to the cross, but no waymarking. Maps claim the height of this summit as 1983m, although it is difficult to reconcile this with other known heights, so it is not a good place to check your altimeter. ▶

The summit involves some quite exposed and unprotected scrambling, for which a short rope is recommended for any inexperienced member of the party.

Return to the small forcella at the foot of the summit, and pick up the onward waymarking a few metres away down the slope. This takes you in a north-easterly direction down an unpleasant scree slope. The paint splashes are infrequent, but after about 100m of descent, you will see an obvious gully up to your right containing a large amount of recently fallen rock and leading up to a narrow forcella, just below which you will spot some fairly new (in 2002) waymarking. Pick your way up the rock fall to the waymarks which comprise a red star and the name '105 Alpinistico'. ▶

The CAI map and Kompass agree on the reference number 105 for this next stage of the route.

This is Forcella della Scala (1850m), the start of the via ferrata, about 4 hours after setting out. The path which drops away to the south-east immediately forks. Take the left-hand (lower) fork, and zigzag steeply down for about 40m until the path traverses to the right (south-west) along an exposed path, protected by a cable largely overgrown with shrubbery. In a couple of minutes you find yourself at the foot of a rather gloomy and damp chimney (about 1810m). ▶

The cable leading up the chimney is worryingly rusty, although this is an indication of how infrequently the route is climbed, not its condition, as the securing bolts are completely solid.

After climbing the chimney, a slightly descending traverse leads, in about 5 minutes, to the top of a gully (about 1795m). The route descends this gully for some 150m – quite strenuous in places, but with more or less continuous protection. The most entertaining pitch is near the bottom, as the cable descends into what appears to be a cave. This is a tight squeeze, and the wall onto which you emerge as you climb down out of the cave is steep and running with water, although a few metal pegs aid your descent. Just round the corner from this wall is a red arrow pointing up

If you want to shorten your day you can leave the gully at about 1400m, on a path traversing off to the right – although it is very difficult to spot, and you will not have completed the route in its entirety.

For a less demanding round of VF Vaio Scuro start from Rif. Campogrosso; this involves a much longer drive from Recoaro Terme, but only around 700m of ascent/descent and a total time of 5½ to 6 hours. It would also be possible to start this round from Rif. alla Guardia and Rif. C Battisti.

the route, and a rusty metal plaque marking the end of the protected part of the itinerary (about 1640m), which will have taken you about 1½ hours.

The gully has now broadened out, and the angle eased, but you have a further 400m of scrambling down the maze of boulders still to come. The route is occasionally way-marked, but it is generally a case of finding the easiest course down between the boulders. ◀

About 300m from the top, a thin tree cover begins. The gully now contains a small stream, which would be more difficult to cope with in wet conditions. The end of the route is at about 1200m, and is marked by a painted sign 'Vaio Scuro Sentiero Alpinistico'. A few paces further you reach a path, waymarked 33, where you turn to the right (west). In another few paces, you reach a shrine to 'Signora dei Sentieri', where the path splits. Your route is uphill, to the right, waymarked 33/105. You now have a fairly long slog up to Rif. Scalorbi, which will take you about 1½ hours; console yourself with the thought that, had you done the route in an anti-clockwise direction, you would now embarking on the traverse of M. Obante, when you are tired, and possibly becoming careless.

At about 1340m, a path goes off to the right, way-marked 105, Campogrosso and Vaio Scuro. This is the tra-versing line which leaves the gully at about 1400m, as mentioned above. Your route continues straight ahead, way-marked 105, Rif. Battisti. After a further 10 minutes or so of traversing, you reach a path to the right waymarked 114, Rif. Scalorbi. Follow this path steeply uphill until (at about 1480m) you again encounter star-shaped waymarking as the route enters a gully and becomes a pleasant scramble. This is Vaio di Pelagatta, and is equipped with occasional old pegs. The gully gives way to a steep grassy slope a little below Passo Pelagatta, just behind Rif. Scalorbi. You now have the easy walk back down the old military road to Rif. Pertica and on to Rif. Scalorbi to reach your car in a further hour.

Circuit of VF Vaio Scuru from Rifugio Campogrosso ◀
From Rif. Campogrosso go west on the road then take the E5 path on the left (path numbers 6/7/33/105). In 15 minutes turn left onto a path signed 'Sentiero delle Mole'; this is path (33), which zigzags down through pleasant woods and in

about 25–30 minutes meets a track at 1160m. To the left is Rif. alla Guardia, but you continue to the right on path 33 (signed Rif. C Battisti 2.15), pretty much on level ground, to pass around the gully of Torrente Rotolon. In 10 minutes you reach open meadows with good views across to Rif. C. Battisti, Passo Ristale and Monte Gramolon (see VICEN 5). In 10 minutes you pass a small house, with the path on fairly level ground, but 10 minutes further on the ascent begins up some quite steep zigzags.

Continuing upwards (10 minutes again) you reach a collection of benches, a signpost and a Madonna 'Signora della Montagna'; the altitude here is 1200m. Turn right uphill on the path signed 33/105 Raccordo Gazza – Vaio Scuro (actually shown as 106 on the map). Before doing this note the route book in a box built into the wall on the left of the Madonna. In 20 minutes' climbing (about 2 hours from Rif. Campogrosso), and at 1330m, follow way-marked path 105 to the right signed 'EEA Campogrosso/Vaio Scuro 3.45'.

▶ In 5 minutes go left up an open stony gully with hands-on scrambling over some of the larger boulders. After about 30 minutes scrambling up you arrive at the first cable at around 1520m. Believe in the red and white arrow and descend the cable (yes, this is the ascent route!) for 20 or so metres. Now follow a marked path as it traverses left and up again for around 25 minutes to a ferrata '*' painted in red on a rock (about 1540m). Some 15 minutes further up (about 1625m) go up a damp-looking gully, and cables lead you up through the gully behind a large chock stone (it's a bit of a squeeze here, so it's best not to have a large rucksack).

This alternative round follows a different fork to the main route during the lower part of the gully.

In a little more than 30 minutes you arrive at the top of the gully and traverse on a narrow path (around 1800m) to the left. In 10 more minutes (care with waymarks) a cable leads up and over a col (1820m) before dropping steeply down the other side. Now a narrow path traverses steep ground with some final cabling (a bit concealed with overgrown small pines); this is the end of the protection.

Waymarks lead to '* 105' painted on a rock in a gully with a large (and fairly new) rock fall. It is now only an hour back to Rif. Campogrosso – first zigzag down steep scree for a couple of hundred metres to meet path 7 (the E5), then turn right and follow an excellent path for about 1.5km back to the road and *rifugio*. ▶

It will have taken you 4½ to 5 hours to the col and *105 waymark, so it's time for lunch and the chance, perhaps (weekends more likely), to watch some really serious climbers on the pinnacles on the northern end of the Guglie del Fumante.

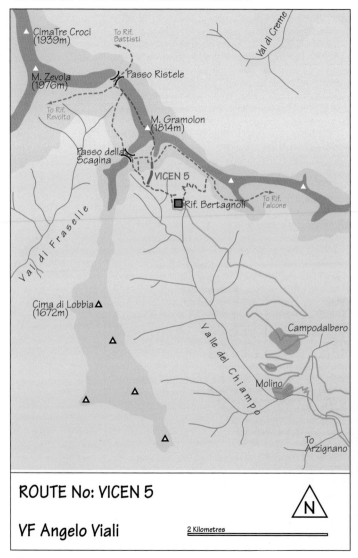

CimaTre Croci
(1939m)

To Rif.
Battisti

M. Zevola
(1976m)

Passo Ristele

To Rif.
Revolto

M. Gramolon
(1814m)

Passo della
Scagina

VICEN 5

Rif. Bertagnoli

To Rif.
Falcone

V a l   d i   F r a s e l l e

Val di Creme

Cima di Lobbia
(1672m)

V a l l e   d e l   C h i a m p o

Campodalbero

Molino

To
Arzignano

ROUTE No: VICEN 5

VF Angelo Viali

N

2 Kilometres

Grade	3
Seriousness	B
Departure point:	Rifugio Bertagnoli, 1250m
Ascent:	650m
Descent:	650m
Via ferrata:	250m
Approximate time:	4 hours
Highest altitude:	1814m, Monte Gramolon

Whilst the route is relatively close to the others in this section, it is approached up a different valley, Valle del Chiampo. This is not a problem if you are taking a hut-to-hut tour, since it is a fairly short walk from Rifs. Revolto and Scalorbi to Rif. Bertagnoli, the starting point. If you are based in Val d'Illasi, however, the drive over from Giazza takes about an hour. As a route from one valley to the other the local Forestry Office recommends driving via the SP17 (S. Andrea, S. Bortolo, to Bolca, then SP36b to Crespadoro and the SP43 to Campodalbero). A good road continues right up to Rif. Bertagnoli, where there is ample parking.

If you approach Rif. Bertagnoli up Valle del Chiampo, take the SS246 north to Montecchio Magiore, join the SP1 to Arzignano, and enter Valle del Chiampo on the SP43 through Ferrazza and Campodalbero. It is a well-appointed *rifugio* (open April to December, 25 beds; tel. 044.4429011), but you would be well advised to avoid weekends, when its character changes and it becomes a very popular place for family lunch.

Walk past the *rifugio* to the little chapel adjoining, where you pick up the path (north-west) signposted to Monte Gramolon. Within a few paces join a wider track, where you turn left to continue up through the trees. After

Whilst few would argue that this is the most exciting ferrata in the area, it does have its moments; it also has the considerable merit of taking you into an area of very attractive mountains and providing a pleasant and undemanding walk.

about 5 minutes, pass a memorial statue, beyond which the path begins to descend slightly round the top of a small gorge with a safeguarding cable. About 10 minutes after setting out, the path crosses over a very broken gully, the upper part of which is signposted 'Viao Milani'. This would make pretty rough scrambling and should not be confused with Sentiero Milani, which you are going to walk on your return.

You are now heading up into a well-wooded gorge. The path continues to Passo della Scagina at its head, but keep an eye out for a steep and eroded scree slope up to the right in a further few minutes. It is easy to miss, but look for a marble plaque a few metres up in the scree, at about 1285m. The cable begins a few metres up the slope above the plaque, which dedicates the route to Angelo Viali. Allow about 20 minutes to here from the *rifugio*. The cable is sound, although frequently not well tensioned, so take care – not only because you might find yourself 'barn-dooring', but also because movement of the cable can dislodge some of the large amounts of loose rock lying around on this route.

The route starts with easy scrambling up the bed of a gully to a 15m ladder (about 1335m). The ladder is initially quite steep and has been damaged by stone falls, so it has a disconcerting wobble. Above the ladder, the cable traverses to the left across a wall. Whilst this is steep, it is sound and well provided with holds. The angle falls back somewhat, and you arrive at a second ladder, slightly shorter than the first and not as 'distressed', but just as steep. The route continues up the broad rocky gully, intermittently protected, but with no real difficulty, save for avoiding kicking loose rocks down onto anyone below.

At about 1420m, you encounter the most difficult pitch of the route, a steep and slightly bulging wall. Its ascent is slightly strenuous, but is aided by a couple of metal pegs near the top. Follow the gully for another few metres until it forks; the cable takes you up the left-hand wall of the left fork. This is initially pleasant climbing on sound rock, but soon becomes very friable. More easy scrambling brings you, at about 1480m, to a box containing a hand-bell! An easy walk up a friable, sandy gully brings you to a pleasant grassy ridge – with a park bench (yes, honestly!). Enjoy a sit down and contemplate the final difficulty of the route; a third ladder just above you (at about 1525m). This one is about 30m in length, and again very steep. An easily angled grassy slope now takes you over a shoulder to the end of the ferrata, where it crosses Sentiero Francesco Milani, way-marked 202, at about 1575m. The route will have taken about 1½ hours to complete.

The way ahead to the summit is now called Sentiero Ezio Ferrari, but is also signposted as VF Gramolon, Madonna della Cima. It is pleasant walking, without protection, so this is the point to pack your gear. The waymarked path passes through dwarf pines and then mixed deciduous trees into a more open area dotted with small rocky outcrops. At about 1710m, look out for a less well-defined path to the right, waymarked, and heading for a wooden pole on the grassy ridge. Follow this new path to the summit of Monte Gramolon (1814m, and about 30 minutes from path 202), a pleasant viewpoint with a large metal cross, a shrine and another bell. A glance at the summit book suggests that most visitors have reached here by the ferrata, although there is a very easy walk up, which you are now about to reverse to return to the *rifugio*.

Follow the waymarked path north-westwards to Passo Ristele (1620m), then turn south on path 202, waymarked Rif. Falcone. Passo della Scagina (with its collection of sign-posts) is now just ahead, but just before you reach it take Sentiero Milani, signposted off to your left (about 1565m); this is still signposted 202 to Rif. Falcone. It is a splendid wartime construction, broad and level as it traverses round the hillside. Within about 10 minutes, a path heads down into the trees on the right. This is path 210, Sentiero Bertagnoli, back into the gorge, which is a quick, but less interesting, route back to the *rifugio*.

Instead, continue on, passing a memorial plaque to Bepi Bertagnoli, and head into a short tunnel. About 20 minutes after joining this sentiero, you come to the point which you passed a couple of hours ago (where path 202 crosses the end of the ferrata). Go straight on for a further 15 minutes until you reach path 207, signposted to Rif. Bertagnoli, to the right down into the woods. Follow this to a gravel road, where you turn left (south), downhill, still waymarked 207. The track enters woodland, passes a welcome spring and brings you back to the *rifugio* about 1¾ hours after leaving the summit.

BRENTA

Maps

Kompass Carta Escursionistica 1:25,000 Sheet 688 (there are also Kompass 1:30,000 and 1:50,000 versions, but the 1:25,000 is the best) or APT Madonna di Campiglio, Passeggiate 1:40,000 Sheet 1 (free)

Tourist Information Office

APT Madonna di Campiglio, Via Pradalago 4, 38084 Madonna di Campiglio, Italy

Tel: (0465) 442000

Fax: (0465) 440404

E-mail: info@campiglio.net

Internet: www.campiglio.net

Tourist Information Office

APT Dolomiti Brenta, 38018 Molveno, Italy

Tel: (0461) 586924

Fax: (0461) 586221

E-mail: info@aptmolveno.com

Internet: www.aptdolomitipaganella.com

Unlike the routes in other sections of this guide, which are accessed from a single valley base, the Brenta Dolomites are accessible from a number of places. It is therefore best to complete the routes over a number of days using *rifugios*, rather than basing yourself in a particular valley, as only a few of the ferrata routes actually lend themselves to day trips.

Although a guidebook could be written on the Brenta alone, this section simply describes each of the ferrata routes, outlines what options are available (with some recommendations for multi-day tours), and indicates where one-day trips are possible. There are many potential variations to itineraries, so look at the routes available, study the map to see how the routes link together, and then enjoy working out your individual itinerary. The weather may impinge on your plans, as will the availability of *rifugio* accommodation and fitness level; because there are so many variables your plans must be flexible, especially where the weather is concerned. The routes below outline the simplest A to B option – the rest is up to you.

There are many villages (and a number of Tourist Information Offices) which surround the Dolomiti di Brenta, but Madonna di Campiglio (1597m) on the western side is recommended as the most convenient base. On the eastern side Molveno (937m) is also a good base, but it is at a much lower altitude, thus making access more difficult – even with the one uplift system from Molveno, approach walks to *rifugios* take longer and involve considerably more ascent.

Madonna di Campiglio has a large Tourist Information Office where English is spoken. Madonna is akin to Cortina in being quite a chic mountain resort, especially in winter, but sports a good range of hotels, guesthouses and apartments, shops, banks, and restaurants to suit all pockets. In September apartments are available quite cheaply in Madonna, thus making it a feasible valley base that would enable you to pick out good-weather windows for two-day trips in the mountains, with an overnight *rifugio* stay and a return to the valley to recover. There are several agencies letting apartments, including Agenzia Immobololiare Campiglio, tel: 0465.443252, email: agenziacampiglio@tin.it, internet: www.agenziacampiglio.it.

On the western side there are campsites at San Antonio di Mavignola, Madonna di Campiglio (Camping Fae, tel/fax:

General view towards the Central Brenta from Passo Groste

0465.507178) and at Carisolo (805m) (Camping Parco Adamello, tel: 0465.501793, www.campeggitalia.it/trento/parcoadmello), and on the eastern side in Molveno adjacent to the pretty Lago di Molveno (Camping Spiaggia, Molveno, tel: 0461.586978, email: camping@molveno.it, internet: www.molveno.it/camping).

The ferratas of the Brenta are all quite high-level routes, generally involving walk-ins of at least 2 hours from the nearest road access points. However, there is a gondola for access from Carlo Campo Magno, just north of Madonna di Campiglio which takes you to a strategic point of attack at Passo del Groste. Another lift also operates from Pinzolo (south of Madonna) to Doss del Sabion, and from Molveno on the eastern side there is a lift system, but no quick access and approach to the central area is generally gained by following path 322.

General Information on the Brenta Group

Geographically the Brenta group (42km in length) extends north from Lake Garda and west from Trento, and is separated from the other Dolomite ranges by the valley of the River Adige. It runs north–south with very little east–west projection, and only at the southern end of the central group, beginning around Cima Tosa, does the range split into two longer branches enclosing Val d'Ambiez. In the Brenta group there are still several small areas of glaciation, all lying on the west side of the main Brenta ridge; some of these have to be negotiated in the course of the ferrata routes. To the west Val Rendenna is a great dividing line between the Brenta and the Adamello and Presanella groups, which comprise a complete contrast of volcanic granite and larger remaining areas of glaciation.

In spite of its grandeur it was comparatively late in being discovered by mountaineers. On 24th July 1864 John Ball stimulated interest for climbers making the first east west crossing via the Bocca di Brenta. The bocca ('mouth'), 2552m, a dramatic gap between Brenta Alta and Brenta Bassa, is still an important pass, crossing in an east–west direction from Molveno to Madonna di Campiglio. As early as the 1930s climbers began to widen the horizontal rock ledges, previously simply scoured from the cliffs by wind and weather, from Bocca di Brenta to Bocca degli Armi, and equip them with pegs, ladders and wire ropes as a protected high-level route.

However, in spite of the ferrata climbing aids, nature is often at its fiercest in the Brenta and can show the mountaineer the superior power of mountains at any time of the season. A sudden drop in temperature with snowfall in high summer, or icing in autumn, can present even the most experienced and expert climber with very serious problems. Plan your days carefully with special regard for route conditions and weather forecasts, particularly when thunderstorms are predicted. In mist be very careful to follow way-marked paths and not to take paths you are uncertain of; Brenta terrain really never allows a pathless descent, so don't be embarrassed to turn back.

Lift Systems
- Madonna di Campiglio, Carlo Campo Magno, Groste 1 and 2; end of June to mid-September
- Madonna di Campiglio, Pradalago; mid-July to end of August (route BREN 13 only)
- Madonna di Campiglio, 5 Laghi; end July to end of August (route BREN 13 only)
- Pinzolo, Doss Del Sabion; mid-July to early September (routes BREN 7, 8 and 9)
- Molveno, Pradel; May to October (0830 to 1300 and 1400 to 1800)

Rifugios in the Brenta Group
Large, good-quality *rifugios* are numerous in the Brenta, but even with the number of bed nights available they become very overcrowded, especially at weekends and in the peak month of August. Below are listed the high- level *rifugios* in the Brenta group, which make useful bases for excursions to link the via ferratas. There are numerous other *rifugios* at lower levels which may also be useful for extended walking trips in the Brenta or as stopping-off points for an approach to the higher mountains. The extremely useful *Guide to the Refuges in Trentino* (including all those in Brenta) is published in English by the APT (Trentino Tourist Board). This can be obtained free from Tourist Information Offices in Trentino or by email from apt@provincia.tn.it.

Members of the Austrian Alpine Club (OAeV) can take advantage of reciprocal arrangements in any of the CAI *rifugios* (not the private ones though). It is easy to join in the UK, and as a member you get up to 50% reduction on the price of a bed and even some meals. Other benefits include emergency rescue cover.

Advance bookings at *rifugios* are essential at peak times (July/August, and weekends anytime), but are advised at all times. Types of sleeping accommodation vary from small two-bedded rooms to large communal mattresses, but whatever you are in a sheet sleeping bag is obligatory. Each *rifugio* seems to have its own meal arrangements on timings, ordering and serving. You can get half-pension deals in the *rifugios*, but choosing from the basic menu, e.g. soup, pasta and sauce, is usually cheaper.

Below are the main *rifugios* in the area from north to south.

Rif. Peller, 2022m
CAI, SAT. Tel. 0463 536221.
Open 20 June to 20 Sept (and 1 Dec to 30 April). 40 beds.
Access by car from Cles, a drive of 17km, with the road (waymark 313) unsurfaced in parts. Walking access using the road takes about 4 hours. This *rifugio* can be used in a demanding two-day excursion of the northern section of the Brenta from Passo Del Groste (see routes BREN 11 and BREN 12).

Rif. Graffer al Groste, 2261m
CAI, Trento section. Tel. 0465.441358.
Open 20 June to 20 Sept (and 1 December to 30 April). 70 beds.
Easily accessed by gondola lift from Campo Carlo Magno (Madonna di Campiglio) to Passo del Groste. Get off at the mid-station and it's a 30 minute uphill approach; or go to the top station, and it's a 20 minute descent.

Rist. Affittacamere Vallesinella, 1513m
Private. Tel. 0465.442883.
Open 15 June to 30 Sept. 30 beds.
Probably somewhere you will leave your car as the access point to the higher *rifugios*.

You can drive here (4km) from Madonna di Campiglio and park for a small daily charge. The car park does fill up, but a minibus taxi service runs from Madonna di Campiglio to Rist. Vallesinella. The shortest fare is from Madonna Sud, at the south end of Via Vallesinella, just after Garni Dei Fiori (D9 on Tourist Office plan of Madonna). It is also possible to get the minibus to/from Madonna North, or even the Groste gondola. Charges for these trips are slightly higher.

Rif. Casinei, 1825m

Private. Tel. 0465.442708.
Open 15 June to 10 Oct. 60 beds, and pleasantly situated in a small glade on the way to the higher rifugios.
Access from Rist. Vallesinella (see above). The approach to the *rifugio* takes under an hour for the ascent of 310m on path 317.

Rif. F.F. Tuckett and Q. Sella, 2272m

CAI, Trento section. Tel. 0465.441226.
Open 20 June to 20 Sept. 112 beds.
Access from Rist. Vallesinella (see above). The approach to the *rifugio* takes about 2 hours, with an ascent of 760m on path 317, passing Rif. Casinei on the way.

An alternative approach is to take the Groste gondola to Passo del Groste and follow path 316 (under 1½ hours).

The *rifugio* is situated under the impressive Castelletto walls, and is a good base for the start of the SOSAT route (BREN 2) or Bocchette Alte (BREN 4).

Rif. Maria e Alberto ai Brentei, 2182m

CAI, Monza section. Tel/Fax 0465.441244.
Open 20 June to 20 Sept. 90 beds.
Access from Rist. Vallesinella (see above). The approach takes about 2–2¼ hours, with an ascent of 670m on path 317, passing Rif. Casinei and then continuing on path 318, the 'Bogani' path.

The *rifugio* can be used as a base for a number of routes: Sentiero SOSAT (BREN 2), Sentiero Detassis (BREN 3), Bocchette Alte (BREN 4) and Bocchette Centrali (BREN 5).

Rif. A. Alimonta, 2580m

Private. Tel. 0465.440366

Open 20 June to 20 Sept. 94 beds.

Access from Madonna di Campiglio is the same as for Rif. ai Brentei above, and then continue for about 1 hour on path 323. Total time from Rist. Vallesinella is about 3–3½ hours.

The *rifugio* is a good starting point for Sentiero O. Detassis (BREN 3), which links to the Bocchette Alte (BREN 4) and Bocchette Centrali (BREN 5).

Rifs. Tosa, 2439m, and Tommaso Pedrotti, 2491m

CAI, Trento section. Tel. 0461.948115, Fax 0461.587003. Open 20 June to 20 Sept. 120 beds in total between Rif. Tosa and Rif. Pedrotti.

You are most likely to reach Rif. Tosa from a ferrata route, as it is situated just a few minutes below the Bocca del Brenta and is a strategic point for the Bocchette Centrali (BREN 5), Sentiero Orsi (BREN 6) and Sentiero Brentari (BREN 8). The nearest access from a valley base is from Molveno along Val delle Seghe, following path 319 all the way. This involves an ascent of over 1500m, for which you should allow at least 5 hours.

Rif. Silvio Agostini, 2410m

CAI, Trento section. Tel. 0465.734138. Open 20 June to 20 Sept. 54 beds.

It is possible to drive about 3km from San Lorenzo in Banale to a parking area at Pont Baesa. The road along Val d'Ambiez is then closed to traffic and is designated path 325. Follow this past Rif. Al Cacciatore (1820m), where the path becomes Sentiero A. Dallago and leads to Rif. S. Agostini. The approach to the *rifugio* involves a vertical rise of 1600m, and you should allow 5–6 hours; this can be made easier by using the taxi service which runs in Val Ambiez up to Rif. Cacciatori from early July to early September. Check details with Taxi Bosetti, San Lorenzo in Banale, tel. 333.3198204.

The *rifugio* is a departure point for climbing the summits of Cima Tosa and Cima d'Ambiez. Ferrata routes approached from here are Sentiero Ideale (BREN 7), Sentiero Brentari (BREN 8) and Sentiero Castiglione (BREN 9).

Rif. XII Apostoli (F.11i Garbari), 2488m

CAI, Pinzolo section. Tel. 0465.501309.

Open 20 June to 20 Sept. 22 beds.

The easiest access to this *rifugio* is to use the Doss del Sabion gondola and chairlift from Pinzolo (good parking here and public bus service from Madonna di Campiglio). From the top of the chairlift (2100m) descend path 357 (a ski piste at first and then a narrow steep path) to Passo Bregn de l'Ors (1836m). Path 307 then heads east along Piano di Nardis and Scala Santa (an easy, short cabled ascent) to the *rifugio* (allow about 3 hours for this). A longer approach can be made from the Val d'Algone road (open to vehicles as far as Malga Molvina), following path 324 until it joins path 307 in Val di Nardis (this involves 1100m of ascent).

Ferrata routes accessible from here are Sentiero Ideale (BREN 7) and Sentiero Castiglione (BREN 9).

Direction of Routes

The routes in the Brenta are generally hut-to-hut trips rather than individual climbs, and as such can be completed in either direction. Each route is described in just one direction; but with the help of a map, it should be reasonably easy to follow the route in the opposite direction.

Character of Routes

The character of these routes could be summed up as ledges and ladders. The ladders can be quite airy, but as long as you take your time and clip on correctly they are a perfectly safe place to be. Ledges, however, are not always protected, even in some very exposed places where you may think they should be! A head for heights, freedom from vertigo and surefootedness are essential.

Timings

Timings are based on the authors' completion of the routes, which seem to correspond reasonably well with those stated in local guides. The timings are guidelines only, and assume a good general fitness and a medium-weight (10–15 kilos) rucksack. A big load will slow you down (as well as being more cumbersome), so try to keep your pack weight down. Also (and this especially applies at the beginning of your holiday) the routes in the Brenta are generally at 2500m and above, where the air is a little thinner, and you may need a couple of days' acclimatisation even if you are reasonably fit on arrival.

Snow and Ice Equipment

The need to carry ice axes and crampons will depend on your own personal experience and ability, weather conditions (particularly day-to-day temperatures and precipitation), and the time of your visit relative to the depth of previous winter snowfalls and the melt rate across the summer. However, all the high-level routes in the Brenta involve some glacier crossing, and whilst it may be warm one day the weather changes very quickly, and soft snow may turn to ice overnight or freezing rain may lead to verglassed rocks. Therefore, although not especially high relative to the Alps, you should consider the Brenta routes in Alpine terms. For the higher-level routes you are advised to carry snow and ice equipment, and this is highlighted in the route descriptions.

Via delle Bocchette
(Brenta Central and South)

The main part of the Via delle Bocchette, in the Central and Southern Brenta, extends from Passo del Groste to Rif. Dodici Apostoli (XII Apostles). The first part, Sentieros Ideale and Brentari, was constructed in the early 1930s. Routes were added over the years, with the final high-level link, Bocchette Alte, being opened in 1969.

The Via delle Bocchette, includes the following routes:
- Sentiero Benini (BREN 1): Passo del Groste – Bocca di Tuckett

Low Level Option: Bocca di Tuckett – Bocca degli Armi via Rif. Alimonta
- Sentiero SOSAT (BREN 2)

High-Level Option: Bocca di Tuckett – Bocca degli Armi
- Sentiero delle Bocchette Alte (BREN 4)
- Sentiero delle Bocchette Centrali (BREN 5): Bocca degli Armi – Rif. Tommaso Pedrotti
- Sentiero Brentari (BREN 8): Rif. Tommaso Pedrotti – Rif. Agostini or continuation Sentiero Ideale (BREN 7); direct to Rif. XII Apostoli
- Sentiero Castiglioni (BREN 9): Rif. Agostini – Rif. XII Apostoli.

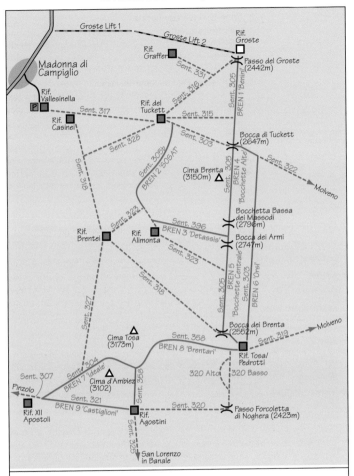

BRENTA CENTRAL & SOUTH

Schematic diagram

Not to scale

There is a northern section of the Via delle Bocchette with the following routes:

- Sentiero Vidi (BREN 10): Passo del Groste – Bocchetta dei Tre Sassi
- Sentiero Costanzi (BREN 11): Bocchetta dei Tre Sassi – Passo di Pra Castron – Rif. Peller
- Sentiero delle Palete (BREN 12): Passo del Groste – Rif. Peller.

BREN 1:
SENTIERO ALFREDO BENINI

Grade:	2
Seriousness:	C
Departure point:	Campo Carlo Magno and the Groste gondola to Passo del Groste, 2442m
Ending at Rif. Tuckett:	
Ascent:	550m
Descent:	650m
Approximate time:	3½–4 hours
Return round from/to Passo Groste:	
Ascent:	700m
Descent:	700m, plus an additional 1½–2 hours
Via ferrata:	1000m (intermittent protection)
Highest altitude:	2900m

Technically this is a fairly easy route with great views, the most entertaining climbing being the last 100m or so as you descend to Bocca del Tuckett.

This route is the first (northern) part of a combination of routes forming the Via Delle Bocchette (see above). As with all the routes in this area it can be quite serious in adverse weather conditions, especially after new snow. There are sections on the route which retain snow throughout the year; these can be crossed quite easily as long as temperatures are high, but an ice axe (and possibly crampons) would be useful in cold conditions, especially for the descent from Bocca del Tuckett.

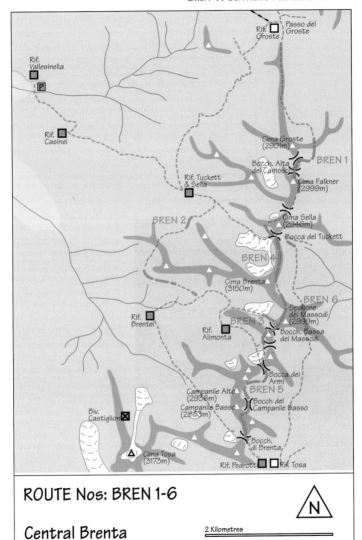

Rif.
Vallesinella
P

Rif.
Casinei

Rif. Tuckett
& Sella

Rif.
Groste

Passo del
Groste

Cima Groste
(2901m)

Bocch. Alta
del Camosci

BREN 1

Cima Falkner
(2999m)

BREN 2

Cima Sella
(2946m)

Bocca del Tuckett

BREN 4

Cima Brenta
(3150m)

BREN 6

Spallone
del Massodi
(2999m)

Rif.
Brentei

Rif.
Alimonta

BREN 3

Bocch. Bassa
dei Massodi

Bocca dei
Armi

BREN 5

Campanile Alto
(2936m)

Bocch del
Campanile Basso

Campanile Basso
(2883m)

Biv.
Castiglion

Bocch.
di Brenta

Cima Tosa
(3173m)

Rif. Pedrotti   Rif. Tosa

ROUTE Nos: BREN 1-6

Central Brenta

2 Kilometres

N

Sentiero Alfredo Benini is most easily reached by taking the Groste gondola from Campo Carlo Magno to the top station at Passo del Groste. A return circuit from Passo del Groste is described below, which can easily be completed in a single day using the gondola both up and down. However, when you look at the map you will realise that various other options can be considered depending on route choice, weather conditions, and your fitness and ability levels. Sentiero Alfredo Benini takes 3–3½ hours from Passo del Groste to Bocca del Tuckett, and (instead of losing height here by descending to Rif. Tuckett) you could continue either on BREN 4 (Sentiero Bocchette Alte) to Rif. Alimonta in a further 5 hours or (more easily) on BREN 6 (Sentiero Osvaldo Orsi) to Rif. Tosa in a further 3 hours. See those routes below for details.

'Mind your head' sign on Sentiero Benini (BREN 1)

From Passo del Groste follow path 305 climbing steadily past the top of a chairlift (closed in summer) with good waymarks to 2562m, where a short descent leads to the junction of paths 305 and 331, which comes up from Rif. Graffer. Continue on path 305 and a few minutes further on is the SAT ferrata sign, although the start of the protection is a good 40 minutes away yet. Follow the waymarked path climbing up over a typical limestone desert of slabs and pavements scattered with broken rock, reaching a memorial plaque for Sentiero Alfredo Benini about 20 minutes further on at about 2720m. As you pass along the east side of Cima Groste, about 15 minutes further on is the first wire protection, leading to a sign 'Bivacco Del Mattino', simply a flat ledge under an overhang and not shown on maps. A short descent now leads to Bocchetta dei Camosci, 2771m, with a great view down west to Madonna di Campiglio 1200m below.

'Tuckett' is painted on a rock and the sentiero continues below Cima Falkner, along a ledge round a number of corners with wires protecting the more exposed parts, climbing (in about 10 minutes) to the high point of the route at about 2900m. A few minutes further on is a plaque, 'Via Delle Bocchette, Sentiero Alfredo Benini 1895–1968 SAT CAI 1972'. Next comes a climb down a rock rib (exposed but with good protection) and then a ledge rises up to a wide path which turns south-west, with Cima Sella immediately in front of you (south) and beyond that Cima Brenta, 3150m. Being about 2 hours from Passo del Groste to here, it's a good spot for elevenses, with a view to the impressive pinnacle of Castelletto Superiore, 2703m, below you to the west (your height at this point is about 2880m).

The route now descends onto Vedretta di Vallesinella Superiore (actually this is much smaller than the 'Inferiore', though higher and hence named 'Superiore'). It's a short and easy-angled snow crossing and there are waymarks where the path is on rock, but in early season there could be much more snow here and route-finding may be more difficult. After descending about 20 minutes to around 2730m a sign points down to the right for Sentiero B. Delle Giacomo and Rif. Tuckett; this is protected path 315 which descends to Rif. Tuckett in less than an hour. Don't descend here as you will miss the best part of the Benini route, which continues to Bocca del Tuckett (although the descent from here can be used as an escape point in adverse weather).

Continue following Benini 305 across rocky but easy ground; there are a lot of waymarks dotted about here so take care in mist, even though the line of the path is generally easy to follow. Eventually some wire protection leads to three easy-angled ladders and then two steeper ones before a short climb on stemples to a ledge. One more steep ladder and a very short one take you to Bocca del Tuckett, with Val Perse dropping down to the east and Rif. Tuckett to the west.

Sentiero Alfredo Benini ends when you reach Bocca del Tuckett, 2648m (about 3–3½ hours from Passo del Groste), and from there you have the options described above in the opening paragraphs.

Descent of Vedretta di Tuckett to Rif. Tuckett

The descent of Vedretta di Tuckett is relatively easy angled; it is a snow slope all the year round, but there is no crevasse danger, although there are some small ones in the lower part of the glacier (vedretta). Early in the season, and at any time of the year in freezing conditions, an ice axe is recommended and crampons advised. Otherwise the angle of the slope is not particularly steep and a well-stepped path will usually be in evidence. Later in the season (especially after a winter of low snowfall) the lower part of the glacier involves walking on hard ice, although a covering of scree actually makes this easier than it may sound. Generally allow about an hour to descend the 380m from Bocca del Tuckett to Rif. Tuckett, 2270m.

To return to Passo del Groste take path 316 from Rif. Tuckett as it makes its way very pleasantly up to the top station of the Groste gondola in 1½–2½ hours. It is also signed 331 Rif. Graffer, the path junction of which is at about 2400m, an hour or so from Rif. Tuckett. Unless you are staying at Rif. Graffer it is easier to follow path 316 all the way to the top station for the ride down to Campo Carlo Magno.

Descending the ladders just before Bocca del Tuckett on Sentiero Benini (BREN 1) (photo: Marion Smith)

BREN 2:
SENTIERO SOSAT

Grade:	2
Seriousness:	B
Departure point:	Rif. Tuckett, 2272m
To Rif. Maria e Alberto ai Brentei, 2182m:	
Ascent:	200m
Descent:	300m
Via ferrata:	200m
To Rif. Alimota, 2590m:	
Ascent:	400m
Descent:	100m
Via ferrata:	200m
Approximate time:	3 hours
Highest altitude:	c.2450m (or Rif. Alimonta)

As the approach to Rif. Tuckett is only 2 hours from the car park at Rist. Vallesinella in the valley, this route makes a good first day towards the higher Brenta routes or a single-day outing that could be done up and down from Rist. Vallesinella in 7–7½ hours. In bad weather conditions it is advisable to use SOSAT as an easier alternative to going up high on Sentiero Bocchette Alte (BREN 4). The ferrata part of the route is actually quite short and comes near the end of the route, starting with a descent into an exposed gully, followed by a climb up a vertical ladder. Nevertheless there are no technical problems, the protection is sound and, being a short day, it's none too serious either. You can, of course, complete the route in the opposite direction.

From Rif. Tuckett follow path 303/305b heading east towards Bocca del Tuckett. In about 10 minutes path 305b, SOSAT, turns right (south) across the glacial moraine of Vedretta di Tuckett, and in a further 5 minutes you reach a short ladder and a plaque for the Via Delle Bocchette. Don't get excited,

Sentiero SOSAT offers a relatively easy and fairly short excursion from Rif. Tuckett to either Rif. Maria e Alberto ai Brentei, 2182m, or the higher Rif. Alimonta, 2580m. The sentiero is named after the working section of the Trento Alpine Society.

179

Via Delle Bocchette warning sign

as the SOSAT ferrata is still about an hour away, and although you will pass an occasional helpful cable there's no real exposure here. The well-waymarked path winds its way, generally west, along the north flank of Punta Massari, zigzagging up and along ledges with quite a lot of drainage, so watch your footing. The path turns south around the west side of Punte di Campiglio to pass through an impressive collection of very large jumbled boulders, some of which would make significant climbing crags were they in a lesser mountainous area. The path has been constructed quite ingeniously as it winds through the boulder field, but take care to follow waymarks in poor visibility. About 1–1¼ hours from Rif. Tuckett, you descend a short, steep, narrow gully with no protection, and about 10 minutes further on you arrive at the SOSAT ferrata.

Cables lead you down through a hole in the rock, with stemples and then a series of ladders and ledges continuing the descent into the chasm of a foreboding gully, with the vertical exit ladder on the opposite side. If there are people coming in the opposite direction (and there often will be) this is a great place for some spectacular photographs. Some of the cabling is old (and also thinner than usual), but it's there when you need it. Cross the gully to climb the vertical ladder (about 20m high, 51 rungs), then walk off to the right on the protected ledge and the ferrata is virtually over. There is a notice at the top of the ladder saying don't throw stones, which you would think is rather obvious!

Continue on a wide ledge, though after about 5 minutes the roof above this ledge is only about a metre high, and tall folk will need to crawl along (also take care if you have a large rucksack). About 20 minutes after this there are another couple of easy cabled sections and two short ladders to descend, and then you reach the SOSAT route plaque, dedicated in 1960. The route then depends on where you are heading for. If it's Rif. Brentei turn to the right to follow path 323, a descent of about 30 minutes. If you are heading for Rif. Alimonta then continue uphill on path 305b to the *rifugio* in 30–35 minutes. Either way, the total time from Rif. Tuckett is about 3 hours.

BREN 3:
SENTIERO OLIVA DETASSIS

Grade:	4
Seriousness:	B
Departure point:	Rif. A. Alimonta, 2580m
Ascent:	300m
Descent:	300m
Via ferrata:	200m
Approximate time:	2½ hours
Highest altitude:	2796m, Bocca dei Massodi

The route can be climbed as a short round-trip from Rif. Alimonta to Bocchetta Bassa dei Massodi, then heading south on the final part of the Bocchette Alte route, Sentiero Umberto Quintavalle, over Cima Di Molveno to Bocca dei Armi and back down to Rif. Alimonta. Alternatively, it can be used as a link from or to Rif. Alimonta and Bocchette Alte (BREN 4) at Bocchetta Bassa dei Massodi, 2790m. However, it is probably best ascended to join the Alte route rather than descending from it, especially at the end of the day when you may be tired. A slightly longer ascent or descent (about 400m) can be added to both of the above options if you stay at Rif. Brentei instead of Rif. Alimonta. Another extended day option would be to climb Sentiero Oliva Detassis (created by the Detassis brothers and named after their mother, Oliva), head south to Bocca dei Armi, and then continue on the Via delle Bocchette Centrali (BREN 5) as a through-trip to Rif. Tosa/Pedrotti. Allow about 5 hours for this option.

Sentiero Oliva Detassis is perhaps the hardest of the Brenta ferratas. It is a steep and very exposed route (reflected in its grade) which goes up a series of ladders; it is definitely not for vertigo sufferers, though the protection is good throughout.

From Rif. Alimonta a poorly waymarked path 396 leads round a rock buttress to the north of the *rifugio* into the glacial bowl of Vedretta dei Brentei. Within 10 or so minutes this meets path 323/305b, coming from the left up from Rif. Brentei, and the SOSAT (BREN 2) route. (Those descending Sentiero Detassis should note that at this junction there are battered signs on the ground for both Rif. Brentei and Rif. Alimonta, but path 396 is neither signed nor waymarked.) A reasonable path now leads into the glacial bowl waymarked towards an old snow patch (early in the season waymarks here may still be covered by last winter's snow). The angle of the slope now becomes very steep, and you go up scree over ice at the foot of the glacier. It is poorly waymarked and finding a good line would be difficult in mist, but you should essentially head for the middle of the slope to left (north) of the steep snow coming down from Bocchetta Bassa dei Massodi. The route starts to the right of black and yellow walls rising above you to the east; there is a big red asterisk painted on the wall, if you have clear visibility. Basically, there's no easy way – you just have to get up to the start of the route the best way that you can!

It's a short, unprotected climb to the first wire and stemples, with steep ladders from that point on. If you have made an early start then the ladders will be cold, with some water seepage, damp or even ice. The first half (100m) of the route is the steepest, and there are more resting places between ladders on the top half. The ascent of the ladders takes 40–45 minutes, a total of about 1½ hours from Rif. Alimonta.

At the top of Sentiero Detassis, with Bocchetta Bassa dei Massodi, 2796m, ahead of you to the right, you have two choices. One is to head north on Via Delle Bocchette Alte (BREN 4 below). The other option is follow the cables (only 2 minutes) to Bocchette Bassa dei Massodi, which is a quite narrow ridge plunging away steeply on both sides, and can be quite intimidating to cross especially if still covered in snow. Cables and ladders on Sentiero Umberto Quintavalle (actually the last, and fairly easy, section of the Bocchette Alte) will complete the circuit if you have planned a short day. You climb about 100m onto the scree-covered plateau, about 2890m, on the north side of Cima Di Molveno, 2917m. Follow waymarks, cables and ladders down to the glacier (commemorative plaque at the end of the route) and Bocca dei Armi and then back down Vedretta degli Sflumini to Rif. Alimonta. (The glacier is not desperately steep, but an ice axe and crampons are recommended as parts of its crossing can involve hard ice as well as snow.) ▶

As mentioned in the introduction, you could continue from Bocca dei Armi on the Bocchette Centrali to Rif. Tosa/Pedrotti (see BREN 5 below).

BREN 4:
SENTIERO BOCCHETTE ALTE

Grade:	4
Seriousness:	C
Departure point:	Rif. Alimonta, 2580m
Ascent:	700m
Descent:	500m
Via ferrata:	4–5 hours intermittent Bocca dei Armi to Bocca del Tuckett
Approximate time:	6 hours (to Rif. Tuckett)
Highest altitude:	2999m, Spallone Dei Massodi

In ferrata climbing terms (in good weather condition) this is a technically straightforward route, but it should not be underestimated, as it is essentially a high Alpine-style traverse, which is reflected in the grade. Good mountaineering skills and experience are prerequisites for the Bocchette Alte; it is most certainly not a place for beginners and should only be attempted in stable weather conditions, as once you are on the route there are no escape options. Early in the season there may be old snow or icing, though because of its sustained altitude this can be a problem at any time of the season. An ice axe and crampons are strongly recommended and a short rope is also advisable. Up-to-date information on route conditions can be gleaned from *rifugio* managers, who in many cases are mountain guides themselves. Despite these warnings, the Bocchette Alte is one of the Brenta group's classic routes, so if you have the experience, and of course good luck with the weather, then go and enjoy it.

This is the highest route in the Brenta group, with a series of high-level and at times very exposed ledges and multiple ladder sections, which take you along the eastern face of Cima Brenta at about 3000m.

If you choose to go north–south and want a long and demanding day the Bocchette Alte can be combined with **Sentiero Alfredo Benini** (BREN 1), using the Groste gondola to Passo del Groste as the access point. From there allow about 3 hours on Sentiero Benini to Bocca del Tuckett plus about 5 hours on Bocchette Alte to Rif. Alimonta in a total of about 8 hours.

Another combination would be to do the **Alte route** from Rif. Tuckett to Bocca dei Armi (about 5 hours) and then continue on the **Via delle Bocchette Centrali** (BREN 5) to Rif. Tosa/Pedrotti in a further 3 hours, thus making a total day of about 8 hours.

The Bocchette Alte is a splendid day out, whether climbed north–south or vice versa. The authors favour the south–north traverse from Rif. Alimonta (or even Rif. Brentei) to Rif. Tuckett; this takes about 6 hours depending on conditions and traffic. This direction not only provides the opportunity to climb Sentiero Oliva Detassis (BREN 3) as the approach to the Bocchette Alte route but, because you are starting at a higher altitude, you get to the high part of the Alte route more quickly. However, the choice of direction is up to you. ◀

If approaching from Rif. Tuckett it's a climb of about an hour to Bocca del Tuckett and a further 5–6 hours on Sentiero Bocchette Alte to Bocca dei Armi and down to Rif. Alimonta. The features on the Alte route being the reverse of those described below.

To include the climb of Sentiero Oliva Detassis as the approach to join the Bocchette Alte at Bocchetta Bassa dei Massodi, see BREN 3 above. Note, that this misses out a short section of the Alte route, Sentiero Umberto Quintavalle, which climbs from Bocca dei Armi up the west side of Cima Molveno on cables and ladders to a scree-covered plateau at about 2890m, just below the summit. Waymarks, cables and ladders then lead down to Bocchetta Bassa dei Massodi, 2796m, a narrow, intimidating pass, especially if still covered in snow. Cross the pass and you see Sentiero Detassis leading steeply down the western side and Bocchette Alte continuing on the west flank of Spallone dei Massodi; this section of the route is Sentiero Mario Cogiola, though this is not signed. Ladders, intermittent cables and some walking sections lead onwards and upwards, with a good view back south across Bocchetta Bassa dei Massodi towards Cima Di Molveno.

About 30 minutes from Bocchetta Bassa dei Massodi a quite long section of cables is followed by a walk (well waymarked) across a fairly flat, high-level limestone pavement on Spallone Dei Massodi, 2999m, the highest point on the route (this peak was also known as Cima Butler in old guides in recognition of the first ascent by an English climber). At the northern end of the high-level pavement is a plaque, 'Alla Scala degli Amici, Gardolo 26/09/69', which commemorates the 'Ladder of Friends' financed by Detassis' friends. Waymarks and cables lead down and round a corner, and a few minutes from the plaque the Ladder of Friends descends to a narrow ledge and short ridge. Intermittent cables (it's quite exposed here on some of the non-cabled parts) and another ladder take you up again, followed by more intermittent cables to Bocchetta della Vallazza, between Spallone Dei Massodi and Cima Brenta, about 30 minutes from the top of the Ladder of Friends. This is quite a wide, level area with no exposure and makes a good spot for a break, with dramatic views to the east opening up down to Sentiero Orsi (BREN 6) and Val Perse.

Now you are at the start of the next section, indicated by a plaque, 'Sentiero Dorotea Foresti I Figli Anno 1968–1969'. It's a walk along a ledge with intermittent cables and continued exposure, especially at some places where it is not cabled. After about 15 minutes you round a corner to a steep, narrow snow gully coming down from the summit of Cima Brenta (an additional hazard here is possible stone fall). Although a wire leads across the snow, this crossing can be problematic early in the season or at any time when cold and icy. Old (but sound) ladders lead up out of the other side of the gully to a ledge with good new cables. About 10 minutes further on a sign (the same as the one before) indicates the end of the Foresti section.

Soon after this yet another plaque, 'Societa degli Alpinisti Tridentini Cengia Carlo e Guiseppe GARBARI 1969', indicates the start of the next section, known as the Garbari ledge. Follow waymarks as they lead down to the right (in mist beware of a decoy path straight on). It's quite a scrambly descent and is not protected, but it is very well waymarked. An easy walk along a ledge follows to some new cables and a very comfortable section, with Molveno and Lago Molveno about 2000m below you to the south-east.

Around 30 minutes after the Garbari sign your high-level traverse is coming to an end, and the descent (about 300m) to Bocca del Tuckett begins. This is the Pedrotti section, and it takes about 45 minutes down a series of cables, broken ground and short ladders – always well waymarked – to Bocca del Tuckett and a quite unusual plaque to Enrico Pedrotti – Coro del SAT, dedicated to the founders of the SAT choir.

Now all you have to do is descend Vedretta di Tuckett to Rif. Tuckett – for details of this see BREN 1 above.

BREN 5:
VIA DELLE BOCCHETTE CENTRALI

Grade:	3
Seriousness:	C
Departure point:	Rif. Alimonta, 2580m
Ascent:	250m
Descent:	350m
Via ferrata:	500m (intermittent)
Approximate time:	3–3½ hours
Highest altitude:	c.2800m (above Bocca dei Armi)

As its name suggests, this ferrata is the central part of the Via delle Bocchette. Constructed in 1936, the route is dedicated to celebrated Trentino climbers whose names are listed on a plaque at the southern end of the route (near Bocca di Brenta).

This really is a classic route as it takes you from Bocca dei Armi along ledges on the eastern side of Cima Dei Sflumini, around Campanile Basso to the west side of Cima Brenta Alte to Bocca di Brenta, above (and quite close to) Rif. Tosa/Pedrotti. It is not particularly difficult in good conditions and is perhaps the best example of all Brenta ferratas, with a series of ladders and ledges transporting you through the most dramatic rock formations you can imagine. However, like the other routes in the Brenta, it can be a very serious proposition when it's cold, and perhaps icy, especially around the Bocca's Campanile Alto and Basso.

Starting from Rif. Alimonta (the highest *rifugio* in the group, and very strategically located for the central Brenta routes), path 323 climbs to the Vedretta Sflumini in 15–20 minutes. The glacier is not desperately steep, but an ice axe and crampons are recommended, as parts of its crossing (10–15 minutes) can involve hard ice as well as snow. There are some narrow crevasses (easily stepped across), and the line of crossing is roughly up the middle of the glacier (with the popularity of this route this is usually quite obvious).

Bocca dei Armi is a quite wide but stunning pass. The route starts from here climbing an initial series of four ladders (the first of which will probably be straight out of the snow early in the season!) to a narrow, airy, but well-protected rock rib. This is actually the highest point reached on the route, with a striking view back down to the approach glacier. Waymarking (not that it's needed most of the time) and protection are good throughout the route, though there are some quite exposed ledges where there is no protection and your head for heights will be tested.

Cabling leads along a ledge for about 100m, with the ledge then continuing without protection. At the next cable, and only about 15 minutes into the route, you get your first view of the Campanile Basso before a short exposed and unprotected part of the ledge. A short ladder descent leads into a chossy gully, which you cross and then walk along the next ledge for about 10 minutes, with a now much closer view of the Campanile Basso in front of you (take plenty of film – you'll need it, as even if it's a bit misty the views are tremendous). The next 20 minutes or so takes you through Bocchetta dei Sfulmini Basso, with intermittent cabling and at one point a very airy and exposed unprotected passage, though the ledge along Campanile Alto is almost a stroll. If conditions are good you may see climbers on Campanile Basso, first climbed in 1899 (just stand in awe and imagine the gear climbers had available to them over 100 years ago!).

You will now have been on the Bocchetta Centrali for an hour or so, generally going along horizontal ledges without much change in altitude, but now you go quite steeply down for about 150m into Bocchetta del Campanile Basso. Early in the season there may well be snow pack here, and at any time of the summer in cold conditions icing can make this part of the route quite tricky. Continuing from here you notice three plaques, one a route plaque 'Sentiero Arturo Castelli'. After a well-protected move around a corner you follow waymarks for a short ascent up a ramp on the northeast side of Cima Brenta Alte. Waymarks then lead you down again and, after a short ladder, good cables lead along a ledge with a helpful little bridge and an overhanging roof which is quite low, making a crouch (or even a crawl) for tall folk. A short walk now leads to the route plaque with the names of celebrated Trentino climbers (Arturo Castelli, Rizieri Costazza, Celeste Donini, Giovanni Strobele, Bruno Detassis and Enrico Giordani). The final ladder leads down to a ledge, followed by a short ascent up the now almost extinct glacier Vedretta Bocca di Brenta to Bocchetta di Brenta. A short walk from here is Rif. Tosa/Pedrotti.

BREN 6:
SENTIERO OSVALDO ORSI

Grade:	1
Seriousness:	C
Departure point:	Rif. Tosa/Pedrotti, 2491m
Ascent:	300m
Descent:	500m
Via ferrata:	200m
Approximate time:	3½–4 hours
Highest altitude:	2648m, Bocca del Tuckett

Sentiero Osvaldo Orsi is essentially a walk with some protection on its most exposed parts. It does, however, take you through some spectacular scenery in the central part of the Brenta group on the eastern flank of Cima Brenta.

This route provides an easier option from Rif. Tosa/Pedrotti to Rif. Tuckett (or vice versa) at a lower level than the Via della Bocchette, and is a way of returning to Rif. Tuckett following completion of the higher level routes (or in the event of bad weather).

From Rif. Pedrotti (the higher of the two *rifugios* at 2491m), follow path 319 Molveno and 303 Sentiero Orsi down to the original Rif Tosa (2439m). In a few minutes' more descent (about 2400m) you reach a path junction, with path 319 heading right (down to Molveno) and Sentiero Orsi, path 303, the left branch. Path 303 traverses past Cima Brenta Alta, rising steadily with Campanile Basso and other peaks towering above you to the west. For about an hour you can enjoy the views as you walk along with little exposure until you reach the route plaque and, a few minutes further on, the first cable. The protection is short, but things are a little more exposed now as you go along a series of ledges with excellent views. You soon reach another couple of cabled sections along the 'Sega Alta' ledge, after which the protected part of the route is for all intents and purposes over (except for a final cable up to Bocca del Tuckett, see below).

However, a couple of minutes after the last cable (which is only about 15 minutes from the first one) you follow waymarking down a fairly steep unprotected gully (the original path appears to have been re-routed here due to rock falls but the waymarking is good). Ten minutes further on you reach a steep snow slope (even in September) filling a gully leading down from Cima Brenta. Although it's only about 20m wide, it is a very exposed crossing with quite an alarming drop off down towards Val Perse, and so an ice axe (and even crampons) are advisable. From here a path leads along with some up, but mostly down, for about 30 minutes (2–2¼ hours from Rif Pedrotti) to a height of about 2500m. Spectacular views are everywhere, none more so than Val Perse falling away to the east with the impressive walls of Cima Roma rising above it.

From here path 303 turns generally west following waymarks, with a steep climb into the upper reaches of Val Perse – not pleasant. The path goes up rocks to the right (north) of an old snow patch (or early in the season perhaps more easily up the snow). Follow waymarks (with no real consolidated path) onward and upward over steep loose scree – nasty! Towards the 'bocca', near the top of the scree there is a cable on the right (north) wall. However, due to the erosion in the gully you would need to be about 10 feet tall to reach it! Part of it is still usable though, and when you can reach the cable it's nice to get off the scree for a few minutes. Consider 30 minutes a good time for the climb to Bocca del Tuckett, which is about 2½–3 hours from Rif. Pedrotti.

Now all you have to do is descend Vedretta di Tuckett to Rif. Tuckett – for details of this see BREN 1 above – a total of 3½–4 hours from Rif. Pedrotti.

BREN 7:
SENTIERO IDEALE

Grade:	3
Seriousness:	C
Departure point:	Rif. XII Apostoli, 2487m
Ascent:	400m
Descent:	460m
Via ferrata:	300m

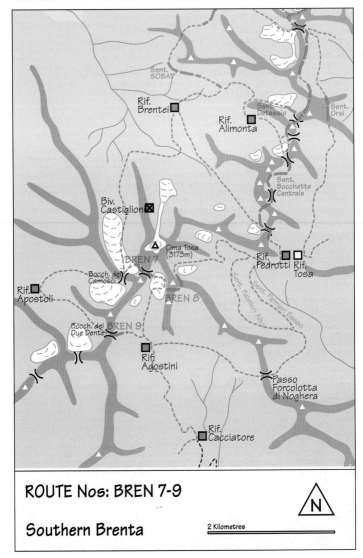

ROUTE Nos: BREN 7-9

Southern Brenta

2 Kilometres

Approximate time:	4 hours to Rif. Agostini, or combined with BREN 8 to Rif. Tosa/Pedrotti 5½–6 hours
Highest altitude:	2871m, Bocca d'Ambiez

This route is described as a traverse from Rif XII Apostoli to Rif. Agostini via Bocchetta dei Camosci and Bocca d'Ambiez, though it would be equally feasible to complete the route in the opposite direction. Sentiero Ideale can be climbed on its own or combined with Sentiero Brentari (BREN 8) to make a through-trip to Rif. Tosa/Pedrotti in what is an only slightly longer day, as you save about 400m descent and reascent to/from Rif. Agostini from the meeting of the two routes on the Vedretta d'Ambiez. The ferrata part of this route up to and down from Bocca D'Ambiez is well protected, but to reach it involves glacier crossings on both the approach to and the descent from the ferrata (Vedretta dei Camosci and Vedretta d'Ambiez). Because of this the route is a fairly serious undertaking, and an ice axe and crampons are recommended at any time of the year.

From Rif. XII Apostoli follow path 304, waymarked R. Tosa, as it climbs first across limestone pavements then onto the

The Sentiero Ideale and Sentiero Brentari (BREN 8) were originally completed in 1932, and they are the oldest part of the via ferrata system in the Brenta Dolomites.

Rifugio XII Apostoli

191

left (north) of the large lateral moraine of Vedretta d'Agola, which leads up to Bocchetta dei Camosci, 2784m; this takes 45–50 minutes. You now have to cross Vedretta dei Camosci on a rising line to the ferrata, which climbs the wall to the north side of Bocca d'Ambiez, on the south side of Cima Tosa. Although the angle of slope on the glacier is not excessive, it steepens towards the end, and so crampons and ice axe may be necessary at any time of the season. Note that a lower level, easier angled track heading north across the glacier is path 327, Sentiero Martinazzi, which goes to Rif. Maria e Alberto al Brentei.

At the end of the glacier crossing there are red-and-white waymarks on the wall which lead quickly up the start of the ferrata. There is a route plaque for Sentiero del Cege, which climbs up ledges, stemples and ladders on quite new and very sound cables to Bocca d'Ambiez, 2871m (about 2 hours from Rif. XII Apostoli). Cross the pass to the cables leading down eastwards towards Vedretta d'Ambiez. There are some places without cables, and the rock is friable, so care is needed, though nowhere is the exposure excessive. About 25 minutes' down-climbing takes you to the glacier Vedretta d'Ambiez. The steepness of the snow slope eases off quickly, but there are some small crevasses and an area subject to stone fall from Cima Tosa up to your left (not a place to hang around!). Rising up to the east is the peak of Punta delle Ideale, after which Sentiero Ideale is named. The glacier crossing takes a line to the north (left on the way down) towards Cima Garbari and the junction with Sentiero Brentari (BREN 8), 40–50 minutes from Bocca d'Ambiez, and about 3 hours from Rif. XII Apostoli. This is the point where path 358 descends to Rif. Agostini below to the south; it is usually waymarked with small red flags stuck in the snow.

The descent from here to Rif. Agostini goes generally south-west across the glacier for a few minutes more before following a fairly steep rocky path heading south along the right (west) side of the valley directly to the *rifugio* in about 40 minutes. ◄

It is also quite feasible (and, if the weather is good, recommended) to continue on **Sentiero Brentari**. For details of that route from the Vedretta d'Ambiez onwards, see BREN 8 below.

BREN 8:
SENTIERO LIVIO BRENTARI

Grade:	3
Seriousness:	C
Departure point:	Rif. Agostini, 2410m, but see BREN 7 above for a suggested combination of the two routes
Ascent:	450m
Descent:	400m
Via ferrata:	600m
Approximate time:	4 hours (or 5½–6 hours if combined with Sentiero Ideale)
Highest altitude:	2860m, Sella della Tosa

In addition to the simple trip of Sentiero Brentari described here, it is possible to link the two routes together as a single day's outing from Rif. XII Apostoli to Rif. Tosa/Pedrotti (see BREN 7); this could be done in either direction.

Sentiero Brentari heads uphill from Rif. Agostini as way-marked path 358 climbing rough, stony ground to Vedretta d'Ambiez in about an hour. As you reach the glacier, Cima Tosa rises up directly above you and Cima d'Ambiez is on your left, with Bocca d'Ambiez splitting the two mountains. Usually there will be small red waymark flags which indicate the safe path across the glacier, but this may not be the case if there has been recent snowfall. The line across the glacier is generally north east towards the walls of Cima Garbari, where the ferrata begins with red-and-white waymarks on the rock. Coming from the left (west) is the route of Sentiero Ideale descending from Bocca d'Ambiez.

The start of the ferrata is the joining point if you were completing both BREN 7 and BREN 8 as a single day's excursion. Both rock and protection are good as you climb away from the glacier using cables, stemples and ladders on the south flank of Cima Garbari. The climb lasts about 30 minutes to a col (not named on the map) between Punta delle Ideale and Cima Garbari at about 2840m. Now follow a series of ledges to the route's high point, Sella della Tosa,

Sentiero Brentari is a scenic route which traverses Vedretta d'Ambiez and high ground around the south-eastern walls of Cima Tosa between Rif. Agostini and Rif. Tosa/Pedrotti. It is a serious route, involving a glacier crossing, and an ice axe and crampons are recommended.

2860m. A further 10 minutes along easy ledges, on the east side of Cima Tosa, with good protection leads to a rickety bridge over a deep gap. This is the end of the protection, and around the next corner a view opens out to the famous Campanile Basso.

Your descent takes you into a vast scree bowl formed by the Vedretta Superiore della Tosa, though today hardly any glacier remains, and although there may be one or two snow patches to cross, for most of the season there's nothing to worry about. Around this scree basin you are enclosed by magnificent rock walls with Cima Tosa to the west, Cima Margherita to the north, and further east Cima Brenta Bassa. Rif. Tosa/Pedrotti is hiding just around the end of the Cima Brenta Bassa massif, but it's still about an hour away. Some of the waymarks around here are a little faded so you need to keep an alert eye, especially in poor visibility, in early season and after new snowfall at any time of the year. About 20 minutes before reaching Rif. Tosa/Pedrotti you reach the junction of path 320 Sentiero Palmeri at about 2460m – see BREN 9 below for details of this path and a suggested circuit back to Rif. Agostini or even Rif. XII Apostoli. The final 20 minutes to Rif. Tosa/Pedrotti goes steadily uphill with a couple of scrambly bits along the way.

Climbing at the start of Sentiero Brentari (BREN 8)

BREN 9:
SENTIERO ETTORE CASTIGLIONI

Grade:	2
Seriousness:	B
Departure point:	Rif. Silvio Agostini, 2410m
Ascent:	450m
Descent:	400m
Via ferrata:	250m
Approximate time:	2–2½ hours
Highest altitude:	2859m, Bocchetta dei Due Denti

The protection on this route is very good throughout the climb, and although some of the ladders are quite steep, they are not especially technically difficult (and freedom from vertigo is par for the course in the Brenta). There is 200m of ladder climbing (about 300 rungs shared out between a sequence of 13 ladders), with some quite reasonable resting places where you can stop to enjoy the view and perhaps get some photographs as well.

An excellent little (in Brenta terms) route which gives a quick and fairly easy link from Rif. Agostini to Rif. XII Apostoli via Bocchetta dei Due Denti.

From Rif. Agostini follow path 321, and within 10 minutes reach the first wire, a little surprise as the sign at the *rifugio* says it's 40 minutes to Sentiero Castiglioni. It is only a short section of cable (just a few minutes) and then, as per the sign, it's another 30 minutes to the start of the route. A well-waymarked path climbs steadily towards Cima d'Agola, which rises above you to the west.

Sentiero Ettore Castiglioni is basically a ladder climb, which progresses as follows. Three ladders to a ledge; ladders 4 and 5 to another ledge with a little bridge; and then ladders 6 and 7 to another ledge and a short gully. Ladders 8, 9 and 10 are all short as they lead up into a wide, open gully – there are a lot of loose stones here so take care for the sake of those below. Ladder 11 is the longest and steepest on the climb as it takes you to the right of a rock prow at the top of the gully. From the next short ledge ladders 12 and 13 take you to Bocchetta dei Due Denti, 2859m, where the view down to Rif

Climbers on the first ladders of Sentiero Castiglione (BREN 9)

XII Apostoli is superb. The time taken to climb the ladders is about 35 minutes. It's worth keeping your ferrata kit on until you pass the one short cabled section on the descent (only a few minutes from the pass).

The descent is relatively easy, as Vedretta di Prato Fiorito has disappeared as far as you are concerned, with the residual glacier being across the scree bowl to the south below Cima Prato Fiorito. Early season, there may be some significant snow to cross here, but at an easy angle. Later on in the year there should only be a couple of easy snow patches to cross. Waymarks are brilliant, and the *rifugio* is reached in about 45 minutes from Bocchetta dei Due Denti.

Although Sentiero Ettore Castiglioni is a short route, you do have to get to it, and it is the southernmost of routes in the Brenta group. As with all the routes in this area you will probably work out your own itinerary, but here are three pointers to help your planning ideas.

1. You could simply climb the route on its own from the south, approaching along Val D'Ambiez via Rif. Cacciatore.

2. You could combine it with Sentiero Ideale (BREN 7) as a return circuit from Rif. XII Apostoli to Rif. Agostini and back, either as two half-days or one long day.

3. Another suggestion (over two days) is to combine BREN 7 and 8 from Rif. XII Apostoli to Rif Tosa/Pedrotti (without the descent and reascent to Rif. Agostini). After an overnight stay in Rif. Tosa/Pedrotti return on path 320,

Sentiero Palmieri, to Rif. Agostini (about 2½ hours), and then complete Sentiero Castiglioni to Rif. XII Apostoli. Note that Sentiero Palmieri has two options at its path junction 15–20 minutes from Rif. Tosa/Pedrotti, an alto (high) option and a basso (low) option. The alto has a few cabled (but easy) protected bits, but does have the advantage over the basso option of saving you about 250m descent and reascent. The high point of path 320 (after the alto and basso have joined up again) is Passo Forcolotta di Noghera, 2423m; it is a good viewpoint. From here after a short descent you follow an undulating traverse towards Rif. Agostini, with views to the south, along Val D'Ambiez, which leads down towards San Lorenzo in Banale. The last few minutes to Rif. Agostini are uphill, with its little chapel standing proudly on a rock to the south of the *rifugio*.

Northern Brenta

The routes in the northern Brenta are less frequented than those south of Passo del Groste. One of them (Sentiero Vidi, BREN 10) is a relatively short route, which makes for quite an easy day if you use the Groste gondola both up and down. The other routes are not technically difficult, but whichever way you complete them, it will involve a long, and probably lonely, day or two in very rugged unspoilt mountains. Stable weather conditions, a high fitness level, map-reading competence and a good level of mountain experience and judgement are prerequisites for these excursions. Sentiero Claudio Costanzi (BREN 11) and Sentiero Delle Palete (BREN 12) are described in less detail than other ferratas, with optional lengths of days for you to consider; they will appeal more to the long-distance walker, who loves challenging mountain days, than to out-and-out ferrata climbers. In addition, an interesting circular route is suggested, Sentiero Val Gelada (BREN 12a), which takes in the protected part of BREN 12 and links to BREN 11 to return to Madonna di Campiglio in a single day's outing.

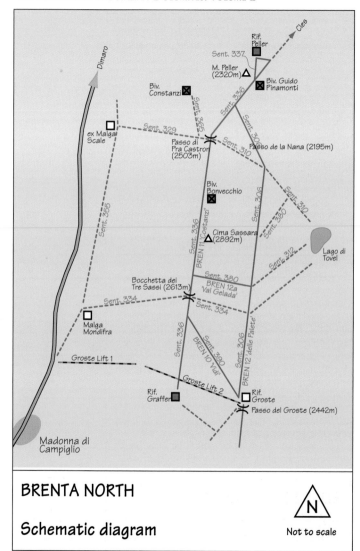

BRENTA NORTH

Schematic diagram

N

Not to scale

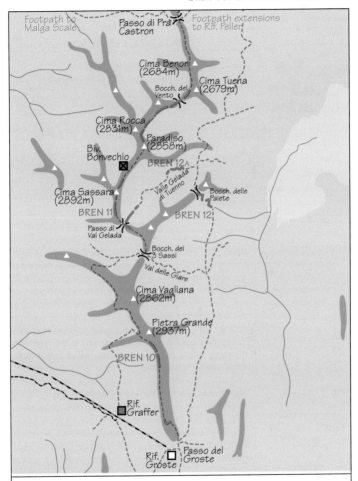

ROUTE Nos: BREN 10,
& protected parts of BREN 11 & 12
Northern Brenta

2 Kilometres

BREN 10:
SENTIERO GUSTAVO VIDI

Grade:	1
Seriousness:	C
Departure point:	Passo del Groste, 2442m
Ascent:	260m
Descent:	550m (to Groste middle station)
Descent:	1050m (to Groste bottom station)
Via ferrata:	500m (intermittent)
Approximate time:	2½–3 hours to middle station, 3½–4 hours to bottom station
Highest altitude:	c.2670m

This route is more of a mountain walk with some protected sections than a climbing ferrata.

Although this is a technically easy route it has a lot of exposure, and while it is perhaps less spectacular than some of the other Brenta routes it does require a good head for heights and sure footedness on narrow, exposed paths on very steep ground. The route makes a good introduction to the Brenta mountains and can be undertaken as a way of getting used to exposure. Unusually, for routes in this part of the world, it has the benefit of being easy to complete from the valley in little more than half a day, which can be useful if the weather is unsettled.

Take the two-stage Groste gondola from Campo Carlo Magno to Passo del Groste, 2442m. Less than 200m northeast from the top gondola station the route is signed 'Sentiero Gustavo Vidi', waymarked as path 390; it follows a rising path across scree to a red SAT ferrata sign in under 10 minutes. From here you zigzag up steep ground for another few minutes to a ledge leading right (about 2560m) and a new route plaque, 'Sentiero Gustavo e Natale Vidi' (Natale, also a mountain guide, was Gustavo's son).

To the left a short climb to a col and rock spur gives a good viewpoint of the main Brenta peaks to the south and a photo opportunity, though you will get similar views higher on the route anyway. Follow the ledge, with good views down on your right to Pra Castron di Flavona and Sentiero delle Palete below, until waymarks lead left up to a superb narrow ridge with great views all around. Going along the ridge, reassuring wires give protection across a narrow rock bridge just before you reach a section of cables at about 2630m (about 40 minutes from Passo del Groste). Easy protected climbing leads to a narrow rock gap followed by a walk along the ridge to the highest point of the day at about 2670m.

The path now turns down to the left on to the west flank of Pietra Grande as it follows a long traverse (descending slightly) across a scree-covered slope with a good deal of exposure as the ground on your left drops away steeply. If you have made an early start this part of the route will not have seen the sun yet, and care is required if it is damp, icy or even (early in the season) snow covered. In about 10 minutes you reach a short cable and the original route plaque, 'Sentiero Gustavo Vidi 1969'. Five minutes further on, a series of easy-angled ladders takes you up about 30m to a ledge at a higher level, and more continuous cables then lead along this ledge to a ladder and a short descent. The protection continues for a few more minutes, with the next feature on the route being a rather impressive wooden bench seat under an overhanging rock with the carved inscription 'In Ricordo Della Guida Alpina Natale Vidi'.

The path is now less exposed and leads (in about 20 minutes) to the flat top of an unnamed grassy outlier from the Pietra Grande ridge, map spot height 2522m. Just over the north side of this ridge is the path

A ledge on Sentiero Vidi (BREN 10)

junction with Sentiero Claudio Costanzi; this is signed ahead for path 336 towards Bocchetta dei Tre Sassi, and to the left 389/336, Rif. Graffer, 50 minutes.

Path 336 continues north to Bocchetta dei Tre Sassi (see BREN 11 below) across a steep hillside of scree, but this is the end of Sentiero Gustavo Vidi, and a direct return to Rif. Graffer completes a relatively easy and pleasant half-day excursion.

Follow path 336 as it heads roughly south-west before zigzagging down to the left to a ledge, then continuing further leftwards along a ledge until more zigzags lead down the side of a steep scree slope to Orto Della Regina (the 'queen's garden'), a large Alpine plateau (at just over 2400m). The natural hollow is renowned for fossils and the variety of floral species which blossom here in succession during the summer months. The queen after whom it was named was Sissi, the wife of King Franz Josef of the Hapsburg Empire in the 19th century.

Continue down path 336 to Rif. Graffer; it takes about 50 minutes, as indicated on the sign where your descent started. From Rif. Graffer it's 20 minutes down to the mid-station of the gondola, from where you can ride down to Campo Carlo Magno. Alternatively, walking to the left of the Ristorante Boch Bar at the middle gondola station and following the ski pistes takes you easily down to Campo Carlo Magno in about an hour.

BREN 11:
SENTIERO CLAUDIO COSTANZI

Grade:	2
Seriousness:	C
Departure point:	Rif. Graffer or mid-station Groste gondola (+20 mins)
Ascent:	1150m (estimated)
Descent:	1400m (estimated)
Via ferrata:	2 hours (1+1)
Approximate time:	10 hours (distance: about 18km)
Highest altitude:	2892m, Cima Sassara

Sentiero Costanzi is a serious long day out requiring high levels of fitness, stamina and mountain experience. Although there are some escape points and emergency bivouac shelters, this is a very committing route, which should be undertaken only in periods of stable weather; it should not be attempted in mist, fog, rain, thunder, snow or icy conditions. Also it is best to consider the bivouacs as places for emergency use only rather than planning to stay overnight, as weather changes may turn the next day into a much more serious proposition. Some of the high-level glacial bowls (in the early part of the route particularly) often hold snow early in the season and, with the most exposed and protected parts of the route being about 2800m, an ice axe and crampons may be necessary.

This route is a very long, remote and complex excursion, with a lot of ascent, descent and reascent in a less frequented part of the Brenta group. It may not be as popular as the routes in the central area, but nevertheless it has some spectacular and rugged mountain scenery.

The route is path 336 throughout from Rif. Graffer to Rif. Peller, and can be completed in either direction. It is described here heading north from Rif. Graffer where path 336 climbs past Orto Della Regina (the 'queen's garden', see BREN 10 above) to reach the junction with path 390, Sentiero Vidi, on the west spur of Pietra Grande, after about an hour. ▶ From the path junction continue on path 336 across a vast scree slope on the western side of Cima Vagliana, which leads around to Bocchetta dei Tre Sassi, 2613m. The time from Rif. Graffer to Bocchetta dei Tre Sassi, which is named after the three jagged rock peaks which stick up from the broken col, is about 2 hours. Here also you will find the route plaque dedicated to Claudio Costanzi No 336 CAI/SAT 1974, and a view down Val Delle Giare to the east.

Note that you can make an alternative start to Sentiero Costanzi by taking the Groste gondola to the top station and using Sentiero Gustavo Vidi (BREN 10) as the approach to this junction point; this adds about 30-40 minutes time to the day as well as perhaps adding to the mental drain of a longer day on exposed ground.

If you wanted an **escape point** already then path 334 goes down to the west into Val Gelada Di Campiglio (see BREN 12a below for details). Note, you could escape east (also path 334) down to join path 306, Sentiero delle Palete and return south to Passo del Groste or even go down to Lago di Tovel (where there is accommodation), though that is not recommended (unless you have planned to go that way) as it will take you 'a long way from home'.

Sentiero Claudio Costanzi continues as waymarked path 336 climbing scree and broken rock to a ledge with the first short cables, though no real exposure, and on to Passo di Val Gelada, 2818m, about 30 minutes from Bocchetta dei

Tre Sassi (again see BREN 12a; this time for a suggested circular route including Val Gelada Di Tuenno). From the pass climb some quite steep scree with waymarks leading onto rocks to reach the first main part of the protection on the route (a ladder and cables). The character of the route unfolds with a narrow, exposed, gravel-covered ridge with no protection, and you need to take care with hand and foot placements as the rock is very friable. More continuous cables now lead around the western flank of Sasso Alto, 2890m, with at one point a low overhang (an inconvenience for tall folk and those with large rucksacks). The cables lead down to a small (unnamed on maps) col with very crumbly rock followed by a short climb to the scree covered Cima Sassara, 2892m, though maps show it as 2894m.

This is the highest point reached on the route, though you now stay around the 2800m mark for quite some time. The path splits to go along the scree on the west side of the mountain, but a well-trodden and waymarked path goes up a ridge to the right to reach the summit in only a few minutes more (about 3½ hours from Rif. Graffer). If the weather is clear then the summit visit is a must, with wonderful views all around. There is a large, quite ornate metal cross (SAT Dimaro, Cima Sassara, 2892m, 16/10/1977) and the views take in: to the east, down towards Lago Di Tovel and Cles; to the south, Pietra Grande and the central Brenta peaks; to the west, the glaciers of Adamello and Presanella; and north the snowy peaks of the Ortler group. From the summit waymarks lead northwards down to Biv. Fratelli Bonvecchio, 2780m (reached about 2 hours from Bocchetta dei Tre Sassi or about 4 hours from Rif. Graffer).

The next 2 hours or so involves some easy walking, cabled sections and some quite airy, unprotected scrambling with a lot of ups and downs. Care is required here in following the waymarks as you pass the peaks of Cima Paradiso, 2858m, Cima Rocca, 2831m, Cima delle Livezze, 2779m, and Cima del Vento, 2761m. Then after passing the west side of Cima Tuenna and Cima Benon the path heads steadily down to reach Passo di Pra Castron, 2503m (the end of the protected part of Sentiero Costanzi), about 6 hours from Rif. Graffer.

From Passo di Pra Castron you have a number of options, as outlined opposite.

1. Continue on Sentiero Costanzi to Rif. Peller; for this allow about 4 hours, giving a total day of about 10 hours. Path 336 goes around the eastern flank of Sasso Rosso (an appropriately named red-coloured mountain), with easy walking leading past Selletta de la Nana and down to Passo de la Nana, 2195m. From here local guidebooks vary in what they describe for the final part of Sentiero Costanzi, though maps show path 336 as the definitive route going to Passo della Forcola 2105m, past Biv. Guido Pinamonti and on to Rif. Peller, 2022m. From Biv. Guido Pinamonti you can take path 337 to go over Monte Peller as a more direct finish.

2. Complete a very long (about 12 hours) circuit back to the bottom station of the Groste gondola at Campo Carlo Magno. To do this descend path 329 westwards into Valle del Vento. Take great care here to follow the waymarked path as it goes through some steep craggy ground as it descends to ex Malga Scale (an abandoned settlement). From here make sure you pick up path 355, which heads south and becomes a jeep track that joins a road leading to Malga Mondifra, past the golf course and back to the Groste gondola station.

3. In an emergency Biv. C.A. Costanzi (12 beds) is about 1km away down path 365 to the north-west.

4. Another emergency descent (about 1½ hours) goes eastwards on path 310 to Malga Tuena and Lago Di Tovel, though this takes you a long way from home.

   This is big mountain country, but if you are looking for a long, quiet, remote expedition away from the Brenta crowds then this is it. Completing Sentiero Costanzi to Rif. Peller (10 hours) with an overnight stay and a return to Passo del Groste (7 hours) on Sentiero delle Palete on day two is a challenge to test most people's stamina.

Possible Day Trip on BREN 11

If you simply want a peak to climb then Cima Sassara is well worth doing and can be climbed up and down (returning the same way) from the middle station of the Groste gondola in 7–8 hours. To do this you need to be there when the lift opens at 0830hrs and do the climb up and down reasonably quickly to give yourself time to catch the return gondola, the last one down being at 1700 hrs.

BREN 12:
SENTIERO DELLE PALETE

Grade:	2
Seriousness:	C
Departure point:	Passo del Groste, 2442m
Ascent:	1450m
Descent:	1050m
Via ferrata:	150m
Approximate time:	7 hours (distance: about 16km)
Highest altitude:	2320m

While this route does not have the same spectacular exposure as the ferratas in the central Brenta (such as the Bocchette routes), it is nevertheless a serious and long day out requiring good mountain fitness and experience.

As with Sentiero Claudio Costanzi (BREN 11), this route is a very long, remote and quite complex excursion, with a lot of descent and reascent in a less frequented part of the Brenta group. The route can be combined with Sentiero Costanzi to form part of a multi-day trip to Rif. Peller and back, in the northern Brenta; or Sentiero di Val Gelada (see BREN 12A below) can be used to link the two routes together into a very interesting single day's outing.

Take the two stages of the Groste gondola from Campo Carlo Magno. From the top station (Groste 2), 2438m, follow path 306 Peller, and in less than 200m Sentiero Vidi (see BREN 10 above) is signed uphill to your left. Path 306, 'Sentiero Palete, Rifugio Peller, Solo per Esperti', heads north, downhill below the impressive east walls of Pietra Grande. Follow this good path (easy walking and good waymarks), and in about 40 minutes the first view (north-east) down to the pretty lake Lago di Tovel opens up. In a further 15 minutes the path levels out at about 2170m, with path 334 coming up from Val di S. Maria (right and east) to Bocchetta dei Tre Sassi (left and west).

Path 306 (also signed 380, Malga Tuena) continues ahead (still losing height) for a few more minutes to a height of about 2140m before starting climbing, easily at first, but then the path becomes narrow and exposed. After about 20 minutes a scramble up takes you to the SAT ferrata sign at

The cabled part of Sentiero Palete (BREN 12)

about 2200m. A single short cable is followed by a scramble up a gully to the start of the main protected section in just a few minutes more at about 2220m. The protection is good, with wire and stemples up an open gully; it goes on for about 15 minutes before a walk leads to a cable on very exposed ground, leading to Passo delle Palete, 2319m, in a further 10 minutes. The length of ferrata protection is about 150m.

Descend following waymarks where, despite the map indicating a via ferrata, there is no protection (and rightly so). It takes 15 minutes to the low point (2160m), where path 312 descends to Lago di Tovel and path 380 ascends left (west) to Passo Val Gelada.

The time taken from Passo del Groste to here is about 2¼ hours, and you are about a third of the way to Rif. Peller, which will take a further 5 hours to reach. To do this continue on path 306 for about 1km until the path splits, with path 380, the right fork, descending to Malga Tuena, and path 306, Sentiero alpinisitco delle Palete, the left fork. It takes about an hour from here on steep ground with some exposure and undulation along the east flank of Campo Della Tuenna to arrive at the junction of path 310 coming up from Malga Tuena to Passo di Pra Castron. Turn right here (east) and follow paths 306/310 for a few minutes until path 306 branches left to pass around the east side of Cima Uomo.

Continue on path 306 for about 3km, passing Cima Dell'Omet, until you join path 336 (BREN 11, Sentiero Constanzi) at Passo de la Nana, 2195m; this is the end of path 306. Follow path 336, generally north-east to Passo della Forcola, 2105m, and on to Biv. Guido Pinamonti. Here you leave path 336 to follow path 337 over Monte Peller (a short ascent of a couple of hundred metres) before descending to Rif. Peller, 2022m. If you have chosen this through-trip you will either have arranged for a kind companion to meet you at Rif. Peller or be faced with returning whence you came the next day.

A serious and demanding **two-day trip** is to complete BREN 11 to Rif Peller on day one and then return south on BREN 12, Sentiero Palete, on day two.

Suggested short-return circuit
For details of a pleasing circuit back to the bottom lift station of the Groste gondola via Passo Val Gelada see BREN 12A below.

Possible long-return circuit
Another return option, creating a day-trip from Madonna di Campiglio of about 10 hours, is to continue from Val Gelada on path 306 until the path junction with path 310. At this point ascend west to Passo di Pra Castron, 2503m, and follow paths 329 and 355 as described in BREN 11 above.

BREN 12A:
SENTIERO ATTREZZATO DI VAL GELADA

Grade:	2
Seriousness:	C
Departure point:	Passo del Groste, 2442m, and Sentiero Delle Palete, Val Gelada, 2160m
Ascent:	700m
Descent:	1490m
Via ferrata:	300m
Approximate time:	7 hours
Highest altitude:	2680m, Passo di Val Gelada

Sentiero Attrezzato di Val Gelada (the 'frozen valley') is path 380; it links Sentiero Claudio Costanzi (BREN 11) to Sentiero Palete (BREN 12) and as such is not usually climbed on its own, although you could approach it from Lago di Tovel.

For details of the approach see BREN 12 above, path 306 as far as its junction with path 380, in 2¼–2½ hours. Now follow the well-waymarked path 380 into Val Gelada towards an impressive glacial head wall to reach the first section of cables in 15–20 minutes, at about 2200m. The protected ascent is about 150m, and starts leftwards along a ledge before pleasant climbing on good rock up a gully takes you up the rock wall and into the large bowl on the next level of Val Gelada at about 2340m. It is an impressive, quiet, unspoilt valley with good waymarks until the final part of the ascent up steep scree moraine on the right-hand (north) side of the valley.

About 45 minutes from the top of the first cabled section you reach some more protection (about 30m only) at the top of the scree at about 2610m. From here a scramble and then a walk leads to Passo di Val Gelada, 2680m, in a further 15 minutes (about 4 hours from Passo del Groste). Painted on a rock on the ground is Sentiero di Val Gelada di Tuenno, which seems to be the only named recognition other than path 380!

This route is a suggested round day-trip from Madonna di Campiglio using the Groste gondola lift from Campo Carlo Magno.

You have now joined Sentiero Costanzi (BREN 11), which continues northwards to Sasso Alto and Cima Sassara, if you are feeling energetic and want to visit a summit. However, to complete this return circuit turn left at Passo Val Gelada to head south on path 336 (also waymarked 380) towards Rif. Graffer. After a short climb there are a couple of cables along a ledge before a descent to the next pass above Val Gelada di Campiglio (to the west), Bocchetta dei Tre Sassi, 2613m (named after the three well-weathered and strangely shaped rock pillars guarding the pass). There is also a route plaque dedicated to Claudio Costanzi No 336 CAI/SAT 1974.

Descend from Bocchetta dei Tre Sassi following way-marks on path 336, and in about 20 minutes (about 2490m) the waymarks for path 334 lead down to the right (west). There is no path signpost, so if you don't want to miss the path (334) you will need to be attentive at this point. You could continue on path 336 back to Rif Graffer, but this route follows path 334 to return to the Groste bottom station at Campo Carlo Magno in a little over 2 hours from the point where path 334 leaves path 336. The descent follows Val Gelada di Campiglio, another impressive glacial valley, and having found the path the waymarks are good. After about an hour on path 334, at about 1950m, Vaglia Nella is painted on a rock and the path goes ahead with single red waymarks. This is another place to watch out for as path 334 continues down to the right with red-and-white waymarks, but again no sign-post! In a further 30 minutes, at about 1750m, a sign for 334/336 points back uphill. Take the right branch here, con-tinuing to follow the red-and-white waymarks downhill to a road in another 10 minutes at about 1650m. Turn left and fol-low the road, passing Malga Mondifra and then the golf course on your right, back to the Groste gondola station at Campo Carlo Magno.

BREN 13:
SENTIERO ATTREZZATO UMBERTO BOZZETTO

Grade:	1
Seriousness:	A
Departure point:	Telecabina Pradalago (gondola) to Rif. Pradalago, 2100m

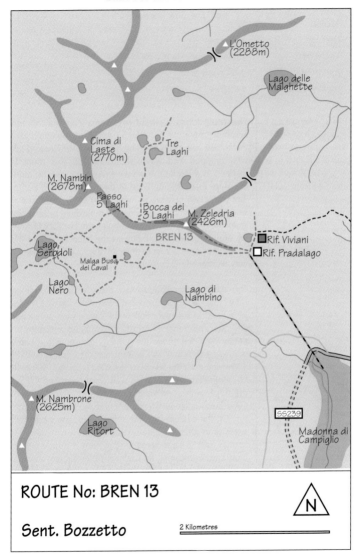

ROUTE No: BREN 13

Sent. Bozzetto

2 Kilometres

N

Ascent:	570m
Descent:	570m
Via ferrata:	150m (in many short sections)
Approximate time:	4–4½ hours
Highest altitude:	2426m, Cima Zeledria

This is a pleasant day's walk which you could do as a loosener at the start of a holiday or as a break from the harder Brenta routes.

This route forms a circuit over Cima Zeledria to Lago Serodoli (one of the Giro dei 5 Laghi), but you could vary this to suit you, perhaps going to the Tre Laghi instead (all well mapped and waymarked). Though this route is mapped as a ferrata it is a very easy route, with no more exposure than Striding Edge in the English Lake District. The protection consists of many short cables, occasional stemples and even some ladders, but nowhere is there any exposure that really warrants clipping on. The rock is granite, and on a clear day, being on the opposite side of the valley, the views across to the main Brenta peaks make it a very worthwhile excursion.

Take the Pradalago gondola from Madonna di Campiglio to Rif. Pradalago (not a *rifugio*, but a bar and restaurant in winter; closed in summer). Follow the signed path 267, Cima Zeledria and Sentiero Attrezzato Umberto Bozzetto, to climb the ridge above the gondola station in a roughly north-west direction. In a few minutes there is another sign and a plaque for the Sentiero Attrezzato Bozzetto 1983 (year of construction). The route is well waymarked and follows the ridge, with good views all around, to the summit of Cima Zeledria (about 40 minutes from the gondola station).

On the descent from the summit there are more short wires, and after 10 minutes follow the waymarked left branch path to Lago Serodoli (the paint is a little faded). Note that 3L (meaning Tre Laghi) is signed straight ahead at this point. A few minutes further on, a ladder takes you down a wall about 5m high before you pass another sign to 3 Laghi, but continue towards Lago Serodoli with more short wires, on a good path, until about 30 minutes after leaving the summit of Cima Zeledria you reach Bocca dei Tre Laghi at about 2370m. From here the path to Lago Serodoli climbs steadily on the north side (right) of the ridge for about 20 minutes to a pass where Passo 5 Laghi is painted on a rock – though this does not appear on maps! Ten minutes from this pass there is another plaque for the Sentiero Attrezzato, and path 226 is signed down to the left, but it is worth continuing ahead to Lago Serodoli, which is only 20 minutes further on and quite a beautiful spot.

Descend from the lake on path 217, signed Lago Nambino/Monte di. Campiglio. After 40 minutes, past the small lake of Lago Nero, a sign indicates 266 Malga Busa dei Caval and Lago Nambino to the left. Follow this path for a few minutes down to Malga Busa dei Caval, where there is another path branch. From here follow path 226 (though the tourist board map shows it as 266), which climbs steadily up and along a steep hillside above Lago Nambino and back to the gondola station in about 45–50 minutes.

Connecting Paths

There are other sentieros which are not ferratas but are nevertheless important links connecting *rifugios* in the system of routes through the Brenta.

Sentiero Attrezzato Dallagiacoma

Path 315 and an early escape route from Sentiero Benini (see BREN 1) to Rif. Tuckett.

Sentiero delle Val Perse

Path 322 and an approach to Bocca del Tuckett from Rif. Croz dell'Altissimo (2½ hours) or Molveno top of Pradel lift (3½ hours).

Sentiero Bogani

Path 328/318 is a low-level path which connects Rif. Brentei to Rif. Tuckett. Allow 1¼ hours.

Sentiero alpinistico D. Martinazzi

Path 392/327/304 from Rif. XII Apostoli via Bocca del Camosci and Vedretta dei Camosci to Rif. Brentei (invloves a fairly easy glacier crossing, but ice axe and crampons advised). Allow 3 hours.

Sentiero Palmeri

Path 320 from Rif. Tosa/Pedrotti to Rif. Agostini via Passo

Forcolotta di Noghera. See Sentiero Castiglioni (BREN 9). About 2½ hours.

Summit Ascents in the Brenta Group

This guide does not include routes that involve rock climbing, and it should be stressed that easily accessible summits on prepared paths do not exist in the Brenta. The builders of the Brenta climbing paths have remained true to the original intention not to open up summits, but to protect only their principal approaches – natural systems of ledges, connecting ridges and traverses. Nevertheless, it is possible under good conditions for more experienced climbers to reach some of the best Brenta summits by their so-called 'normal routes', with difficulty around UIAA Grade II. Descent is usually on the same route. If you are interested in climbs in the Brenta, details can be obtained from local guides and *rifugios* or by purchasing the appropriate climbing guide. The Italian Guidebook covering the Brenta is *Guida Dei Monit D'Italia, G.Buscaini – E.Castiglioni DOLOMOTI DI BRENTA, C.A.I.* An English climbing guide is produced by the Alpine Club, *Dolomites, Selected Climbs*, by Ron James.

A fairly tame family of chamois, some equipped with radio transmitters, live high on M. Agner (AGORD 5 and 6)

TRENTO

Maps
See each route summary

Trentino Area Office
APT Del Trentino, Via Romagnosi 11, 38100 Trento, Italy
Tel: (0461) 830000
Fax: (0461) 260245
E-mail: info@trentino.to
Internet: www.trentino.to

Tourist Information Office
APT Di Trento, Via Manci 2, 38100 Trento, Italy
Tel: (0461) 983880
Fax: (0461) 984508
E-mail: informazioni@apt.trento.it
Internet: www.apt.trento.it

Trento is the capital both of the region of Trentino–Alto Adige and the province of Trentino. The Tourist Information Office provides comprehensive information in English, including a *Guide to Mountain Refuges in Trentino*. There is also a local Tourist Information Office for Trento, where you can obtain details of the many churches, castles and museums in the area as well as information about the First World War and the history of Alpinism in the area.

Trento was the location of the Council of Trent in the 16th century, when the Catholic church, alarmed by the Reformation in north-west Europe, met to plan counter-measures. The city houses a monument to Cesare Battisti, an Italian national hero, an activist for the incorporation of Sud-Tirol into Italy. In the First World War he fought on the Italian side, but was captured by the Austrians and executed as a traitor.

The centre of the city is mainly pedestrianised and has impressive medieval, Gothic and Renaissance buildings, and boasts a full range of facilities for visitors. There are three campsites within easy reach of Trento, the best one being at Terlago, just 12km from the Trento Centro exit of the A22 autostrada (Laghi di Lamar campsite, Localita Vallene, 38070 Terlago, tel. (0039) 0461.860423, fax

(0039) 02.700538636, email: campeggio@laghidilamar.
com, internet: www.laghidilamar.com).

Trento North – Mezzocorona (Fai Della Paganella)

Maps
TRENT 1, 2, 3 Kompass Wanderkarte 1:50,000 Sheet 96 and SAT Mezzocorona 'Monte di Mezzocorona' 1:40,000

These three routes are in the proximity of Mezzocorona. Both Mezzocorona and Mezzolombardo are small residential towns in the heart of the Val d'Adige wine growing area. Unfortunately, neither is geared towards tourism, though there are a few small hotels in the area. Mezzocorona can be reached by bus or train from Trento.

If you have a car a good place to stay is Fai della Paganella. Fai, at 957m altitude, is just over 10km from Mezzolombardo. There is a helpful tourist office, a selection of hotels and a large number of apartments to rent. Although Fai has been developed due to its connection to Andalo for skiing, it maintains a small-village charm and tranquillity. Fai can also be reached by bus from Trento.

TRENT 1:
BURRONE DI MEZZOCORONA

Grade:	2
Seriousness:	B (in dry weather)
Departure point:	Mezzocorona, 217m
Ascent:	700m
Descent:	700m
Via ferrata:	350m
Approximate time:	3½–4 hours
Highest altitude:	891m

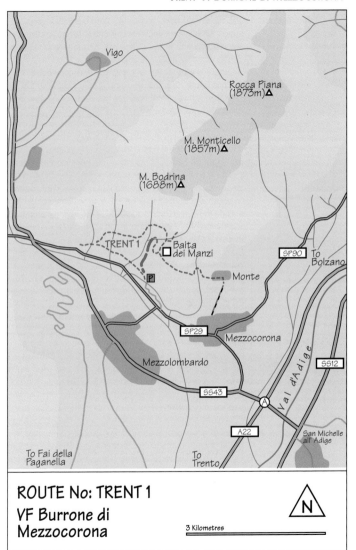

ROUTE No: TRENT 1
VF Burrone di
Mezzocorona

3 Kilometres

This route is a wonderful excursion up the spectacular gorge known as Burrone di Mezzocorona. It is an interesting and photogenic route, with easy access, and is only a short day. Being at a low altitude, it will be a very hot undertaking in the middle of the summer.

The climbing is never technically hard but the ascent is sustained, with some exposure, and unless it has been dry for some time parts of the climb will be damp and slippery. Before climbing this route you should take good note of the weather forecast for the day, and what has gone before over the preceding days. The Burrone is not somewhere to be caught in a flash storm half-way up, as the gorge can be a dangerous place to be when its waterfalls are in spate.

The route starts 2km from the centre of Mezzocorona; in fact it is signposted at the bottom of Via alla Gotta (the road leading up to the Funivia di Monte Mezzocorona). However, if you have a car it is possible to drive to the start of the route below the gorge. Leave Mezzocorona on the SP29 towards Mezzolombardo and look for the hydroelectric station just outside the village. Immediately after the hydro station (and 50m before the SP29 road turns left to go over a river bridge) there is a right turn with a signpost indicating the route '505, Burrone Giovanelli Inizio Sentiero Km 0.5 Weg Angfang'. Follow this narrow road which turns left, straightens and then has an S-bend by a house before reaching a parking area with some picnic benches and another clear signpost for the start of the route.

Path 505 climbs up through trees towards the gorge. After a couple of minutes the path crosses a small bridge over to the left (looking up) side of the gorge to another route sign '505 Burrone Monte ore 2.20 Mt 891'. Cables lead around the edge of the gorge into a large and spectacular bowl. This section was added to the original route in 1982, and climbs up a wall on the right side of the waterfall on two vertical iron ladders for 20–25m. Cables then lead off to the right along a narrow path on steep ground. The path zigzags up, with occasional waymarks, until about 30 minutes after setting off you climb a short ladder across a ravine to more cables. These last for 50m or so before more zigzags lead in a further 10 minutes to a memorial plaque and one explaining the original construction of the route in 1906. The height climbed to this point is about 220m.

Cables now lead you along a ledge into the gorge. The roof over the ledge is quite low, and tall folk will have to watch their heads (or even crawl along for a few metres). A short ladder leads down into the gorge, which is crossed to another set of ladders climbing about 20m, with amazing views above directly up the gorge. At the top of these ladders a short bridge leads to the heart of the gorge and past a Madonna and child statuette. Ten minutes' walking leads right into the gorge as its passage narrows and its giant walls tower above you.

As the gorge opens out again (about 530m) waymarks lead up and left, with a waterfall on the right. Climbing from this point is quite straightforward, though there are still occasional cables, stemples and more short ladders, albeit at easier angles, so it would be best to leave your ferrata kit on. At about 700m (and 1½–2 hours from the car park) a sign '505 Monte' shows the path leading rightwards up through beech

View of the Burrone di Mezzocorona (TRENT 1)

woods. The remaining ascent from here is a walk on good paths. Follow zigzags uphill and 5 minutes after the first '505 Monte' sign cross a track and continue upwards following clear waymarks. More '505 Monte' signs and waymarks lead to the main track just below Baita dei Manzi in a further 20–25 minutes. The sign here shows '505 Burrone Giovanelli ferrata EEA' pointing down the ascent route, 'Monte 505 0.30' to the right, and to the left 'Strada Longhe'. Just around the corner, in the direction of Monte, is Baita dei Manzi, signed at 858m (though some maps show it as 876m). The ascent takes 2–2½ hours, and Baita dei Manzi makes a great place to stop for a break. There is a large shelter, picnic benches and even a water fountain to drink from.

There are two options for descent.
1. If you have left a car at the bottom of the gorge, then you can return to it in 1–1½ hours by going back to the

sign below Baita dei Manzi and following 505 Strada Longhe heading west. It is a gravel road which is block-cobbled lower down, and you follow this road all the way down to vineyards and a crossroads junction, where a sign indicates that the car park and start point is 200m ahead.

2. If you started in the village of Mezzocorona (or wanted to ride back down there in the cable car) take the gravel road from Baita dei Manzi on path 505/504 to the hamlet of Monte, 891m (about 30 minutes). The cable car is open all year round, with a more limited service from 1 October to 31 March. There are gaps in the summer operating times during the day, so check this before you set off. Note that if you have a car parked at the bottom of the gorge and you use the cable car for descent, allow 30 minutes to walk from the bottom of the cable-car station back to the car park.

TRENT 2:
SENTIERO ATTREZZATO FAVOGNA

Grade:	2
Seriousness:	B
Departure point:	Strada del Vino, 1km north of Rovere della Luna
Ascent:	800m
Descent:	800m
Via ferrata:	350m
Approximate time:	5½–6 hours
Highest altitude:	about 1100m

This is a good-quality lower-grade route, with wonderful panoramic views of the wine-growing areas around Mezzocorona.

The return walk back from the ferrata completes a really good circuit. From the route book it can be seen that this route can be completed at any time of the year, with entries even for New Year's Eve and New Year's Day! Note, however, that it may be too hot to climb it in the middle summer months.

The route is signposted and accessed directly from the road-side of the Strada del Vino (SP90), with parking for four or

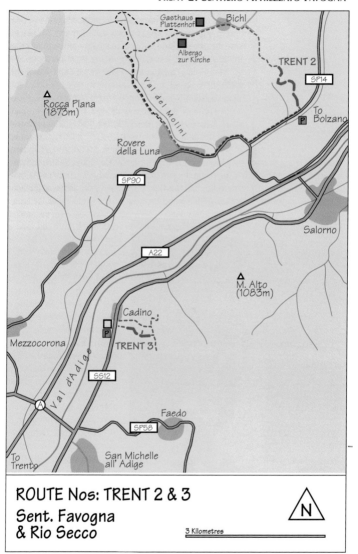

ROUTE Nos: TRENT 2 & 3
Sent. Favogna
& Rio Secco

3 Kilometres

five cars (about 3km from Magre to the north, and just over 1km if approaching from Rovere della Luna to the south). Note that the roadside signpost at the start of the route faces north, so be on the lookout if driving from the south. You will also realise that you are on the fringe of the Sud Tyrol, as the route signs are AVS (Alpenvieren) and not CAI (Club Alpino Italiano) or SAT (Societa Alpino Trentino).

A climb of less than 10 minutes zigzags up through woods before an easy rock scramble leads to the first short section of cable at about 300m. A short walk then leads up to the route plaque, '17-10-1976, Klettersteig Fennberg, AVS S.Unterland'. Start up a chimney (quite steep), with the cables being thinner than usual and not tensioned particularly tightly, but the rock is good, and there are some foothold pegs as well; this section is the hardest climbing on the route.

View to from near the top of Ferrata Favonga (TRENT 2) (photo: Marion Smith)

Following the first moves you climb over and onto a big wedged chock-stone into an easy gully and a break in the cable. A couple of minutes uphill walking leads to the second interesting feature of the route, a wall with a series of stemples but no side-wire (to clip the stemples you will need large ferrata karabiners). Another point to note is that the first stemple is about 4m up the wall, but the holds on the rock are very good to climb up to it. A ledge trends rightwards from the top of the stemples to a 10m ladder, more stemples and a second 10m ladder followed by a step across a gully. A 5 minute walk upwards and rightwards (with some exposure on a narrow path) leads to more cabling, a slight descent and a corner with another 10m ladder. At the top of the ladder there are some loose pebbles, so take care.

The timing to this point from the road is about an hour, and the cable ends again before a 2 minute walk to the next cable, leading into a wide gully with pleasant scrambling (and, if you have started reasonably early, some shade). About 15 minutes further on (at about 550m) the cable ends, and for the next 45–60 minutes you walk uphill, with one irrelevant short cable. The path is occasionally narrow and exposed, but waymarked throughout.

You eventually arrive at a big yellowish wall with a large ledge and overhang. Follow waymarks left (south) along the ledge for about 5 minutes, then more cables lead across an exposed ledge into a large corner. Go up the corner and then across to the right, where you will find the route-book box. Climbing here is easy, but the situation is spectacular, with good views down to the valley. A new box for the route book in 2001 celebrates 25 years of Klettersteig Fennberg 1976–2001, AVS Section Unterland Otsstelle Kurtatsch/Magreid.

The ferrata is almost over, but not the climb. After a couple of minutes, and the last cabled climbing, you once again walk uphill on a waymarked path, which in a further 15 minutes levels out through shady woods. Continue to follow waymarks and (about 3 hours' ascent from the road) you reach a road at the hamlet of Bichl Lindenhof.

Continue down the road for 6 or 7 minutes until it forks. To the right of the right fork path 3 is signed; this leads east, and if followed leads down to Magreid. Whilst this is a descent option, the route described here completes a circuit heading west towards Plattenhof and onwards to Rovere. Therefore at the fork in the road follow path 3 (the road to the left) westwards and soon arrive at some picnic benches – a good spot for lunch maybe? However, just around the corner is Gasthaus Plattenhof, an even better place for lunch!

Continue down the road from Gasthaus Plattenhof to a T-junction, where you turn left. In 100m take the right fork in the road, and in a further 100m reach Albergo Zur Kirche. On the right is the church of St Leonard and a path to the Biotopo Lago di Favogna, if you want to linger for a while. Various places are signed here, but continue along the road signed Wiggerspitz and Aichholz (Wiggerspitze is a peak to the west, and Aichholz is the German name for Rovere della Luna.) About 15 minutes further on the road forks again, and 50m along the right fork (waymark on a tree) a sign post indicates Path 519 ahead, and the descent path on the left 'AVS Aichholz, Rovere della Luna'.

Go down the path on the left, passing a waterfall and going over a bridge before descending, on a good path, down a pretty (and shady) gorge. In about 30 minutes a sign indicates that you have joined path 507. Continue downhill to the left, and in 5 or 6 minutes 'Rovere della Luna 502 bis' is signed, and in a further couple of minutes signed again. Follow the path down hill; it becomes quite stony before opening out onto a track at about 460m and the start of vine-yards. Simply follow the track down Val del Molini, which becomes a road passing over a bridge and continues down past flood defences into Rovere della Luna. Continue down through Rovere (one or two tempting bars on the way) to pick up the Strada del Vino and walk back to the start of the route. Descent from Gasthaus Plattenhof to Rovere is 1¼–1½ hours, plus a further hour or so back to the car park.

TRENT 3:
VIA ATTREZZATA RIO SECCO

Grade:	5
Seriousness:	B (in dry weather)
Departure point:	Cadino, 215m
Ascent:	410m
Descent:	410m
Via ferrata:	300m
Approximate time:	3 hours
Highest altitude:	625m

A hard route with some strenuous climbing up a spectacular gorge.

Although this is a relatively short day, it is a serious under-taking and another of those gorge routes for which you should take good notice of the weather. The ferrata does have an emergency escape route, but this is 1¼ hours into the 2 hour ascent. Helmets and ferrata gear are obligatory, according to the sign at the start of the route, courtesy of SAT Section San Michele all'Adige. The sign also has a detailed diagram of the route. Additional recommended equipment includes gloves (because a lot of the cables are often damp) and two long tapes (or a short rope) for two quite airy, unprotected gorge crossings.

The route is easy to find, leaving San Michele all'Adige heading north on the SS12 road towards Bolzano. Just after the sign for the hamlet of Cadino (at Km mark 398.8) there is a ristorante on the left side of the road with a large car park; you can park here, though it is polite to enquire first with the proprietor. On the opposite side of the road there is also parking for four or five cars in a lay-by, next to a small chapel at the start of the route.

Go up behind the small chapel to a stream crossing; if the water flow gives you trouble at this point, then consider going no further! Zigzag up, and in 2 minutes reach a path junction with the sign for the return path, '489E', to the left and 'Via Attrezzata Rio Secco 490E' directly ahead.

Passing the waterfall on Via Attrezzata Rio Secco (TRENT 3) (photo: Marion Smith)

Continue to zigzag up to reach a small seat and the first cable about 15 minutes from the road.

The cables lead down into the gorge, which you cross to climb a steep wall with some welcome well-chiselled footholds, and then traverse rightwards towards a waterfall, where it is difficult to avoid the swirling spray. Another steep corner climbs up left on drier rock to a ledge leading to another steep corner. It's just over 30 minutes to here, with a vertical height gain from the road of about 150m (spot height 360m). Cables zigzag up and then down to cross the gorge and traverse along the wall on the right. Now some strenuous climbing leads towards a waterfall followed by an exit right (passing some ingeniously threaded cable) to easier ground. After a break in the cabling, the route zigzags up for about 5 minutes to the next cables leading back towards the gully.

The next section is particularly strenuous, with an exposed move around a corner followed by a climb up a gully with very smooth limestone (polished by years of water action) for foot placements. Another steep climb leads to an unprotected step across the gully; this is one of the points where a long tape, or short rope, is recommended to provide some security against slipping on the shiny wet limestone. The route is strenuous again up a steep wall, then a walk leads to a sign 'Rientro in Emergencia' at about 500m. If you are in need of escape, go off to the left and follow a narrow path back down the steep hillside to the road.

Continue the route up the gully on slippery rock to quickly reach the second dodgy unprotected leap (wider than the first one, and two long tapes or a short rope are useful). Now an unprotected 5 minute scramble/walk along the gully leads to a sign 'Facile', giving the option of avoiding a strenuous wall if you are getting tired. Even if you take the short, easy diversion there is still some hard climbing to come. A second 'Facile' sign (the downhill one!) and the rejoin point are passed, and above this you reach a corner with a shrine and 'double wrapped' route book (unusually the book is in two boxes, perhaps an indication of the amount of water on this route!). The height at the route book is 540m.

Cables continue upwards to arrive at a step across water which (in case you still have dry feet) seems to have been designed for you to get your feet wet almost at the end of the climb! A final steep climb leads to the end of the route and a SAT sign at about 570m. Waymarks and a small cairn indicate the exit from the gully uphill on a zigzag path through the woods to a signpost reached in 5 minutes, at 625m. To the right, path 408 is signed 'Cadino Alto/Faedo Rif. Sauch', but to return to the road follow the path left signed '489E Cadino Rientro Attrezzata'.

Descent on path 489E is relatively simple, and although the path is narrow it is good, and has some protected parts. After about 15 minutes' descent there are some cables for handrails, with one short, steep down-climb. Less than 10 minutes further on, with great views over the Adige valley to Paganella and Brenta, cables lead along an exposed ledge above a wall of about 10m, which is climbed down on ladders. A further 20 minutes' easy descent leads back down to the road, and perhaps a beer in the ristorante (a relaxing way to contribute towards use of the car park!).

The descent takes about 45 minutes, as per the SAT signboard, but to complete the climb in the guideline time of 2 hours (15 minutes approach, and 1 hour 45 minutes ferrata) requires a good level of fitness and ability to climb without too much rest. Even so, the round-trip takes about 3 hours.

Trento East

Maps
TRENT 4 Kompass Wanderkarte 1:50,000 Sheet 75 and TRENT 5 Kompass Wanderkarte 1:50,000 Sheet 101

These two routes, to the east of Trento, are both easy days. TRENT 4 is close to Trento, with TRENT 5 about 30 minutes' drive away at Levico Terme, a thermal resort with a variety of available accommodation.

TRENT 4:
SENTIERO ATTREZZATO GIORDANO BERTOTTI

Grade:	1
Seriousness:	A
Departure point:	Parking Colmo, 850m, above Passo Cimirlo, 733m
Ascent:	500m
Descent:	500m
Via ferrata:	60m

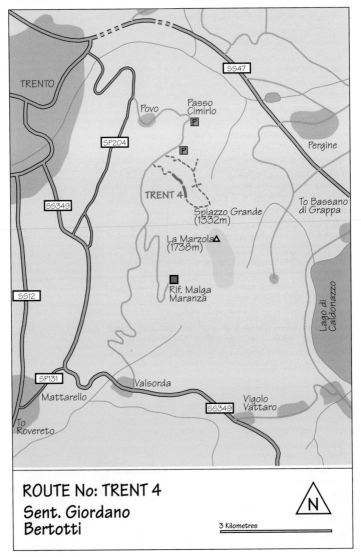

ROUTE No: TRENT 4
Sent. Giordano Bertotti

3 Kilometres

Approximate time:	2½–3 hours
Highest altitude:	1332m, Spiazzo Grande

This is a pleasant – if short – route, which could provide an easy day out after a hard day, a wet-day option, or simply a late afternoon/evening trip, with good views down to Trento and across the Adige valley to Monte Bondone on its western side. From the summit of Spiazzo Grande the panorama of Trento is quite spectacular.

This is a very easy ferrata, which those with a good head for heights could climb without using any equipment.

Drive east, uphill, out of Trento to Povo and continue to Passo Cimirlo, 733m. There is a large car park here, but you can save time, some road walking, and a height gain from Passo Cimirlo of 120m by driving south-west along a good but narrow minor road towards Maranza, and in 1.3km there is a small parking area on the left for five or six cars; this has a sign 'P Colmo'.

Walk along the road, continuing in a south-westerly direction, and in 350m there is a sign on the left for path 427 'Sentiero del Brusadi, Bivio 411, Chegul – Marzola' (this is your return path). Less than 100m along the road is a sign 'Croce Chegul, Sentiero Attrezzato 418 Giordano Berlotti', which is the path you take. The path climbs quite steeply up through mixed deciduous trees and small pines, passing a sign after 5 minutes, with path 418 continuing upwards. Some 15 minutes after leaving the road, the trees open out and a large rock pinnacle appears on your left. Continue upwards to reach a wooden carving and a metal box housing the route book, courtesy of SAT Povo, attached to a large boulder. In a further 10 minutes' ascent you arrive at the protected climb, which only takes 10 minutes. There is 15m of cable, then 15m of easy-angled ladders, followed by a further 30m of cable and a short walk to the summit cross of Croce del Chegul, 1244m.

Leave the summit of Croce del Chegul to the east over an old wooden bridge and past a gravestone dedicated to a Trentino student who fell to his death on 23 September 1898 (this gives a spookier feeling than the more usually encountered shrine or Madonna). Follow red-and-white markers through a thickly wooded area, climbing a little across the plateau of Spiazzo Grande. In 5 minutes you carry on past a sign for path 411 to the left and path 418 to the right to arrive at a main path junction in a further 5 minutes. Follow the left fork, 'Cimirlo', on a wide track which zigzags down through the woods. After 25–30 minutes you reach another junction – path 411 continues down to Passo Cimirlo, but you take path 427 to the left signed 'Sentiero del Busadi' and 'Strada Cimirlo – Maranza'. The path traverses, climbs a little and then descends, steeply at times, back to the road, where you turn right to arrive back at the small car park.

TRENT 5:
SENTIERO CLEMENTE CHIESA

Grade:	1
Seriousness:	A (but see comments regarding water conditions)
Departure point:	Albergo alla Vedova (500m), 2km south of Levico Terme
Ascent:	750m
Descent:	750m
Via ferrata:	1000m
Approximate time:	5 hours
Highest altitude:	1255m, Albergo Monterovere

The scenery on this route is spectacular, through a wild and romantic gorge, with many rapids and one spectacular waterfall.

Since its character derives from the water scenery, this route would be of limited interest after a lengthy spell of dry weather. However, there is a fine balance to be struck between the spectacular and the potentially dangerous! There are no less than nine river crossings to negotiate, only one of which is bridged.

Approach from Trento on the SS47 to Levico Terme. Then head south on the SP133 to Lochere, where there is ample parking. Whilst Lochere can also be reached by bus from Trento, the service is infrequent, and those dependent on public transport should walk from Levico Terme, which is much better served.

Walk south up the road, waymarked 233 for Val Scura, as far as the first right-hand hairpin bend, where you take the path leading straight ahead. A few metres further on, you

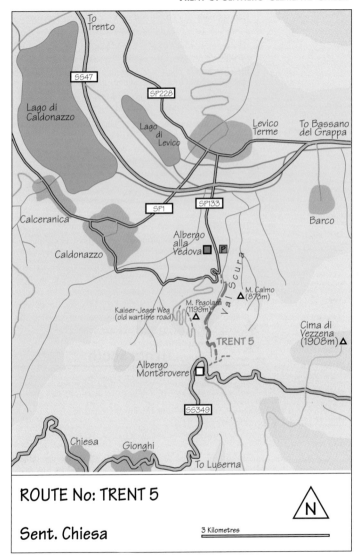

ROUTE No: TRENT 5

Sent. Chiesa

3 Kilometres

pass the SAT via ferrata sign and a notice warning of the extremely friable nature of the rock in the gorge. Continue up the gorge, which soon closes in to form steep, high walls on either side. The path meanders through woods, crossing the river several times before the first ladder is encountered (at about 830m).

The route continues without difficulty, protected on the more friable sections. Several ladders, a rickety bridge below an overhanging wall, and several river crossings are encountered before the waterfall comes into view. A final short ladder leads to a steep scramble out of the gorge (at about 1220m) to the end of the route.

Walk through the trees to a small clearing with a scatter of timber buildings and onto a short grassy slope up to the Albergo Monterovere (1255m) on the SS349, which you will reach about 3 hours after starting out. The lovely wooded plateau you have now reached is known as Spiazzo Alto.

To return to your starting point, walk north along the road leading back to Lochere. This is the Kaiser-Jeger Weg, named after the Tiroler Kaiser-Jeger who built it during the 1915–18 war. Little of the original route remains, since it has been largely obliterated by the improvements required for modern traffic. Numerous short cuts can be followed, all well signposted, to cut out the many hairpin bends in the road. The descent to your starting point will take about 2 hours.

Trento South

Maps
TRENT 6, 7 and 8 Kompass Wanderkarte 1:50,000 Sheets 75 and 101
Trentino Tourist Map 1:20,000 Monte Bondone

These three routes are on Monte Bondone, Trento's skiing mountain in the winter. TRENT 6 and TRENT 7 are high-quality routes in excellent mountain surroundings. TRENT 8 is an easier ferrata, but a demanding day out. Some accommodation can be found around the ski developments of Monte Bondone, though in the summer, except for August, it is relatively quiet.

TRENT 6:
SENTIERO ATTREZZATO PERO DEGASPERI, MONTE BONDONE

Grade:	3
Seriousness:	C
Departure point:	Hotel Baita Montesel, 1480m
Ascent:	700m
Descent:	700m
Via ferrata:	450m
Approximate time:	5–5½ hours
Highest altitude:	2096m, Il Palon

There are some very exposed paths on the approach to this route, where surefootedness and complete freedom from vertigo are essential (these narrow paths could be quite dangerous in wet conditions). The route is south facing and there are no water courses, so carry ample supplies of drinks, especially in the summer months when it could be very hot.

Take the SS45 road out of Trento and then follow the minor road towards Monte Bondone via Sardagna. The gradient of the road is never particularly steep, but the climb uphill negotiates numerous bends, many of which turn back through a full 180 degrees. Continue on the road up through Sardagna and Vaneze, and a couple of bends after Norge you reach the start point at Baita Montesel, 1480m – the first sign you see while driving up the road being 'Albergo'. There is plenty of parking, both in front of the *albergo* and in a lay-by across the road. You can also get to here by bus from Trento.

From Baita Montesel head east on a good track across grassy ski slopes signed '690 Dos de la Cros'. In a few minutes continue past a sign for the via ferrata and go straight ahead, past a track on the right, to a signpost for 'Dos de la Cros'. A little further on, and 10 minutes from the start, path 690, Sentiero Attrezzato, is signed. Now follow a narrow path as it traverses across a very steep grassy hillside; this is the place where you need a good head for heights and to

This is an excellent middle-grade ferrata, once you get to it, that is!

233

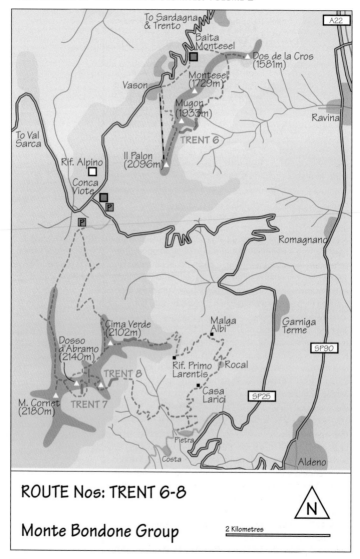

ROUTE Nos: TRENT 6-8

Monte Bondone Group

2 Kilometres

N

take due care. After 10 minutes the path goes into woods (although still on steep ground, exposure decreases) and goes downhill, passing an SAT ferrata sign before zigzagging down and traversing through the woods.

Views down to Trento and the Adige valley open up 1200m below, with Il Palon towering up ahead. The path continues downhill until, in a few minutes, more exposed traverses lead back into the woods and the descent bottoms out at about 1430m. Now zigzag up for a few minutes to reach the first cable, about 45 minutes from Baita Montesel.

The cable leads down a 45 degree ramp (with a Madonna statuette in the rocks half-way down), which ends with an easy down-climb followed by further traversing again without cable. In a couple of minutes a short cabled move round a corner, another traverse, and then waymarks lead you up a rocky rib with more intermittent cables and unprotected walking on the now familiar narrow, exposed path. After about 5 minutes the path zigzags up an obvious line, an open gully to the right, and in a further 10 minutes (at about 1610m) you reach the start of the ferrata proper, after 1½–1¾ hours from the start on the occasionally nerve-racking path. There is a shady ledge here which makes a good place for a break to recharge your batteries.

The ferrata starts up a ramp rising leftwards to the route sign 'SAT Sezione Sardagna, Sentiero Attrezzata PERO PITOR Guida Alpina, Nato 1876–1966, 18.7.1976'. Now you have 20 minutes of good, well-cabled climbing with fine views until a break in the cabled protection. Waymarks lead upwards, right and up again to the next cables in 2 or 3 minutes. The route continues upwards, with very pleasant open climbing on reasonable but not always 100 per cent solid rock, so a little care is needed to avoid dislodging stones onto those below. This part of the climb lasts about 30 minutes until you reach the short crux moves of the climb, with stemples and pegs helping you up a steep crack ending with an interesting two-rung iron step onto easier angled ground. A further 20 minutes of well-cabled, easy, but still pleasant climbing leads to the route book at about 1920m. From here there is only 10 more minutes of cabled protection to the end of the route at 1960m.

You have the option to visit the summit of Il Palon (see below), signed to the left 'path 690 Palon M2098 ore 0.20', or to descend straight away by following the path to the right, signed '690 Vason ore 0.45'. Note that the descent path 690 to Vason is not shown on maps, but is a good, easy-to-follow path.

Ascent of Il Palon, 2096m: If the weather is good and the views clear then the ascent to the summit of Il Palon is worth the extra effort. You already have views to the Brenta and Adamello, but even with the trappings of the ski lifts and radio masts the summit views from Il Palon are amazing. To the south-west is a very good panorama of the Tre Cime del Bondone (see TRENT 7 and photo on p. 243), which shows what a good round that is. Additionally, on a clear day you

Climber on Sentiero Attrezzato Pero Degasperi (TRENT 6)

can see the Stubai and Zillertal ranges of Austria, along with many high dolomite peaks, including Marmolada, Pelmo and Civetta. Note that Il Palon is shown as 2091m, 2096m and 2098m (not the place to reset an altimeter!)

The ascent from Baita Montesel to the summit of Il Palon takes about 3½–4 hours. In August, if you can stand the heat during the climb, you can enjoy the use of the chairlift back down from the summit of Il Palon to Vason. Otherwise, to descend from the summit, which takes 1–1½ hours, retrace your steps back to the sign post at the end of the ferrata (about 15 minutes).

Now follow signed path 690 (not way-marked), which zigzags down through small pines then beech shrubs to an avalanche fence. Turn left here, go down again through a second avalanche fence and out onto the ski piste to follow a track down by the side of the chairlift to Vason at 1650m. Baita Montesel may not be open, so you may decide to take the chance of a drink in Vason. Continue on a track to the right, again following a ski piste, back to your start point at Baita Montesel, 1480m, in a further 15 minutes.

TRENT 7:
VIA FERRATA GIULIO SEGATA

Grade:	5
Seriousness:	B
Departure point:	Conca Viote SP85 Monte Bondone, 1565m
Ascent:	600m
Descent:	600m
Via ferrata:	100m
Approximate time:	4½–5 hours
Highest altitude:	2140m, Doss d'Abramo; 2180m with Monte Cornet option

The Tre Cime del Bondone comprises Monte Cornet (or Cornetto on most maps), Dosso d'Abramo and Cima Verde. VF Giuilo Segata is relatively short, but for most of its 100m is vertical and strenuous. The sign at the start of the route gives warning of its seriousness and makes it clear that any climbing is totally at your own risk.

A good map (scale 1:20,000) for Monte Bondone is available free from the Trentino Tourist Board; you can get a copy from the bar at the front of the large car park at the road junction of the SP85 (good toilet facilities here too). It is also possible to park at the start of path 607, on the right 400m down the SP25 road from the bar towards Garniga. Although the Trento Monte Bondone map shows no vehicular access down the track at the start of path 607, there are no restriction signs on the ground, and there is a car park 400m down the track just before spot height 1554m.

A first-class day out in the mountains which combines the excellent horseshoe of the Tre Cime del Monte Bondone with a short but very hard via ferrata.

From the road, path 607 is signed 'Costa dei Cavai, Monte Cornetto' on a track to the right. Follow this track (driveable), and in 400m go through a small car park where 'Monte Cornetto 1h 30 minutes' is signed again. The path goes up an open meadow leading to the long, broad ridge coming down from Monte Cornetto. Climb the well-way-marked path and after 50 minutes, at about 1940m, it levels out, with a good view of Dosso d'Abramo to the south-east. Continue up path 607 towards Monte Cornetto, and in 15 minutes, after passing a sandy-coloured buttress of loose rock, you reach two tall, pointed cairns at about 2020m and a sign 'Cima Cornetto, Bivio Sent 636-617, 607'. Continue uphill, and in a further 10 minutes (about 2100m) you have an option to go straight to the via ferrata by following the path to the left signed 'Cima Verde 1h, Piani Delle Viote 2.30 hours'. ◀ Continue on the path to the left (south-east) for 10 minutes to another sign at about 2150m, 'Via Ferrata Giulio Segata al Dosso D'Abramo' to the right and 'Cima Verde 1h 636, Piani Delle Viote 2.30' to the left.

Follow the narrow path to the ferrata as it traverses (narrow in places) around the south-east flank of Dosso d'Abramo. In 10 minutes, at about 2050m, is the start of the ferrata route, indicated by a sign which, roughly translated, reads 'We accept no responsibility, it's all up to you!'

Go straight up through an overhanging chimney and a hole in the roof, then make a short move right, followed by another piece of strenuous vertical climbing, relying heavily on the cable, good balance and good foot placement. Now you know it's a hard route, having completed the first 20m of vertical, then the route moves out to the right onto a big ledge. Follow the ledge to the right to a point where the route again goes vertically up a gully, but a cable also continues straight ahead along the ledge. ◀

To continue the ferrata simply continue vertically up again for about 40m until you climb into the final chimney (it is obvious even in dry weather that the route takes drainage at this point). The final 10m climbs the chimney (overhanging in places again) to come out in the open on the grassy summit plateau of Dosso d'Abramo (about 45 minutes of via ferrata climbing and 2½–3 hours from the start). ◀

If you want to complete the Tre Cime del Bondone, the ascent of Monte Cornetto takes an extra 15 minutes up and 10 minutes back down. You return to the same point on the route.

At this point you have a choice, but you have only completed the first third of the ferrata, which still has another 50m of almost vertical climbing. If you are not happy after the first section, continue along the ledge until you meet a wire coming down from a gully on your left – the escape route.

The summit of Dosso d'Abramo (2140m) is 5 minutes away on the left, and the cross (2138m) a couple of minutes away on the right is a good spot for lunch.

Steep cables on Via Ferrata Giulio Segata (TRENT 7)

Descent is down a gully facing south-east between the top of the ferrata and the cross, following cables for about 40m (easy ferrata Grade 1 climbing) down to meet the cable on the escape ledge. When reaching the ledge turn left, and 10 minutes into the descent you reach a sign (at about 2090m). To the left is 'path 636 Monte Cornetto', to the right 'Sentiero Alpinistico Coraza 638 Cimone – Pietra 4' (the ascent route of TRENT 8 below), but the path you want is the one straight ahead, '636 Cima Verde, Piani Delle Viote'. You are now on a good path, and after passing a col at about 2040m you reach the sign for 'Cima Verde, 2102m' in about 30 minutes. It's a short return climb to the summit, worth it

239

Note that **Rifugio Alpino Frateli Tambosi** at Viote is not a *rifugio* in the traditional sense of the term. It is the property of the province of Trento and is an annex of the Alpine Botanical Garden of the Trentino Museum of Natural Science (tel: 0461.948050). The garden boasts over 1000 species of Alpine plants.

for the extra views, and then you continue down on path 636, signed 'Piani Delle Bondone 1h 30'. Note that another sign at this point indicates 'Sentiero Attrezzata Sparavei 630 Malga Albi ore 1.20 Garniga Terme 2.20' (the descent route of TRENT 8 below).

Follow path 636, a grassy ridge, leading down through small pines for over 30 minutes until (about 1640m) you reach a wooden sign 'Sentiero Naturalistico'. From here continue down a good path following red-and-white waymarks. A few minutes further on (now out in the open), path 636 branches right waymarked red and white along the side of the wood, but carry on straight ahead past sign 'Sentiero Naturalistico 3 Cime (alt. 1620 metres)'. Go across the meadow to follow a path at the side of a fence back to the ridge coming down from Monte Cornetto to join path 607, which you climbed earlier in the day. Turn right and follow this back to the car park in about 1½ hours' descent. ◀

TRENT 8:
SENTIERO CORAZA/SPARAVEI

Grade:	1
Seriousness:	C
Departure point:	Covelo, 523m; Pietra, 708m
Ascent:	1450m
Descent:	1450m
Via ferrata:	100m
Approximate time:	8–9 hours
Highest altitude:	2140m, Dosso d'Abramo

A day that involves a very easy ferrata, but which is very demanding in terms of height gain/loss and length of day – a bit of a slog!

As with route TRENT 7, Sentieros Coraza and Sparavei also take in the summit of Dosso d'Abramo, 2140m. However, the TRENT 8 routes are on the eastern side of the mountain and do not readily link to enable them to be climbed with TRENT 7 in a single day. Though VF Giulio Segata could be included with this route, it would demand another level of fitness (as well as being a high-grade ferrata); that route is best included in the Tre Cime del Monte Bondone round.

The best way to complete this day is in a clockwise direction starting with Sentiero del Coraza to Dosso d'Abramo, then continuing to Cima Verde and descending Sentiero del Sparavei back to your starting point in Pietra. The route description highlights the point at which you could traverse off to include VF Giulio Segata to make a really major day out. For details of that ferrata see TRENT 7.

Approach Pietra from Aldeno taking the SP25 road which climbs up towards Cimone and Garniga Terme. About 300m after passing the Km 5 marker on the SP25, turn left signed 'Loc. Pietra', and in only 100m turn left again on an unsigned road which leads up to Pietra. When you get to the tiny village of Pietra take the left fork to pass below the village rather than going into its narrow streets. At the end of the village (only about 150m!) is a small car park for seven or eight cars. It is also possible to continue out of the village for 200m, where there is parking for a couple of cars by a bridge, with a sign for Sentiero Coraza.

From Pietra follow the narrow road (red-and-white waymarks of path 638), Sentiero del Coraza, towards Spagnoli. Just over 300m after the small parking area mentioned above, turn left up a cobbled track just before a waymark on the wall (this is the second, not the first, track on the left from the bridge). In 10 minutes you are at Spagnoli, and a sign indicates 'Sentiero Coraza Baita Fratta ore 1.00, Pala Grande ore 4.30'. Only 20m further on is a right fork, path 630 Sentiero Sparavei Cima Verde ore 3.45' (this is the descent route). Take the left fork for Sentiero Coraza up through beech woods to cross a wide gorge. Continue climbing (in fact, that's what you are going to do for the next 4 or 5 hours!). An hour after setting off you get an open view back down to Baita Fratta, just before you arrive at Baita Fratta (no more than an open and very basic shelter). Another path 638 sign indicates 'Dos d'Abramo 3.30'. About 15 minutes from Baita Fratta is some more open ground, and 15 minutes further on, about 1440m, a big gorge.

A narrow path goes along the right side of the gorge and crosses over to the left. Continue up for 30 minutes to a small brow at about 1680m; this goes to the right, then keeps on going uphill. Five minutes further on a rock pinnacle rises above you, which you pass on the left, at about 1740m. In another 5 minutes '638 Sentiero Coraza' is signed with Pala Granda 1.30 (also shown as maps as Pala Grande and even

Pala Grande is an amazing viewpoint and a good place for lunch, as it is about 3½–4 hours' climbing from Pietra. There is a large cross with a sign 'VF Cimone 1994', plus two palm prints and a dedication with the name Sylvia in the cement. The original sign on the cross for VF Cimone is dated 26.9.65.

To climb **VF Giulio Segata** descend to the left to the start of the route at 2050m. It takes 45–50 minutes to climb it (see TRENT 7 for details).

Pala G). Turn right across a narrow ledge (about 1820m) to the first wires (about 1840m). The protection is only 40m or so, followed by a short walk to more wires up a gully leading to a wall in front of you.

Go left along an exposed ledge (no wires), and then more wires lead down and across a gully before continuing left to traverse along another exposed ledge. About 30 minutes from the first wire, go down again on another ledge (very exposed, no wires). In about 5 minutes you reach a big gully and a sign 'Baito Coraza 1880m, 638 Pala Granda 0.30'. Go up the gully following waymarks then right across a grassy slope to the summit of 'Pala Grande 2017mt'. Interestingly a sign points down saying 'Sentiero Alpinistico procedura con attenzione'. ◀

From Pala Granda continue up the lovely rising, grassy ridge (generally heading east) and in less than 10 minutes reach another signpost with Dosso d'Abramo rising up in front of you. This is the traverse point for the Giulio Segata ferrata. ◀ From here the ascent of Dosso d'Abramo takes a further 15 minutes up a fairly easy, cabled gully (also the way back down to this point) for a total ascent of 5–5½ hours. To continue directly to Cima Verde (and this is the way you need to go if you do visit the summit of Dosso d'Abramo), go right (north-east) on path 636 to Cima Verde, about 30 minutes from here.

From the summit of Cima Verde, 2102m, follow the signed path '630 Sentiero Attrezzata Sparavei Malga Albi ore 1.20'. Be careful to look out for red-and-white marker pegs on the second of two ridges heading down generally east, as the ridge south of east is misleading and quickly leads onto steep, exposed, friable ground; you'll soon be back!

After the marker pegs path 630 is a waymarked path zigzagging down loose shaley ground until the rock changes back to limestone as you enter the small pine belt (about 5 minutes). Continue down to a short wire, turn right and traverse to the second (and last) wire with a down-climb of about 15m. Follow more zigzags until, about 35 to 40 minutes after leaving the summit of Cima Verde, you reach a sign 'Pro Loco Garniga Terme 1750 mt, 630B/12' to the left and '630 Sentiero Sparavei Malga Albi ore 0.45' to the right. In less than 30 minutes, at about 1555m, there's a great view down to Trento and the Adige valley, and then

about 15 minutes further on you reach Rif. Primo Larenti Custode Forestale, Forestali e Amici Dedicano 1977, a *rifugio* belonging to the foresters (not open to the public).

Path 630 now becomes a forestry road and, still waymarked, follows the main track down to Malga Albi at 1264m. Continue down the road (still path 630, and waymarked red and white), passing a house on the right and a parking sign. Then continue down the main track for 15–20 minutes until, at about 1120m and a bend in the road, you arrive at the small hamlet of Rocal, 1112m. Turn right here and follow a good track past the houses. After about 10 minutes pass a solitary house on the right (about 1040m), taking a left fork in the track. Five minutes further on pass Casa Larici, 999m, as shown on the map. Unfortunately the waymarking has now ended, and with the track going back into trees it is difficult to work out where to go. However, you are only 15 minutes away from Spagnoli, which is reached by keeping to the most obvious main track (an old cobbled mule track), which zig-zags down to the junction with path 638 and Spagnoli, which you will recognise from the ascent. Retrace your steps from here, turning right down a track, now waymarked again. Turn right and follow the road back down to Pietra in a further 10 minutes, about 3 hours from the summit of Cima Verde.

General view of the Tre Cime del Bondone

RIVA, LAKE GARDA

Maps

Kompass Wanderkarte 1:25,000 Sheet 690 or Kompass Wanderkarte 1:50,000
Sheet 101 Lagir Alpina 1:50,000 Gardasee
Trentino Carta Toristica Alpi Di Ledro 1:33,000

Tourist Information Office

APT Riva, CAP 38066 (TN), Italy
Tel: (0464) 554 444
Fax: (0464) 520 308
E-mail: info@gardatrentino.com
Internet: www.gardatrentino.com or www.garda.com

After 300 years in ruins, Arco castle has now been partially restored

Lake Garda is a major tourist area. In high season, July–August, it is probably best avoided, not just for the crowds and high prices but because of the temperature – climbing via ferratas can be very hot work. Conversely, the lower altitude of the area means that many of these routes can be climbed over a greatly extended season, even into the winter months.

There are many places around the lake that you could use as your base. Riva is the largest town at the north end of the lake and has good tourist information, but you might prefer to get away from the congested lakeside, in which case Arco, Dro and Ledro are good alternatives. This is also a major climbing area, with a bumper Topo guide published by SAT Arco; many tracks exist for mountain biking, and the lake provides good sailing and windsurfing opportunities. The Tourist Information Office can help with advice about the wealth of accommodation, including campsites, which the area possesses.

RIVA 1:
VIA ATTREZZATA RINO PISETTA – M. GARSOLE

Grade:	5
Seriousness:	C
Departure point:	Sarche di Calavino, 249m
Ascent:	700m
Descent:	700m
Via ferrata:	500m
Approximate time:	5–5½ hours
Highest altitude:	967m, Monte Garsole

This is a quality route, amongst the hardest outside the higher Dolomite mountains. The 5C grade reflects the technical quality and length of route requiring a high level of fitness and stamina and therefore it should only be attempted by experienced ferratists. The total ascent takes at least 3 hours, with a good 2 hours being on the ferrata itself.

This is a steep, strenuous and sustained 'sports' route. It is well cabled on the harder sections, but is exposed throughout, and there are very few other aids, just occasional pegs which serve as footholds.

The route starts (and is clearly signed) from the left-hand side of a Fiat garage at the Trento end of the village of Sarche. It is possible to park at the right-hand end of the garage forecourt, but confirm this before doing so. The Riva to Trento bus service passes through Sarche, so it is possible to do this route using public transport – check times locally.

Follow the waymarked path as it zigzags up through the woods then levels out, passing a sign for the Biotopo Lago Di Toblino. In just over 5 minutes a red arrow on a rock points uphill; take this path and follow red-and-white painted waymarks uphill. There are a number of 'decoy' paths so take care to follow the waymarks, and if in doubt just keep going uphill. About 20 minutes from the road, at about 400m, the path goes up some scree and then left into woods again, where you will see a sign for 'Via Attrezzata Rino Pisetta'. Continue uphill, and in a further 20 minutes the

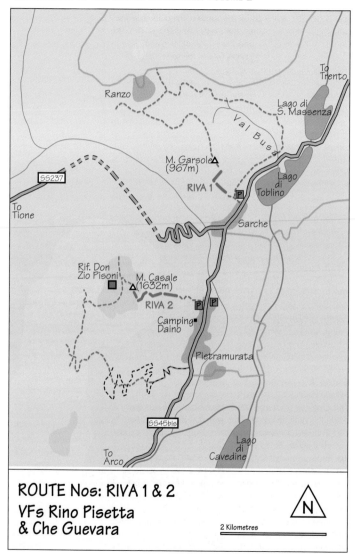

ROUTE Nos: RIVA 1 & 2
VFs Rino Pisetta
& Che Guevara

2 Kilometres

path goes left, followed by a scramble on rocks in a tree-filled gully leading to an open ledge and the start of the route. This is at 570m, and there is a rather elaborate iron route sign and a warning notice about the seriousness of the route. Allow 45–60 minutes to this point.

The route is initially very steep, vertical even, but the cables are sound. Climb the first steep wall (about 10m) onto a ledge and then move down to the left. Now climb another longer (15m) steep wall and crack, with some of the hardest moves of the day, before continuing up and left on easier ground. This first section takes 10–15 minutes, and at 600m you reach a sign 'Rientro Emergenza'. If you are struggling with the climb already, the emergency return goes off to the right; this is the only escape point on the route, and after this you have a further 350m of height gain before the summit.

Near the top of Rino Pisetta looking down to Sarche (RIVA 1)

The route continues to the left, onto a ledge and up again with another good move. About 15 minutes after the escape point there is a strenuous hand-traverse followed by a rest point. You then go up again and hand-traverse again before another very hard move takes you to a large ledge at about 670m and 35–40 minutes from the start of the route. It's a great spot, and there are even some small trees which give shade, so it's worth taking a break here.

The ledge goes along to the left followed by another steep climb, but 10 minutes from the ledge (about 700m) the climbing becomes easier. Now watch out for a short section of friable rock which leads up to another ledge on the left.

You will now have been climbing for about an hour, and some easy climbing now leads up a broken gully, and in a few minutes more the cable ends at about 740m. After a short walk (a couple of minutes) the cable starts again, with easy climbing at first, but at about 800m you come to a steep wall of excellent rock and the last of the really hard climbing. Above this a short walk followed by more cable leads to a metal sign 'Per El Nino, Per Sentiero Pu Vizim' and the route-book box.

Above the route book more easy cabled climbing takes you to another break in the cable at about 880m. Waymarks are now sparse, but it's easy to follow the line of a rising broken rib for a couple of minutes until a red arrow and more red waymarks indicate the path which zigzags up towards the summit. However, there is one final airy cabled section along a broken ridge to Monte Garsole, 967m, where there is a very welcome bench seat. It's a splendid place to have a break, enjoy the tremendous views of the Sarca valley and reflect on a wonderful climb. Allow 3–3½ hours for the total ascent.

The descent follows the signed path to Ranzo; this heads north from the summit of Monte Garsole pleasantly down through shady woods. After about 15 minutes (about 800m) Ranzo is signed again and the main path downhill is indicated by red waymarks. In a few more minutes pass an area with some picnic tables and a water tap and trough, and 100m further on at a fork in the paths take the right-hand main track, leading down towards the road into Ranzo. At the Ranzo road (about 30 minutes from the summit) Sarche is signed to both the right and the left. Take the right turn and follow the road towards Ranzo for just a few minutes until you reach a sign for Sarche in front of house number 72. Turn right and go down the metalled track (also waymarked path 613) which leads down Val Busa. Go down this main track, passing a track going off to the right, and then pass a gate and wire fence where the track changes to gravel. In just over 20 minutes of descent from house number 72 (at about 480m), Sarche is signed down to the right of the main track. A path zigzags down through the woods and in 5 minutes comes to a road at about 430m.

There is no sign or waymark here, but to return to Sarche you need to cross to the southern side of Val Busa, so turn right on the road and almost immediately you see an ENEL (hydro-electric) tunnel entrance on the right and a concrete bridge. Go over the bridge and follow a good path signed 'Via Attrezzata Rino Pisetta, Sarche'. The path goes uphill for about 10 minutes and at about 480m you take the path down through the woods on the left, signed 'Via Attrezzata, Sarche'. In a few minutes there is a lovely open view down to Lago Toblino, and 5 minutes further on a 'Pericol, Gerfahr' sign (i.e. 'danger'). From here the path traverses a narrow exposed ledge (the reason for the 'danger' sign?) with some cables serving as a reassuring handrail. The path turns uphill on some cut rock steps before continuing to traverse the narrow ledge again with a cabled handrail. You then reach a sign down to the left for Sarche (and a way-mark ahead for 'Via Attrezzata') at about 420m. Follow the zigzags downhill back to Sarche – they are not always well waymarked but you should have no trouble finding your way down this last 10 minutes back to the start point.

The total time for descent is less than 2 hours.

RIVA 2:
VIA FERRATA CHE GUEVARA

Grade:	3
Seriousness:	C
Departure point:	SS45 bis, Pietramurata
Ascent:	1370m
Descent:	1370m
Via ferrata:	1000m
Approximate time:	7½–8½ hours
Highest altitude:	1632m, Monte Casale

You are advised to make an early start on this climb for two reasons, firstly to ensure you get a parking space and secondly because the route faces generally south-east and is in the sun for most of the day. It is not really a route to climb in the middle summer months, when it can be really hot, but whenever you climb it make sure that you take plenty of fluids to drink. Walking poles are useful for completion of the top part of the ascent and for the descent.

This is a brilliant ferrata route, but quite a big day. It is not especially technically hard, but it is a serious undertaking due to length of climb and lack of escape route.

249

When approaching from the south on the SS45bis go to the north end of Pietramurata, and just after the Km 133 marker there is a lay-by on the right and a left turn into a side road on the left, just before the sign indicating you are leaving Pietramurata. If you are coming from the north, it's a right turn just after arriving at Pietramurata; there is a car sales Autoveicoli garage on the corner of the turning. Parking is available for a number of cars in the side road in front of a large quarry and in the lay-by on the main road. There is a good campsite in the village at Camping Daino, Viale Daino 17, 38070 Pietramurata, Trento, tel. 0464.507451 or 507270.

The start of the approach to the route is obvious, as 'Via Ferrata' is painted on a rock on the first bend of the side road. Go past the painted boulder up the track, and in 50m a red waymark indicates a path on the left through small pine trees. Continue up following the northern edge of the quarry (**do not** follow old waymarks which turn down into the quarry). The path goes upwards to climb above the quarry onto open ground at about 550m in little over 35 minutes, and then turns left to traverse along above the quarry (heading south), where you reach the first of a number of rocks with the spot height painted on them; this one is 'Quota 550m'. The first cable then goes up to the left, with pleasant, easy climbing on good rock for about 100m; this is followed by a walk, three stemples, a short unprotected scramble and three more stemples. Now follow a traverse path at about 620m which leads around to the main wall of the route. There is a large * painted on the rock and a scramble around to the left of a large pinnacle to the start of the route proper, with 'Via Ferrata Ernesto Che Guevara Quota 675m' painted on the rock. There is also a sign on the rock indicating that it is dangerous to climb the route in the winter. This approach to the ferrata takes an hour from the road.

You start the ferrata climbing excellent rock, followed by a short traverse and more climbing. After about 20 minutes, spot height M 735 is painted on the rock and views begin to open out to the north-east. Follow the cables, traversing again and then climbing a series of short walls and ledges, then more short walls with occasional stemples as footholds to arrive at a big ledge with 'Quota 820m' on the rock. After a short wire a zigzag path goes up to 'M860' (about 45 minutes from the start of the ferrata) and then cables lead you

Note: A change was made to the starting point area in 2004. A path from the car park in front of the quarry now heads south around the works and up to a new set of cables. This path eventually joins the original route below the ascent of the main slabs.

past 'Tiramisu' painted on a rock at about 880m. At this point be aware, as several bent stemples suggest that this area suffers from rock fall. Also you now encounter loose rock and some old loose cabling, and so (though exposure is minimal) extra care is required. More old cables and broken ground then lead to better rock, and at about 1000m there is a horizontal cable leading off to the left on a ledge. This doesn't go anywhere but appears to have been put there simply to make a picnic spot, and – almost 2½ hours since you set off – this can be recommended as a wonderful place to take a break and enjoy the situation and the views.

Continue up on good rock again to a ledge at about 1080m, and in about 20 minutes some easier angled climbing is followed by a walk up through a vegetated area and some shade at last. There are some more cables at about 1150m, and then a short walk leads up to the route book at about 1200m, some 3 hours from the road and after 2 hours on the ferrata itself. Most of the ferrata climbing is over, but continue uphill, and in about 30 minutes (at about 1360m) there is a great viewpoint to the south towards Arco, Lake Garda and Monte Baldo. At about 1450m there is a short (8m) climb, and after another climb you arrive on the plateau of Monte Casale. It is an amazing viewpoint, with Brenta and Adamello to the west, Paganella and Catinaccio to the north, and Monte Bondone, Monte Baldo and Lake Garda to the south. Walk north to a large cross, which is below the summit of Monte Casale but is a good place for lunch, or

The start of Via Ferrata Che Guevara (RIVA 2)

251

take a short walk to the summit at 1632m, where the splendid views can be confirmed on an orientation chart set on a stone plinth (and there's a picnic bench as well!). Allow a total time for the ascent of 4–4½ hours.

From the summit of Monte Casale descend the grassy slopes on a bearing just south of west to Rif. (Capanna) Don Zio Pisoni in about 5 minutes (the *rifugio* is open from early June to late September; there are a small number of beds). Now follow a waymarked track signed '408/426 S. Giovanni Pietramurata', and in 10 minutes, after descending a good track through alpine meadows, pass a sign pointing back the way you have come to 'Rifugio Don Zio 15 minutes'. Turn left here, and 20m further on your path is signed '408/426 Pietramurata ora 2.30'. Go along this track – passing a sign 'Le Quadre 1460m', then a sign 'Aqua Del Duson, 1370m' on your left – until, about 30 minutes from the summit of Monte Casale, path 426 branches. To the right 426 is signed 'Malga Poia', but you take the left branch signed 'Pietramurata 408/426'. In a further 5 minutes (at about 1350m) you reach the start of a steep descent. Path 426 goes down to the left to Pietramurata, with 'Attenzione pericolo danger' on the sign!

The path is protected with several hundred metres of wire as it leads steeply down through shady woods. It is generally damp terrain, even in dry weather, and would be very slippery if it was wet. Although there is no technical climbing the wire serves as a very useful handrail. At about 1120m a short ladder (6m) goes down a steep gully and the cable ends. The angle of slope is still quite steep as you descend almost straight down through the woods – at least it's shady and cool if the weather's sunny. Simply keep following waymarks downhill as you head towards Pietramurata. The steepness eases from about 1000m (after about an hour down the path through the woods), then at about 800m you cross a forest track and continue on a path waymarked down through the woods. In a couple of minutes cross the forest track again and then, at about 670m, cross the road twice more.

Follow waymarks crossing the forest road several more times until, at about 460m, there is a barrier across the road. From the barrier follow the road left and round a right-hand bend to pick up a waymarked path 50m ahead on the left.

Ten minutes from the barrier follow blue waymarks left and follow the forest road – the end is in sight! Go round a left bend and downhill to cross the road. 'Per 426' is painted on a rock, and a path on the right runs downhill parallel to the road (or just follow the road). When the path ends follow the forest road back to its end, where there is a Pietramurata signpost and a small parking area; it takes about 2 hours to here from the start of the steep descent at spot height 1350m.

Continue down to the main road coming out by a bus stop and zebra crossing by the SS45bis 132 Km marker. Head north, and almost immediately you see the New Entry Snack Bar – time for a drink, maybe? All that remains from here is a walk along SS45bis road for just over 1km back to the start point, a total descent of 3–3½ hours.

RIVA 3:
SENTIERO ANGLONE/SCALONI

Grade:	1
Seriousness:	A
Departure point:	Dro
Ascent:	500m
Descent:	500m
Via ferrata:	100m
Approximate time:	3 hours
Highest altitude:	580m, path 428 bis Coste Dell Anglone

Even beginners should not need ferrata belay equipment on this route, although there is a sign at the beginning of the Anglone route warning of falling stones, so a helmet would be a good idea.

The start is from the village of Dro from a car park on Via Capitelli, off the main square and shown on the Garda Trentino Tourist Walking 1:30,000 map. Go (north-west) along Via Capitelli, which bends to the right to meet another road in 250m. Turn left and in 100m signs to the left indicate Sentiero Campagnolo/Sentiero Scaloni – Ceniga – Arco

Sentieros Anglone and Scaloni can hardly be called ferratas, but they combine to make an easy day which could be climbed in quite bad weather conditions as a loosener or even on a day off.

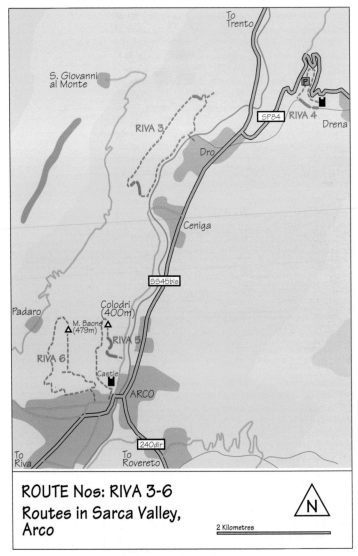

ROUTE Nos: RIVA 3-6
Routes in Sarca Valley,
Arco

*Descending
steps on Sentiero
Scaloni (RIVA 3).
(photo: Marion Smith)*

(this is your return route). Follow the road as it bends to the right, and in 100m 'Sentiero Anglone S. Giovanni Al Monte 425' is signed. Go along this side road as it veers left after a house on the right to another sign for 'path 425 Sentiero Anglone' on a track which goes round to the right. Continue on this track for about 10 minutes to the next sign on the left, '425 S. Giovanni ore 3.40'. There is no indication of Sentiero Anglone at this point, but this is the path you take; it zigzags up through olive groves then trees to arrive at an SAT VF sign and a notice 'Attenzione Caduta Sassi' at about 220m.

A series of steps cut in the rock leads up to a ledge with a handrail and more steps, before you walk up to about 300m and a good viewpoint back to Dro and Arco. Steps and a wire lead up a gully, and after about another

20 minutes' walking there is a sign for 'path 425 San Giovanni' at about 460m. There is no sign for the path on the left, which is the one you take, but '428 bis' is painted on a large rock at the start of the path. The time from the car park in Dro to here is about 1 hour.

Follow path 428bis as it traverses generally south-west along the Coste Dell' Anglone, and in just over 5 minutes you get a view back towards Riva and Lake Garda before going back into woods to walk through a sunken gorge. Some 20 minutes from the start of path 428 you reach a sign '428 Ceniga' at about 570m and meet a forestry road. Follow the road slightly uphill (waymark on a tree) ahead on the right for about 500m (10 minutes) until waymarks appear for a path on the left. Go down this path through the trees, and in a few minutes pass two water troughs carved in the rock under a big overhang. Now there is a short ascent, but watch out for paint marks on a rock as the path turns right and zigzags uphill and back to the right before turning back left and heading generally south-east. Path 428bis lasts about 50 minutes before it joins the main path 428 at about 560m signed '428 Ceniga/Scaloni'. Turn left down hill with views across towards Drena and the gorge of route RIVA 4 see below.

The route was re-cabled, and new wooden steps provided, in 2003.

◀ In less than 10 minutes' descent you reach a large wooden triangle and here, though not obviously, turn right (spot height 507m on the map). The path goes through trees then comes out into open ground with a couple of exposed ledges and the first cable at about 500m. Some carved steps and a short zigzag are followed by a walk down to about 400m, where more steps lead down to the route-book box. Zigzag down more steps to a set of old wooden steps (with views to Dro and the Marocche, an amazing geomorphologic landscape and glacial wonder of 187m³ mass of boulders). Descend a second set of wooden steps and a ramp, with 1909 carved on a rock. More walking and more carved steps are followed by a cable, a short (3m) metal bridge and steps down to an SAT VF sign at about 300m. Ten minutes' easy walking then leads down to a track which trends right and then left by a big wall to a T-junction with the main track, Sentiero Campagnola, at about 180m.

Turn left and follow Sentiero Campagnola (also signed '425 S. Giovanni') back to Dro and the car park in about 25 minutes, making a total round of about 3 hours.

RIVA 4:
SENTIERO ATTREZZATO RIO SALLAGONI

Grade:	4 (see note below right)
Seriousness:	A (but see note in text below)
Departure point:	Picnic area on the SP84 Dro to Drena
Ascent:	200m
Descent:	200m
Via ferrata:	200m
Approximate time:	1½–2 hours
Highest altitude:	380m, Castello Drena

This is a quite artificial route using cables and large stemples to climb walls smoothed by thousands of years of water. At times it is strenuous, but the cabling is good so that an ascent can be made even in damp conditions. However the route should **not** be climbed if there has been heavy rain or sudden storms are forecast. The grading of 4, A assumes dry conditions in stable weather – the seriousness would be increased to B or even C in anything other than optimum conditions.

The start of the route is easily reached from a large car park by a picnic area on the SP84 from Dro to Drena. After a zigzag bend in the road at the Km 18 marker, pass a sign 'Localita Lavini' and a hard-surface sports pitch and the car park (free) is on the right. There is a bus stop here as well, so it would be possible to do the route using public transport but check bus times locally with the tourist office. There are picnic areas on both sides of the road, but stay on the east side and go through the picnic area heading east for 30m to locate a wide track signed 'Passeggiata per Il Castello'.

Follow this track as it heads generally south, and in about 200m there is a large ENEL (hydro-electric) tunnel entrance. Continue on the main track as it forks slightly right and downhill, and in 100m 'Sentiero attrezzata Rio Sallagoni con arrivo al Castello' is signposted. 'Passeggiata' is signed uphill to the left; this is the return route used in descent. In a

This is an excellent adventure, climbing the canyon up to Castello Drena (the canyon was used as an emergency exit from the castle in days gone by).

Fairly tall and fit ferratists may find the grade of this route easier than is suggested, but shorter climbers will struggle to reach the cable on the main (overhanging) traverse, making it really strenuous.

The start of the canyon of Sentiero Attrezzato Rio Sallagoni (RIVA 4) (photo: Marion Smith)

further 100m on the main track there is a sharp right bend, with a red waymark painted on a rock and a path leading up to the left (this is a return path from an escape point on the route, mentioned below). Follow the road down to the right and in only 10m you will see, on your left, a roofed notice board and a sign to the start of the Rio Sallagoni route. From here a path leads directly into the bottom of the canyon, only 15 minutes from the car park.

It is an impressive place as the walls tower up on either side. The route climbs the wall on the left as you look up the canyon, steeply at first using large stemples for your feet and the cables to haul yourself up. Some of the cables and footholds at the start may be damp even in dry weather. After the steep start the route levels out, with a step onto a large boulder, to continue up the left side of the canyon with a spectacular waterfall on the right. After a difficult traverse around an overhanging bowl pass underneath a large chock-stone to arrive at a junction in the cable. Going up stemples on the left is an escape route which, with a 5m climb, leads to a path down which you could descend back to the main approach track. However the route continues ahead along the left wall going around another large overhanging scoop before switching to the right wall to pass beneath some giant chock-stones to an open part of the canyon (the really hard work is over: 15–20 minutes of climbing, with 30 minutes more ascent to come).

There are paths on both sides of the stream, but unless you are feeling incredibly sporty take the right-hand path which zigzags up to a scary wire bridge coming across from the left side. There are some other wires here which are apparently used by guides taking people canyoning. Continue on the right side of the now more open canyon with some wire protection and stemples, and walk uphill until signs point the route down to the left and a small wooden bridge ('Castello' and an arrow painted on a rock and 'Privato' indicated to the right ▶). An easy path leads up to and around the castle to arrive at a fence directly next to the castle entrance. The castle was built in 1175 by the Counts of Arco, destroyed in 1703 by the French General Vedome, and restored between 1984 and 1988; it has a small museum and is worth the minimal entrance fee for a look around. Opening times are 1000–1800hrs every day except Monday from March to October. Between November and February opening times are the same, but the castle is open only on Saturday and Sunday.

To descend follow signed path 'Passeggiata' half way up the castle drive. This leads down to the SP84, where you cross the road and take a path (to the right of a roadside picnic table) which runs alongside a wall with the road above. This again leads down to the SP84 at the Km 16 marker, where you turn left to head back uphill for 50m to locate a path on the right signed 'Passeggiata per Le Marocche'. Follow this path down through the woods, initially with blue markers which change to red ones as you near the end of the path. Rejoin the main track which you started out on, turning right, slightly uphill to go back to the car park. The total time for the descent is less than 30 minutes, and could also be achieved by following the road, though the path is more pleasant and much shorter.

The 'Privato' sign has been removed, so the upper stretch of gorge can now be explored. This is much easier, and is equipped only with stemples and belay pegs, apparently for canyoning trips. This is certainly not suitable for wet weather, and you will probably end up with wet feet, even in dry weather! Emerge from the gorge a few hundred metres south-west of the castle at a small drainage plant. Rejoin the main route by walking up the drive to the road.

RIVA 5:
Sentiero Attrezzato dei Colodri

Grade:	2
Seriousness:	A
Departure point:	Arco
Ascent:	315m
Descent:	315m

An easy but really pleasant route on good rock, with good situations surrounded by impressive rock walls which give some extreme climbing at world-class standards.

Via ferrata:	150m
Approximate time:	2–2½ hours
Highest altitude:	400m, Cima Colodri

This route faces the morning sun, and although the ferrata is usually climbable all the year round, it can be very hot in the middle of the summer. It is an ideal route for beginners, for a short evening sortie, or just a 'day off' from bigger things.

You can approach the route from the centre of Arco in 20 minutes following a minor road on the east side of town below the castle (Via Paolina Caproni); this runs along the west bank of the Sarca river towards Ceniga. By car, either use a car park in Arco (some with 5 hours' limit and small charge; not the disc car parks, which are only 1 hour), or follow the same road northwards to a parking place about 1km after Camping Arco. The route starts 10 minutes from the road opposite Camping Arco. Intermittent waymarks lead up through a 'Percorso Vita' (unusual in that it is specifically a training area for climbers) on a path that zigzags up through boulders and exercise stations.

The route takes only 40–50 minutes to climb, plus a 5 minute walk to the large cross on the summit of Cima Colodri. Initially climb up to the right, before a rightwards traverse leads to a ledge with views down to the campsite. Now zigzag up towards the vertical walls above, before the route goes left to follow an ascending line on good rock below the rock walls. Protection is good throughout, as are the views. Two short climbs, with small stemples, lead to a short (8m) corner and steep wall; there are some pegs on the wall but the rock is good – so try to climb the wall without using the pegs. Above this pitch is the top of the climb (at about 315m), and a walk over a deeply fluted limestone pavement to the summit cross.

Descent from the summit would be possible by reversing the route back to the start, but a more scenic way is to walk down and perhaps visit Arco castle on the way. Follow waymarks to the north which, although their general direction of descent is west, lead almost immediately down the right (east) to pick up a good path through the woods; this path curves

*Climber on Sentiero
Attrezzato dei Colodri
(RIVA 5)*

round to the left, and in a few minutes reaches a Y-junction of paths (at about 295m) and sign 'Cima Colt'. For a longer day you could take the right fork to Cima Colt (consult map); otherwise take the left fork on a good path (known as Sentiero de Secci, and equipped with a number of interpretation boards) which descends to a road at the little church of S. Maria di Laghei, 230m in just 20 minutes from the summit.

To return straight back to Arco the well-paved road, called Via Crucis (after the stations of the cross), winds down to the town in about 30 minutes. However, to visit the castle, take the asphalt track branching off to the left a couple of hundred metres from S. Maria di Laghei (opening hours 1000–1900hrs April to September and 1000–1600hrs

October to March; there is a modest entrance fee). After visiting the impressively sited ruins, pick up the signed path down to the old town.

RIVA 6:
VIA DEL 92 CONGRESSO, MONTE BAONE

Grade:	*
Seriousness:	* (see explanation in text below)
Departure point:	Arco
Ascent:	400m
Descent:	400m
Via ferrata:	0m
Approximate time:	2½–3 hours
Highest altitude:	479m, Monte Baone

This route has been included as a warning as much as anything else. Although it is shown on maps with conventional via ferrata crosses, it has no protection at all.

Via del 92 Congresso is a UIAA Grade II/III rock scramble, mostly on very good limestone, but at times very exposed. Strangely enough there are cables on the 'Rientro' descent route even though that is very easy, with nothing like the climbing or exposure encountered on the ascent. Having said that, if you have a good head for heights and enjoy a good scramble then the ascent of Monte Baone, 479m, makes an entertaining short round of about 3 hours. If anyone is nervous about exposed free-climbing, take a short rope with you.

There are three different maps available free from the tourist office in Arco. All of them show Via del 92 Congresso as a ferrata route. The best of these maps is 'Garda Trentino, Carta Escursionistica Wanderkarte 1:30,000'. This is far superior to another Garda Trentino map at 1:27,000 and a local Commune di Arco 1:10,000 map, both of which are somewhat pictorial.

To approach the route follow the signs in Arco to 'Parco arciducale' ('the arboretum') on the west side of Arco (about 10 minutes). From the arboretum continue up Via del Calvario, which has footpath signs 'M Colodri M400-Colt 430-Baone 480'. In 2 minutes up the road there is a sign for

'Via crucis di Laghel' ('crosses of Laghel'), followed by a fork in the road. Take the left fork, and in 25m (by one of the crosses) a road goes off to the left signed 'Monte Baone 479 Percorso Alpinisitico 2h 15m 92 Congresso'. That's what the route is – Alpinistico!

Follow the road generally west away from Arco and then as it winds uphill, in 7 or 8 minutes, there is a 5 tonne weight restriction sign and a red-and-white waymark on the wall. Continue on the road (now gravel) and in 2 minutes follow a waymarked path which leads left from the road. In about 5 minutes this path meets a gravel track with a sign for Arco pointing back the way you have just come. Turn right on the track and almost immediately on the right is a way-mark, a low wall and up on the rocks a sign 'Attenzione Caduta Sassi'. Altitude at this point is about 190m; there is no sign, but this is the start of the Via 92 Congresso.

After a short set of zigzags the waymarks lead up a wonderful rib of solid limestone with easy, unprotected scrambling. There is no escape until very near the top (explained in text below), so before climbing anything make sure you would also be happy to reverse it. After 10 minutes of climbing, the ground levels out at about 260m and a short descent leads to easy ground. Next is an exposed rightwards traverse. The rock is good, but the situation airy, before some less exposed slabs and a short walk (with good waymarks) leads to another exposed traverse. Continue up a short (3m–4m) vertical wall on good holds (altitude just over 300m). Now there is more easy scrambling and shaded walking until (about 370m) a very exposed ledge traverses rightwards for about 15m, leading to another short vertical wall.

You are near the top now, and this is the one **escape point** mentioned earlier. To avoid the exposed ledge scramble up through trees to the left until you see some cairns, which lead up through broken ground until you can traverse easily back to the right to pick up the red-and-white markers again above the exposed ledge and climb.

Continuing the climb after the exposed ledge to yet another ledge and an easier scramble to about 400m, and the difficulties are over. A further 10 minutes' walking with some scrambling gets you to the summit of Monte Baone, where the sign indicates an altitude of 480m, though maps show the height as 479m.

A broken sign indicates the path to Padaro/Chiarano; the descent follows a path through the woods until, in about 10 minutes, you come to a sign pointing left through a gap in a wall to 'Padaro/Rientro Sentiero 92 Arco'. In 30m there is a T-junction, where you turn left again going slightly uphill and heading south/south-west in the direction of Chiarano. In about 5 minutes the path reaches a fence enclosing a large garden and then meets a road. To the right the road is signed to Chiarano and Arco, but continue on the road, which bends left around the perimeter of the garden, for about 250m, where, just before the road comes to a dead end, there is a blue marker on a wall on the right. Turn right here on an indistinct grassy path, which soon becomes more obvious and in 5 minutes leads to a road where 'Rientro Sentiero 92 Congresso' is signed down to the left.

Go down the path to the left and soon, with power lines overhead, the first wires appear to aid the descent. Although the angle of the slabs is easy, they could be slippery if wet. Continue down for 10 minutes (more cables and some walking) until at about 270m the path reaches some olive terraces and turns left. Pass a small house and follow a wall and waymarks before cabled ledges lead down to the road just east of the impressive slabs of the climbing area of Falesia di Baone. Time for descent of the 'Rientro' is about 20 minutes.

At the road go left, and almost immediately right off the cobbled road onto a gravel track. In 50m the track is again cobbled for a steep down-slope and in less than 10 minutes leads to a T-junction (signed 'Falesia di Baone'). Turn left and follow the road, above the arboretum, back to the end of Via Lomego and the arboretum gates (2¾hours for the round).

RIVA 7:
FERRATA DEL CENTENARIO SAT (VIA DELL'AMICIZIA)

Grade:	3
Seriousness:	A
Departure point:	Riva del Garda

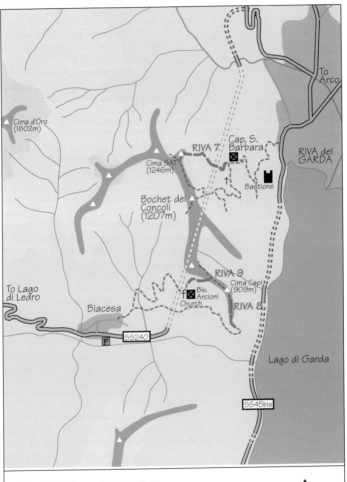

Cima d'Oro
(1802m)

Cima SAT
(1246m)

RIVA 7

Cap. S.
Barbara

RIVA del
GARDA

Bastione

Bochet dei
Concoli
(1207m)

To Lago
di Ledro

RIVA 9

Cima Capi
(909m)

Biacesa

Biv.
Arcioni
Church

RIVA 8

SS240

Lago di Garda

ROUTE Nos: RIVA 7-9
VF Centenario SAT,
Sent. Susatti & Foletti

N

1 Kilometre

Ascent:	1200m
Descent:	1200m
Via ferrata:	600m
Approximate time:	4½–5½ hours
Highest altitude:	1246m, Cima SAT

This is a stunning route with fantastic views down to Riva and the northern end of Lake Garda.

This route could be climbed at almost any time of the year, but faces the sun and could be very hot in midsummer. Not a technically difficult route, but given the exposure on the part of the route that includes some long ladder climbs, it is not suitable for beginners or people who suffer from vertigo.

Parking in the centre of Riva is difficult and metered, so unless you are staying in the town it is advisable to park on the outskirts and walk to the start. The route is on the western side of Riva, with Cima SAT towering above the lake. The approach starts opposite the end of Via Bastione, with clear waymarking for path 404 Capanna S.Barbara/Cima SAT and a large diagrammatic map at the beginning of the path. It is easy to locate Via Bastione, as it is the main road running west to east above the harbour and old town, with the Bastione fort as a landmark above the town. Bastione was built by the Venetians in 1508, and razed by the French in 1703 at the same time as Arco, Drena and Penede in the War of Spanish Succession.

Your ascent to the ferrata follows path 404 S.Barbara/Cima SAT. Climb a narrow road as it zigzags up to Bastione, then continue to zigzag up and, after a short (200m) cemented stretch, path 404 S.Barbara/Cima SAT forks to the right (a left fork indicates 'Sentiero Attrezzato Fausto Sussati' – see RIVA 8). About an hour from Riva you arrive at the small refuge of Capanna S. Barbara (560m); this is rarely open, but is a good spot to take a break. In a further 5 minutes, at a newish small building, 404 bis Via dell'Amiciza/Cima SAT climbs to the right and 404 heads up to the left 'Chiesetta S.Barbara'. (This is where you rejoin the path from your descent route later in the day.) It is only a couple of minutes more to the start of the route.

The first half of the route is a little broken with short sections of cable, but it works upwards all the time – a short cable, a walk, a short cable, a gap, a longer cable, followed by a walk on an exposed ledge (on a good path) to the left. You are only 10 minutes into the route now and already the views are great. After a longer section of cable (50m), a gap and an exposed ledge, the path zigzags up (with an occasional scramble) following grey waymarks and then a steady uphill walk to the foot of an imposing steep wall and the first of a series of ladders (30 minutes on the route, and about 2 hours above Riva). Each ladder is listed below, and the number of steps is hopefully reasonably accurate! Heights have been estimated on the basis of the number of steps.

- **Ladder 1**: 73 steps, about 21m in height.
- **Ladder 2**: 48 steps, about 15m.

One of the ladders on Ferrata del Centenario SAT (RIVA 7)

Depending on other people on the route allow 15– 20 minutes for the first two ladders, and then a 15 minute walk (some cables) to the start of the next (big!) set of ladders.

- **Ladder 3**: 24 steps, about 7m in height.
- **Ladder 4**: (the big one) 136 steps, about 40m.
- **Ladder 5**: 32 steps and 10m in height.

The ascent of ladders 3, 4 and 5 takes 25–35 minutes.

A path now zigzags up through some woods, and in 10 minutes you see the Italian flag on the summit of Cima SAT and the final ladders above you. However, the path goes to the left of the final rocky buttress and even seems to be avoiding it altogether, but in a few minutes traverses back right onto the rock and the final three ladders to the summit of Cima SAT.

- **Ladder 6**: 32 steps, about 10m high.
- **Ladder 7**: 24 steps, 7m in height.
- **Ladder 8**: 8 steps, 2m high. ▶

The views are spectacular the whole way up, but none better for a photograph than the top of the penultimate ladder and summit flag (a metal one!). For the total ascent from Riva to Cima SAT allow 3–3½ hours.

Note that, after the initial descent from the summit, it is possible to return to Riva by a route going to the right (north) to follow waymarked path 418 to the junction of path 402 and then turn right to return to Riva in about 3 hours. We favour the more direct route as described above; this seems to be the one most used locally.

A protected descent (cable and stemples) leads from the summit to a path (west) signposted 404 to the left. In 5 minutes (path traversing and rising slightly) another signpost is reached left, 404, with right 413 giving two options of descent. The most direct route, path 404, is recommended. Although it almost continually descends steep and potentially exposed ground, it is wonderfully engineered and a super path throughout.

Descend 404 passing 'Chiesa di Guerra 1915–1918' and then pass some old barrack buildings and more steep zigzags. About 25–30 minutes from the summit another path junction is reached, left 404, right 405 – follow 404, and in a further 5 minutes reach yet another junction! 413 goes straight ahead, and your path is 404, down to the left, but you may be tempted by the notice of 'Acqua Min. 5' for a watering-hole detour. ◀

Continue on 404 to another junction, 405 Sentiero Attrezzata Fausto Sussati (about 50 minutes of descent from the summit), and in 7–8 minutes there is a wonderful viewpoint. A short section of cable (a useful handrail) now protects a slippery section of dirty rock before, with the chapel in view, arriving at a final ladder and some stemples (46 steps – 12m). From here it is 10 minutes down to the chapel, and 5 minutes more back to the Capanna S. Barbara *rifugio* and the final return via Bastione back down to Riva. Total descent is about 2 hours.

View down to Riva from the penultimate ladder of Ferrata del Centenario SAT (RIVA 7)

RIVA 8:
SENTIERO ATTREZZATA
FAUSTO SUSATTI, CIMA CAPI

Grade:	2
Seriousness:	A
Departure point:	Biacesa village, 450m
Ascent:	480m
Descent:	480m
Via ferrata:	200m
Approximate time:	4½ hours
Highest altitude:	929m, Cima Capi

The old Riva–Biacesa road has been replaced by a new tunnel, which means it is no longer possible to access the route from the lakeside on path 405, despite what some maps show (the best map to use is a Garda Trentino publication, 'Riva del Garda Monte Rochetta Monte Brione', at 1:10,000). The best itinerary for ferratists starts at Biacesa. The more interesting part of Sentiero Susatti is climbed to the summit of Cima Capi, with the descent by Sentiero Foletti (RIVA 9). This is the almost universal choice of visitors, but if you have time further exploration of these lovely hills is well worthwhile. In addition to the northernmost part of Sentiero Susatti, there are extensive areas of First World War fortifications and tunnels to explore (torch needed). There is a very limited bus service from Riva to Biacesa, but access is much easier if you have a car.

There is a small car park (adjacent to a children's playground) on the left-hand side of the road as you enter Biacesa from Riva. From the car park walk up the road towards the village and turn right by the bus stop, where a signpost indicates '417 Bochet dei Concoli 460 Chiesa S Giovanni 0.50 Cima Capi'. Go past Osteria dei Magasi (a good place for a coffee) and in 100m, at the top of the road, turn right (with another signpost for path 460). Follow the road for 300m and then take the left fork (again clearly waymarked) onto a roughly

An easy, but splendid, route to the summit of Cima Capi, with extensive views over Lake Garda. The itinerary described here is, in fact, about half the entire route. There is a little-used extension, northwards, towards Bocca d'Enzima which, whilst protected, is little more than an exposed stroll.

paved track. After 200m another waymark is reached – the path to the left is the descent route (or would be the ascent if you were climbing RIVA 9 Mario Foletti). Take the right fork, signed 'Ferrata Cima Capi' (this is actually Ferrata Fausto Susatti). The path here is also known as Senter del Bech, path 470, which is indicated on some maps. The path is quite narrow in places as it contours across a steep wooded hillside. After passing an unnecessary wire (handrail only), with a drop to your right, the track leads to another signpost.

Do not follow 'S. Attrezzata Laste 40 mins' (signed ahead) but take the path to the right signed 'Pozze Alte and Cima Capi'. About an hour after leaving the village there is an impressive viewpoint (about 570m) down to Lake Garda, almost 500m below, with an old wartime lookout and fortified firing position built into a large overhanging rock face. The path continues past some trenches, and 5 minutes further on is yet another sign – '405 Cima Capi' to the left (the way to the ferrata) and to the right '405 Val Sperone and Riva', but Riva has been crossed through and a note made on the sign saying no exit to Riva (see earlier information regarding road closure). About 10 minutes further on a few metal pegs aid climbing up a 3m gully, and in a further 10 minutes an SAT Ferrata sign and the beginning of the cabled

Climbers on ridge to Cima Capi with Lake Garda below (RIVA 8)

route is reached at a height of about 720m, about 1½ hours from Biacesa.

The climb has several sections of cables with wonderful views to the lake. Scrambling is easy here, but in airy, exposed positions, with Cima Capi rising straight in front of you. After climbing past a cave (another wartime lookout point) and some more cables the ferrata is almost over, ending at about 860m and yet another lookout point. A final short cable just below 900m is followed by a walk to the summit, passing wartime trenches all the way along the summit ridge, with views to Biacesa, Riva, the lake and the alluvial plain formed by the Sarche river. Different maps show the summit of Cima Capi as anything between 907 and 929m, so it is probably not the best place to recheck your altimeter. The total time for the ascent is 2–2½ hours.

Descend from the summit continuing on path 405, and in little over 10 minutes at about 880m a path junction is reached. Path 405 continues ahead signed '405/404 S.Barbara/Riva 1.30' and, depending on your transport arrangements, you could continue on this path and follow it back to Riva. However, the circular route described here is the recommend option. To the left 'Sentiero Attrezzata Mario Foletti' is signed, along with 'Chiesa San Giovanni 1.15'.

Path 460 goes through a series of built-up wartime trenches and past a big cave, and in 10 minutes you reach a plaque advising the start of the ferrata (about 895m). Traverse with the help of a wire across an easy slab, and then the wire goes up to the right (a path straight on is a decoy). Go along a ledge with good views back to the summit of Cima Capi before descending into a gully, where you get a view down to Bivacco Francesco Arcioni. The wire ends at the bottom of this easy gully and the path continues in a few minutes to the bivouac at 845m. This is an amazing little place where drinks (beer, wine and soft drinks) can be obtained on an honesty basis. The bivouac is open from 0800 to 1800hrs, but must be booked if used outside these hours.

From the bivouac continue on path 460, passing the small church Chiesa San Giovanni and winding down through woods back towards Biacesa. Stay on the main waymarked track, which joins path 417 in about 10 minutes (at about 700m). Continue down the track towards Biacesa for a further 15 minutes, and just below 500m is an artist's studio with a garden full of interesting, and in some cases amusing, artefacts. From here the car park is about 15 minutes away. Allow a total time for your descent (depending on how long you linger at the bivouac) of 1½–2 hours.

RIVA 9:
SENTIERO ATTREZZATO
MARIO FOLETTI, CIMA CAPI

Grade:	1
Seriousness:	A
Departure point:	Biacesa
Ascent:	500m
Descent:	500m
Via ferrata:	100m
Approximate time:	4 hours
Highest altitude:	929m, Cima Capi

Although this can be completed as a route in its own right, it is also recommend as the descent in a round-climb of Cima Capi from Biacesa, climbing Sentiero Fausto Susatti first. (This round is explained in RIVA 8 above.)

To climb this route on its own, you can either descend the same way back to Biacesa, or from the summit of Cima Capi take path 405/404 back to Riva via Bocca d'Enzima and Chiesa San Barbara. For both these options, the ascent of Sentiero Mario Foletti is simply the reverse of the descent described in RIVA 8.

Follow path 417 out of the village of Biacesa up past Osteria dei Magasi. At the second left fork (about 460m) follow path 417, until just below 700m it forks left. At this point take path 460 (the right fork) and continue up to Chiesa San Giovanni and Bivacco Francesco Arcioni (845m). Follow the sign and waymarks to Sentiero Attrezzato Mario Foletti for a few minutes to the first wire (simply a handrail up an open gully). Continue, and more wires lead along a ledge with views to Cima Capi before a short step down leads to a traverse across a big slab and the end of the ferrata, indicated by a plaque just below 900m. Pass a big cave and then some built-up wartime trenches to a signed junction. The summit of Cima Capi is just a few minutes away to the right, and the continuation path

405/404 path to Chiesa San Barbara and Riva is to the left. Total time for the ascent to the summit of Cima Capi takes about 2 hours, and the return descent 1½–2 hours.

RIVA 10:
SENTIERO MAURO PELLEGRINI/FIORE MORA

Grade:	1
Seriousness:	A
Departure point:	Pieve di Ledro
Ascent:	1225m
Descent:	1225m
Via ferrata:	100m
Approximate time:	7 hours
Highest altitude:	1748m, Cima Caset
(Note: figures assume parking at roadhead and visit to summit of Monte Corno)	

The protected sections on this route are both short and easy, and only the most inexperienced via ferratist would feel the need for self-belay equipment – a good head for heights and sure-footedness should be sufficient.

This route is included because of the quality of the mountain walking it offers.

Whilst Pieve di Ledro, at the western end of Lago di Ledro, has ample parking, if you start walking from here you need to add about 170m of climbing on to what is already a fairly long day. It is better to drive up to Val di Maria, the limit of public access, at about 830m, where roadside parking is limited but usually possible. If you are reliant on public transport, then in addition to the extra climb you have to make an early start from Riva, since the only bus which is suitable leaves at 0800hrs. The return is at 1733hrs, but check times locally for any variation.

Take the road opposite the Hotel Sport, and drive south past the entrances to Camping Azzurro and Camping Al Lago. About 500m further, turn right into via del Roccola, which is also signposted to S. Martino, Bocca Spinera and Malga Giu, waymarked 456. Drive uphill until the road splits; both routes are closed to public access, but there is a

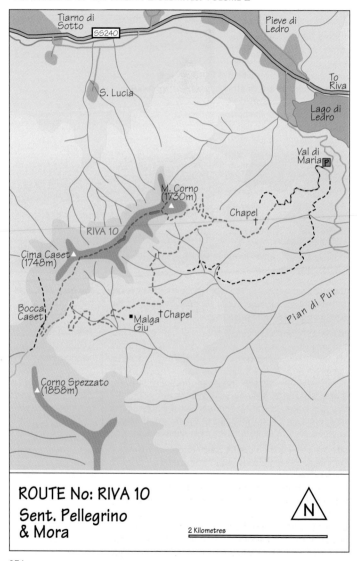

ROUTE No: RIVA 10
Sent. Pellegrino & Mora

2 Kilometres

reasonable amount of roadside parking (830m). Start walking up the right-hand road, which soon becomes very steep. After about 30 minutes (about 1105m) turn off left (south-west) onto a path waymarked 456. A further 20 minutes' walking brings you to a grassy ridge, where the chapel of S. Martino stands (1228m). Path 456 continues straight ahead, back into the woods, soon passing a decorated spring (now dried up) and a cave. A further few minutes brings you to a junction (at about 1330m) just below Bocca Spinera. The route to the left, waymarked 456 to Malga Giu, is the route on which you will return later in the day.

Take the path straight ahead, waymarked '456b, Monte Corno and Bocca Caset'. In about 10 minutes, at about 1400m, keep an eye out for a less well-defined path off to the left. Whilst it is signposted (again, to Monte Corno and Bocca Caset), it is easy to miss. Follow the painted waymarking on an indistinct path, until (at about 1480m) you reach a rock wall. The path now swings to the left (south-west) along the foot of the rocks. After about 20 minutes, the path takes a sharp right turn and climbs up the left-hand side of a broad, grassy rake, the first significant break in the rock wall. The rake leads you to the ridge (at about 1655m) a few metres from the sentiero, which is just to your left (allow about 2 hours to this point). ▶

Return to the ridge and the start of the sentiero, marked with a memorial plaque to Mauro Pellegrini and Fiore Mora, members of the Ledrense section of SAT. You immediately encounter a 30m cable safeguarding an easily angled but friable gully. You now follow a lovely airy path on an ingenious course through the many towers and pinnacles of the ridge.

The distinctive rock window on Sentiero Pellegrino/Mora (RIVA 10)

Before you start on the sentiero you should visit the summit of **Monte Corno**, 1730m, 15 minutes to the right. This grand viewpoint is reached by the way-marked path, and was an important lookout position for the Italian forces facing the Austrians across the valley.

After about 50 minutes (at about 1720m) you scramble through a distinctive little rock window, and shortly after reach the second length of cable, which protects a slightly airy traverse and a friable groove. The route continues through the rocky outcrops, soon passing just below a small ruined lookout post on the crest of Cima Caset, 1748m, with a roomy dugout underneath. Another 20 minutes brings you to a further memorial plaque, marking the end of the sentiero (at about 1660m), which you should reach about 2 hours after its start.

The path continues on a gently descending traverse for a few minutes before it turns sharp left back into the trees. Continue down until (at about 1590m) you join a gravel road which comes up from your right. About 100m further on, there is a gravelled track on the left. Whilst neither signed nor waymarked (indeed, a barrier post discourages you), this is the route you should take. Drop steadily, with views of Malga Giu below you until, after about 30 minutes, at a sharp right-hand bend (about 1345m), take the path off to the left, waymarked 456 to Bochet di Spinera and Pieve di Ledro.

This old wartime route meanders beautifully through the trees along the 1300m contour line. You reach the junction with your outward route in about an hour. Retrace your steps to the valley, allowing about 2½ hours for the descent from the end of the sentiero.

RIVA 11:
VIA FERRATA SPIGOLO DELLA BANDIERA

Grade:	3
Seriousness:	A
Departure point:	Albergo Colomber, 405m
Ascent:	580m
Descent:	580m
Via ferrata:	100m
Approximate time:	3½ hours
Highest altitude:	1165m, Rif. Pirlo alla Spino

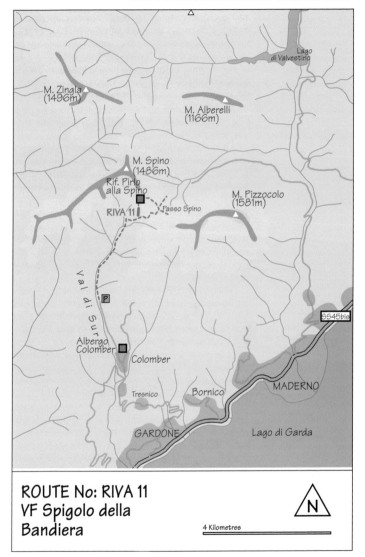

ROUTE No: RIVA 11
VF Spigolo della
Bandiera

N

4 Kilometres

This pleasant little via ferrata is in a lovely setting. Whilst it has recently been completely re-cabled, the inadequate waymarking has not been improved, so it is in danger of becoming Lake Garda's best-kept secret.

The approach is from the pleasant little lakeside town of Gardone. The drive up from the lake can be confusing through the maze of narrow little lanes, so take care to turn off the main road at the correct point, which is opposite the Hotel Villa Capri. Wind up through the village of Tresnico to the track which is signposted to Albergo Colomber. Whilst this point can be reached by a local bus, it is a very limited service, so public transport is only an option if you are planning a stay up in these hills. The beautifully located Rif. Pirlo alla Spino, at the top of the ferrata, is a good choice, although only open from June to September (however, a well-equipped bivouac room at the rear is permanently available). Another option is the Albergo Miramonte, a few hundred metres before the turn-off to Albergo Colomber.

Take the track to the left (west) of Albergo Colomber, which leads into the Val di Sur. This has a rough, but good, surface, and you can drive up to an altitude of about 590m, where it narrows to footpath width. There are quite a few parking opportunities during the final kilometre, including right at the end.

Follow the path northwards, through woodland, climbing quite steeply in places. There are a good many side tracks which can be confusing, and the waymarking is less than ideal. The *rifugio* is variously referred to as Rif. Spino and Rif. Pirlo, and the ferrata is referred to only a couple of times (and not where you need it!). However, stick to the path waymarked 1 until, after about an hour, you arrive at an obvious junction (at about 950m). The ferrata is signposted straight ahead and Passo Spino to the right, and the *rifugio* can be approached by either path. Be sure to identify this junction correctly, because the path to the ferrata is not far ahead and can easily be missed. About 10 minutes later (at about 1025m) you come to a rock wall about 3m high, with a faded red-and-white waymark. There are two trees growing closely together to the immediate left of this wall, and a faint path running off to the left. Whilst there is nothing to indicate it, this is your route.

Follow the path up through the trees for a few hundred metres towards the foot of the buttress which can just be glimpsed through the vegetation. You reach the start of the route (at about 1045m), with a sign confirming that you have

indeed reached Via Ferrata Spigolo della Bandiera. The route begins with a leftward rising traverse, initially across a short wall, then onto a gently angled slab. It then goes straight up the front of the buttress, which is broken and quite vegetated. There are, however, a series of steeper steps until you reach an easily angled and quite vegetated area which leads up to the only slightly difficult passage of the route, an overhanging block about 4m high. This is surmounted with the aid of a bit of muscle and a metal foothold (although the latter is hardly necessary). A series of short rock steps now lead to the top of the buttress (at about 1095m). A 5 minute walk brings you to the *rifugio* (at 1165m), in a lovely position overlooking Val di Sur.

The start of VF Spigolo della Bandiera is hidden in thick woodland (RIVA 11)

When you leave the *rifugio*, take the path a few metres east of the end of the terrace which, after a couple of hundred metres of descent, brings you back to the faint path which you followed to the start of the ferrata. Retrace your steps to the motorable track, which you will reach in about 1½ hours.

ROVERETO

Maps
Kompass Wanderkarte 1:50,000 Sheet 101, 1:20,000 Brentonico, Monte Baldo, from Tourist Information Offices and Lagir Alpina, Lago di Garda 1:50,000

Tourist Information Office
APT Rovereto, Via Dante 63, 38068 Rovereto, Italy
Tel: (0464) 430363
Fax: (0464) 435528
E-mail: roverto@apt.rovereto.tn.it
Internet: www.apt.rovereto.tn.it

The historic town of Rovereto

Rovereto is a busy town in the Adige valley, and although it caters for the tourist, it has a distinctly local feel to it. If the bustle and buzz of the town appeal, the tourist office can help you find an apartment or hotel accommodation. You might, however, prefer to stay in one of the quieter villages, such as Brentonico, in the surrounding hills. The nearest campsites are a few kilometres downstream at Ala, and up in the hills to the south-west at Polsa and S. Valentino. Its location in the Adige valley means that Rovereto is well connected to the region's public transport network, and local services also radiate from the town.

Most of the routes in this section have a major historical dimension and traverse areas of intense activity during the 1915–18 war. One, however, ROVER 4 Monte Albano, is a classic of modern 'sport via ferrata' construction.

Rovereto stands at a point where the River Leno flows into the Adige, and has been a location for fortified buildings since prehistoric times. The Romans used the site of the original for their own fortress, which was in turn replaced on the site during the 15th and 16th centuries by the Venetian castle, which remains to this day. The town remained a Venetian outpost until it became part of Austro-Hungarian Empire in 1509, under whose control it remained until the post-First World War settlement.

The many rich buildings in the town, some of which bear the Venetian lion of St Mark, are testament to its long-standing prosperity. The lovely historic centre is a maze of narrow streets and arcades. Its eastern end is dominated by the castle, which is the home of the Museo della Guerra, an extensive collection devoted to the history of warfare throughout the ages. The concentration is, inevitably, on the two world wars, with much of the material relating to the 1915–18 campaigns fought above the town on Monte Pasubio.

ROVER 1:
SENTIERO GAETANO FALCIPIERI/CINQUE CIME ATTREZZATA, MONTE FORNI ALTI 2023m

Grade:	2
Seriousness:	A
Departure point:	Bocchetta Campiglia, 1216m
Ascent:	1270m
Descent:	1270m
Via ferrata:	approx. 800m intermittent cable on a 3km ridge
Approximate time:	7 hours
Highest altitude:	2040m, Cimon del Soglio Rosso

Note: Torch essential for return by Strada delle 52 Gallerie

It is quite a long day, if the route described is done in its entirety, although it is possible to reduce it almost by half by leaving the sentiero after the main summit to pick up the

This is a quite outstanding itinerary, combining a superb mountain tour with exploration of some of the region's most impressive feats of wartime construction.

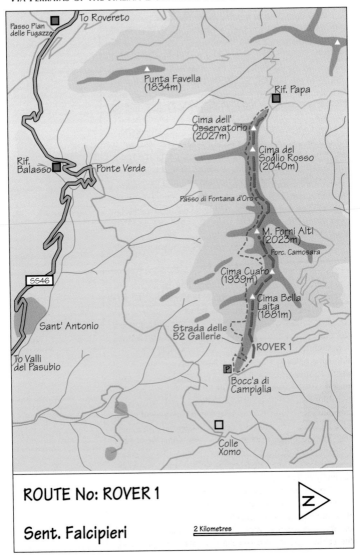

Passo Pian
delle Fugazze   To Rovereto

Punta Favella
(1834m)

Rif. Papa

Cima dell'
Osservatorio
(2027m)

Cima del
Soglio Rosso
(2040m)

Rif.
Balasso   Ponte Verde

Passo di Fontana d'Oro

M. Forni Alti
(2023m)

Forc. Camosara

SS46

Cima Cuaro
(1939m)

Cima Bella
Laita
(1881m)

Sant' Antonio

Strada delle
52 Gallerie

ROVER 1

To Valli
del Pasubio

Bocc'a di
Campiglia

Colle
Xomo

ROUTE No: ROVER 1

N

Sent. Falcipieri   2 Kilometres

Strada delle 52 Gallerie to return to the starting point. The route is also known as Cinque Cime Attrezzata after the five summits it traverses – Cima Bella Laita (1881m), Cima Cuaro (1939m), Monte Forni Alti (2023m), Cimon del Soglio Rosso (2040m) and Cima dell'Osservatorio (2027m). Many of the waymarks you will see refer simply to '5C'.

From Rovereto follow the SS46 road over Passo Pian delle Fugazze (1162m). Continue east over the pass towards Valli, as far as Ponte Verde (901m). From here, take the minor road off to the left to Colle Xomo. Then take the left turn to Bocchetta di Campiglia (1216m), the start of the route, where there is ample parking. Unfortunately, it is not possible to reach this point by public transport, so a car is essential unless you want to try hitching, which could be perfectly feasible, since this is the starting point for the popular walk along the Strada delle Gallerie, which is your return route after completing the sentiero.

A few paces north of the car park a waymarked path leads up into the trees and climbs steeply, soon passing a memorial plaque dedicating the sentiero to Gaetano Falcipieri. Some unprotected scrambling leads to a few stemples and the first cable (about 1320m). This protects easily angled climbing up broken and well-vegetated rock, which is followed by a meandering course through trees from outcrop to outcrop. Short lengths of cable protect the few slightly exposed passages. A short tunnel takes you through a buttress, after which follows about 15 minutes of gentle climbing through the trees, encountering several easy rock scrambles along the way. The first significant obstacles, two 20m rock buttresses, are reached at about 1560m. These are quickly followed by a 15m ladder, after which you embark on rather more sustained, but never difficult, climbing. The route now reaches its first peak, Cima Bella Laita (1881m), by which time the route's character has changed from its gentle, vegetated beginning into something quite distinctly mountainous.

A pleasantly airy, unprotected traverse leads in about 10 minutes or so to the second peak, Cima Cuaro (1939m). The descent which follows is slightly awkward, but well protected. You now reach an area of rather more friable rock, and the cabled descent into Forcella Camosara (1875m) needs

Strada delle 52 Gallerie runs just below the intermittently protected ridge, the line of Sentiero Falcipieri (ROVER 1)

care if there are other parties below you. The route gradually gains height, generally following the ridge, with some slightly exposed, unprotected walking along a narrow crest at one point. The summit of Monte Forni Alti (2023m), with its metal cross, is reached some 2½ hours after setting out.

Follow the quite steep and eroded track down into a little col (about 1965m) with a sign down to the left (south) of a low rock wall to Strada delle Gallerie. If time is short or the weather deteriorating, this is the first of several opportunities for you to head for home. It is also a potentially confusing spot, since the sentiero is unmarked and none too obvious; climb the slope straight ahead of you to reach the crest of the ridge, and you will soon pick up the waymarks again. From now on the route generally undulates along, or just below, on the north side of the ridge, frequently only just above the Strada delle Gallerie, which is following a course closely to your left. You very soon come to Passo di Fontana d'Oro (1875m), another opportunity to leave the sentiero and return on the Strada.

Your next landmark is the fourth summit, Cima Cimone del Soglio Rosso (2040m). This stretch of the route comprises lovely airy walking, not protected, but perfectly straightforward. A few minutes later you reach the last peak of the ridge, Cima dell'Osservatorio (2027m). This is topped by a round metal structure, which (as the name rather suggests) carries a series of metal sighting tubes aimed at surrounding peaks. Within a couple of minutes Rif. Papa comes into view down the steep scree slope. It will have taken you about 5 hours to reach this point (at 1928m), and you still have to traverse the entire length of the Strada delle Gallerie to return to your car. A torch is vital for this last leg of the itinerary; many of the tunnels are lengthy and are very uneven underfoot, so don't even think about setting out to walk the Strada without one. The first tunnel is only a couple of minutes from the *rifugio*; the entrance is hardly inviting, with its half-barrier and signs forbidding mountain biking (frequently ignored).

The couple of hours it will take you to return to your starting point involve easy walking, but take you through some dramatic mountain scenery. The route is one of the great achievements of mountain warfare construction, apparently completed in less than a year and still largely intact (in summer 2002 a stretch of track between Gallerie 41 and 40 was closed, and a diversion in place due to a landslip). Each of the 52 tunnels is individually named and bears a plaque displaying, in addition to its name, its number and length. Pride of place, in terms of distance, goes to Galleria 19, no less than 318m long and called simply 'Re'. The prize for the most impressive tunnel must, however, go to Galleria 20, named after General Cadorna, which is a complex descending spiral. The other tunnel worthy of special mention is Galleria 8, which has a side tunnel, 'Galleria Radiale e Cannoniere', which contains a number of artillery firing positions, one of which still has a cannon in situ. Galleria 1, the last you pass, is named Zappa – disappointingly after a certain Capitain Zappa, rather than the musician!

ROVER 2:
SENTIERO FRANCO GALLI,
MONTE CORNO BATTISTI (1760m)

Grade:	1
Seriousness:	A
Departure point:	Anghebeni, on SS 46, 15km from Rovereto
Ascent:	1240m
Descent:	1240m

Via ferrata:	200m
Approximate time:	5½ hours
Highest altitude:	1760m, Mont Corno Battisti

Note: torch essential for a thorough exploration of wartime tunnels, although not vital for the basic itinerary

Monte Corno Battisti is a mountain awash with historical interest, this having been a major fortified position for the Austrian forces during the 1915–18 war. The route described makes for quite a tiring day, and has only a relatively short section protected by cable.

This splendid itinerary visits many old tunnels and fortifications, although there are many others to be found if you have time to explore more thoroughly. The protected sections are entirely straightforward, and only the most inexperienced via ferratist would feel the need to carry self-belay equipment. The route is also well waymarked and signposted.

The starting point is Anghebeni, about 15km from Rovereto on the SS46. There is a good-sized car park opposite the Carabinieri station at the eastern end of the village. For those using public transport, there is a limited bus service from Rovereto.

From the car park (about 635m), walk 50m up the road (south-east) to a turn-off on the left, waymarked as path 102 and signposted to Ca d'Austria, Bocchetta di Foxi and Rif. Lancia. The metalled surface soon gives way to a rough, stony track. You are now on a major military supply route for the fortifications on Monte Corno Battista (your return route will utilise the entire length of this military road). After about 20 minutes (at about 750m), at the ruins of an old wartime command post, turn left on path 122b, signposted to Sella di Trappola. For the next 15 minutes follow the rough, stony track steeply up through the trees until (at about 860m) you take a much more pleasant little path on the right, waymarked but not signed, which climbs in more comfortable zigzags. At about 1410m you arrive at a ridge, still in trees, which links Monte Corno Battista with its subsidiary, Monte Trappola.

The path levels out and follows the line of the ridge, passing a couple of caves on the left, until you round a corner and get your first sight of the impressive rock walls of Monte Corno Battista. In a few minutes you arrive at Sella Trappola (1434m), and continue past a tunnel entrance which provides access to several observation positions, followed

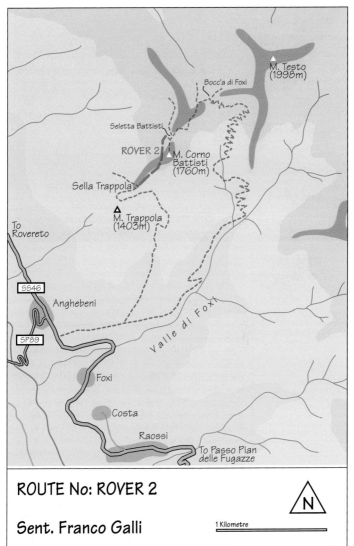

ROUTE No: ROVER 2

Sent. Franco Galli

1 Kilometre

N

Wartime tunnels and military insignia on Sentiero Galli (ROVER 2)

quickly by about 20m of cable to safeguard the ascent of a broken groove.

At the top of the cable, the route enters a short tunnel, which splits just inside the entrance; take the right-hand route, which is easily negotiable without a torch. You then pass the ruins of an old stone structure and a further tunnel before (at about 1490m) you reach a very short length of cable up a broken groove. A flight of steps now leads to a further tunnel; again no torch is needed. The track then divides at a boulder, although the two are linked very shortly by a tunnel. You now arrive at a diversion off to the left, signposted as a 'Panorama'. The view is well worth the two or three minutes it will take you to climb a flight of concrete steps, traverse a cabled gangway and pass through a tunnel to a super little belvedere.

The path continues to the foot of a rock wall, which it follows through the trees, passing two more tunnels before entering a third. On emerging, you climb a flight of concrete steps under an overhanging roof. At about 1625m, the route enters a further tunnel and ascends a steep flight of concrete steps inside. This climbs about 20m, but three windows provide sufficient light. The route briefly emerges onto a broad ledge, with a cement plaque set into the wall at the entrance to the next tunnel. This also contains a steep flight of steps, at the top of which the route turns to the left to join a cable which leads to a narrow ledge. Just before you emerge from the tunnel, you can take a right turn up a further flight of steps (although these would certainly require a torch to explore), which are chained off after about 20m of climbing. At this point, a signposted escape route descends to the left and rejoins the route at about 1655m. If you have a torch, then this diversion is the more interesting option.

Cables now zigzag up the slope to a col (about 1720m). The look-out post on the summit of Monte Corno Battisti, at 1760m, is now a short stroll up to your right (south). It will have taken about 3 hours from the village, plus whatever time you have spent exploring the wartime artefacts en route.

When you leave the summit, retrace your steps to the col to pick up path 122, signposted to Bocchetta di Foxi. Within a couple of minutes, at Seletta Battisti, you pass an outdoor altar with several commemorative plaques, including one to the celebrated Trentino patriot Cesare Battisti. After a short climb your path contours pleasantly, firstly to the east, then north into trees. You now follow a grassy ridge before dropping to the col, Bocchetta di Foxi (1720m). You now follow path 102, which turns back sharply to your right (south) for the long descent on the easily graded zigzags of the old military road on which you set out at the start of your day. Allow about 2½ hours from the summit back to Anghebeni.

Military insignia on Sentiero Galli (ROVER 2)

ROVER 3:
MONTE CORNETTO

Grade:	1
Seriousness:	A
Departure point:	Passo Pian delle Fugazze, 1162m
Ascent:	700m
Descent:	700m
Via ferrata:	80m
Approximate time:	4–6 hours
Highest altitude:	1899m, Monte Cornetto

No direct vehicular access to Passo Campogrosso by northern approach.

Although not a ferrata in the climbing sense, Monte Cornetto is a good summit with an easy ascent and good views.

This route is included for comprehensive ferrata coverage; it is a wartime route with limited, occasional protection.

From Rovereto follow the SS46 road to Passo Pian delle Fugazze, 1162m (plenty of parking, and also accommodation at the Albergo; see www.albergoalpasso.it). On the road which leads uphill south-west from Passo Pian delle Fugazze, pick up the start of path 45 on the left signposted 'Sellata Nord Ovest (NO) 1h 10min and Monte Cornetto 2 hours' – you will probably better these times. Path 45 is good underfoot as it climbs steadily up to Sellata NO through pleasant woods in about an hour. At Sellata NO path 45 takes a left waymark, and it would be possible to climb Monte Cornetto this way, thereby missing the ferrata-designated ascent. However, follow path 46 towards Malga Boffetal for a few minutes until the path for Monte Cornetto leads up to the left and Malga Boffetal is straight ahead.

Follow the old wartime track (well engineered but subject to some rock slippage in places) as it winds its way up through eight tunnels with short sections of chains (unusual for the Dolomite ferratist) for protection. Apart from one move around a corner there is virtually no exposure, and with a reasonable head for heights you will probably not need any ferrata equipment. The tunnels are quite short and high, so although a torch and helmet could be

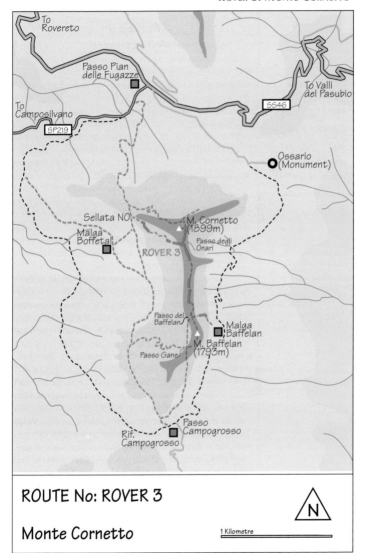

ROUTE No: ROVER 3

Monte Cornetto

N

1 Kilometre

useful, with care these are not essential. In 30 to 40 minutes from Sellata NO you arrive at Passo degli Onari, 1772m (you will return here after climbing Monte Cornetto to continue south along the ridge). From Passo degli Onari the wartime route continues to the summit of Monte Cornetto along ledges and through four more tunnels with the assistance of another short (10m) chain. The summit has extensive views of the Piccole Dolomiti.

For a short day descend from the summit back down path 45 to Sellata NO and retrace your ascent back to Passo Pian delle Fugazze from there. However, the recommended route retraces your steps to descend from the summit back to Passo degli Onari. From here you could retrace your steps back down path 46, but it is better to continue the day by heading south along a superb ridge (path 14) towards Passo del Baffelan; this is also known as Sentiero d'Arroccamento. The path along the ridge is superbly engineered as it winds its way on ledges through rock pinnacles and along a further nine tunnels, with two more short chains for protection.

It takes 50 minutes from Passo degli Onari to Passo Baffelan, where again you have a number of options. Passo Campogrosso, with a 6km walk back to Passo Pian delle Fugazze, is 45 minutes away. You can descend to the west via Passo Gane (20 minutes) then descend to Malga Baffetal, or even ascend Monte Baffelan. However, a more exciting descent goes down to the east on Boale del Baffelan with the warning 'Sentiero Attrezzato per Esperti' and takes 20 minutes; this leads down to Malga Baffelan. Actually the path is steep and loose in places and has some exposed scrambling down with no protection! The only 'attrezzato' is a 10m vertical chain (and a couple of pegs for footholds), which you use to swing down a steep corner. Once down in Malga Baffelan follow the metalled road northwards (no vehicular access) back to Passo Pian delle Fugazze in about an hour.

ROVER 4:
VIA FERRATA MONTE ALBANO

Grade:	5
Seriousness:	C
Departure point:	Mori, 200m
Ascent:	460m
Descent:	460m
Via ferrata:	350m
Approximate time:	4–5 hours
Highest altitude:	660m, Monte Albano

This is a quality route indeed; it is one of the hardest routes you will find outside the higher Dolomite mountains and should only be attempted by experienced ferratists with fitness and stamina. Because of its quality and accessibility it is a very popular route (especially at weekends), and some of the rock is very shiny.

This ferrata is a 'sport' route. Steep, sustained, but always well protected, it is exposed throughout.

Approach the route directly from the village of Mori, where parking can be difficult. There is a car park in the centre of town, but note that a weekly market on Thursday takes this over. You can reach Mori by regular bus services from Rovereto or Riva. Monte Albano is clearly visible rising to the north of Mori. Head through the old part of Mori to the last road running east–west before the rising steep ground; this is Via Villa Nuova to the west and Via di Roma to the east. About 150m from the point where Via di Roma becomes Via Villa Nuova, Via Monte Albano heads up above Mori towards Santuario di M. Albano (a sanctuary, and still a very favourable place of repose). Via Attrezzata Monte Albano is clearly signed. Walk uphill for 15 minutes on a cobbled road to Parco di Arrampicata. Here you will find picnic benches, information boards for the ferrata and some boulder climbing areas. Follow signs towards the Via Attrezzata Monte Albano on a path which zigzags up through trees for 5 minutes to the start of the route. Note that as you leave the picnic area, 'Rientro Attrezzata' is shown to

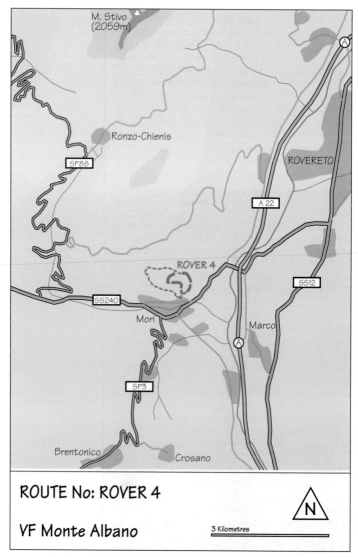

ROUTE No: ROVER 4

VF Monte Albano

3 Kilometres

the right (east); this is the more difficult descent route (described below) and could be used as an easier ascent at about ferrata grade 3. There is only one escape (see diagram), a traverse along a ledge between the first two pitches – after that you either go up or come down again!

The first 6m of the climb are not protected – is this a deliberate ploy to test if you are 'up for it'? Climb a gully on very shiny holds, with some dirt fall as well, until you can reach a peg to pull up on onto a ledge and clip onto the ferrata protection. Once on the cable – follow it! The route is very committing and requires strenuous effort from start to finish, plus good technique, stamina and a head for heights. Protection is excellent, with good cables, but nothing more

Climber on steep wall pitch of Via Ferrata Monte Albano (ROVER 4) (see diagram on p. 296)

SCHEMATIC DIAGRAM OF PITCHES ON VF MONTE ALBANO

This route has earned the reputation of being one of the finest, and hardest, 'sport' via ferratas in the region. This is evidenced by the fact that each of its seven pitches is individually named, as indicated on the diagram below.

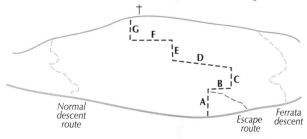

A Via dell'Edera

B Traversata del Guto

C Camino delle Gemelle

D Traversata deghli Angelli

E Camino del Cobra

F Passagio dei Diedri

G Parete del Chiado

than the occasional peg for additional help. Gloves are highly recommended because you will frequently need to use the cable to haul yourself up with. Although the route becomes easier from pitch D, be warned that the final section (G in the diagram) is steep and strenuous. Allow 2½–3 hours for the ascent.

Once clipped on go up **Via dell'Edera (A)**, a steep corner (10 minutes' climbing), to a large ledge (a rest); this also signs the 'Rientro emergencia', the only escape route on the climb. From here climb a short wall before traversing to the right on **Traversata del Guto (B)**, holding onto the cable, with occasional pegs for security for your feet, but otherwise on shiny vertical rock! Again there is a rest point before a 10m vertical wall, **Camino delle Gemelle (C)**, then continue up to a small bridge. Climbing time so far is about 75–90 minutes. After another short step, the next section, **Traversata deghli Angelli (D)**, traverses to the left on slightly easier ground. Continue the traverse (passing a small sign 'Inizio Pala Della Madonna') with a little climbing before arriving at an impressive pillar about 20m high, **Camino del Cobra (E)**. The pillar climbs easier than it looks, before you continue your leftward traverse, climbing down **Passagio dei Diedri (F)** over a broken ledge leading to a corner. Now climb steeply up for 8m before a traverse leads to the route-book box. After this, the last corner is a sustained vertical (and slightly awkward) climb, **Parete del Chiado (G)**, to the end of the route, a wooden fence and a welcoming bench to rest on.

Climber traversing on Via Ferrata Monte Albano (ROVER 4)

Above the end of the ferrata walk up a way-marked path along olive grove terraces to a sign '675 bis Rientro Attrezzata/675 Sentiero di Rientro'. Continue walking for 5 minutes, then make your choice. The easier route, Sentiero 675, goes to the left walking down to the start of the route in about 40 minutes. The route described here is the Attrezzata descent, which continues to the right and takes 1–1¼ hours to descend. Take Rientro Attrezzata back to ferrata land, and climb again before traversing right to begin the descent. It is easy at first, but then goes down vertically for 6m before reaching an easy but exposed sloping ramp. Simply follow the cable to its end in about 30 minutes, then zigzag down on a waymarked path (including a bit of pot-holing through a tunnel in some fallen boulders) before reaching the picnic bench area in about an hour. This descent route (which can, of course, be climbed) is nowhere near as shiny as the main route, suggesting most people use the walking descent anyway.

To complete your day, walk back down the cobbled road to Mori and a well-earned celebratory drink.

ROVER 5:
SENTIERO ATTREZZATO
DEL VIPERE AND CORNA PIANA

Grade:	1
Seriousness:	A
Departure point:	Passo San Valentino, 1314m
Ascent:	230 or 500m
Descent:	230 or 500m
Via ferrata:	50m
Approximate time:	1 or 3 hours
Highest altitude:	1540m, Corna Bes, or 1735m, Corna Piana

A very short and easy route which is included for comprehensive ferrata coverage.

Extended mountain day option
Go north to Passo Canelette, 1617m, from where you can, if you have more time, also climb Monte Altissimo di Nago, 2079m, which has a magnificent panorama of Lake Garda and is renowned for rare alpine flowers. To return from Passo Canelette follow the 'Generale Graziani' road back to Passo San Valentino. If you want to enjoy the Alto Piano di Monte Baldo, Rifugio Graziani at Passo Canelette is a good place to stay (tel: 0464.867005).

The ferrata is only 15 minutes from the road, and takes a further 15 minutes to Corna Bes – you could climb up and down this route inside an hour. An extension to Corna Piana and other peaks is suggested to make this a 'mountain walking day' rather than a climbing one.

Approach the route on the minor road from Mori via Brentonico, or from Avio in the Adige valley, to Passo San Valentino. A few hundred metres west of the pass, along the road which leads to Passo Canelette, you can park opposite a picnic area. Path 650, signed on the right, climbs steeply through the wood and zigzags to the foot of the rock wall where the ferrata, indicated by a plaque 'Sentiero Attrezzata Delle Vipere', begins. The route traverses diagonally to the right along a fairly wide ledge, with intermittent cable protection, across the rocky wall to a summit at about 1540m in 30 minutes.

For a longer walk follow path 650 which descends north-west to Malga Bes, 1511m, before following an old wartime path which climbs the southern flank to the summit of Corna Piana, 1735m, in about 1½ hours. ◀

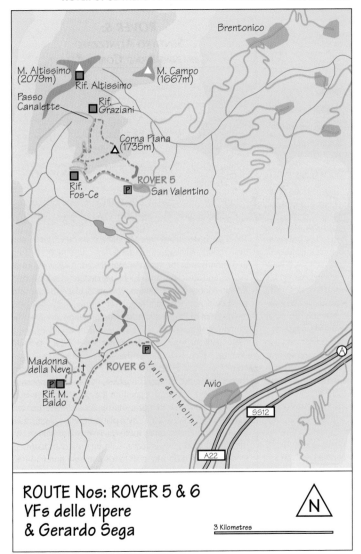

Brentonico

M. Altissimo
(2079m)
Rif. Altissimo

M. Campo
(1667m)

Passo
Canalette

Rif.
Graziani

Corna Piana
(1735m)

Rif.
Fos-Ce

ROVER 5

San Valentino

Valle dei Molini

Madonna
della Neve

ROVER 6

Avio

Rif. M.
Baldo

SS12

A22

A

ROUTE Nos: ROVER 5 & 6
VFs delle Vipere
& Gerardo Sega

N

3 Kilometres

ROVER 6:
SENTIERO ATTREZZATO
GERARDO SEGA, MONTE BALDO

Grade:	2
Seriousness:	C
Departure point:	Madonna della Neve, 1070m (or Valle dei Molini, 300m)
Ascent:	600m
Descent:	600m
Via ferrata:	300m
Approximate time:	4–5 hours
Highest altitude:	1300m

An esoteric but excellent route with tremendous views, a limestone gorge and big walls. Despite its easy accessibility and proximity to a very popular area, the ferrata is in a fairly solitary location and has a committing but peaceful feeling.

The route is described from Madonna della Neve, giving the best 'round'. Although this adds 17km (30 minutes) driving in comparison to the Valle dei Molini start, it saves 400m of ascent and descent, and 2½ hours on the climbing day. Rifugio Monte Baldo, 1100m, is a good place to stay, and you could start the walk here as it is only a few hundred metres from Madonna della Neve (information at www.*rifugio*montebaldo.it or tel. 0464.391553). This would also be a useful base for Ferrata Delle Taccole (see ROVER 7 below).

From Madonna della Neve descend almost 400m before the ascent to the ferrata. Follow waymarks down a tarmac road towards Avio; this becomes a gravel road, where after passing an outdoor centre a path leads down to the left signed '652 Avio, 685 Sentiero Gherado Sega, 652 Mulateria' (note the route spelling). Follow this path down into a wooded gorge, and in 250m a path junction is reached where path 661 goes off to the right and 652/685 branches left, continuing down the spectacular gorge. After 30 minutes of descent a flood warning sign is passed, and 100m further on 685 Gerardo Sega is signed. Your spot height here is about 700m (the **alternative start** from Valle dei Molini at 300m joins the route here, ascending path 685 from the Km 3 marker on the road up from Avio (SP208) – but is an unnecessary slog).

Assuming you have descended to this point turn left following waymarks to cross the stream fed by Cascata Prefesa (**warning:** this may be a problem after heavy rain). A short detour to view the waterfall is worthwhile before continuing on path 685, which traverses and climbs the steep wooded hillside with occasional waymarks. About 30 minutes from the waterfall the trees start to thin out and the path zigzags uphill to a wide ledge under a large yellow overhang – beware of stone falls around this point. The start of the route, 840m, with a commemorative plaque, '13.1.1912 – 18.11.1970, Gerardo Sega S.A.T Avio 1.5.1976', is now less than 5 minutes away along a stony ledge. Allow 1¼–1½ hours from Madonna della Neve.

A 6m ladder leads into a loose corner, with new cables giving excellent protection as the route traverses left along an

Ladders at the start of Sentiero Attrezzato Gerardo Sega (ROVER 6)

airy ledge where you can already appreciate the verticality of the gorge! About 20 minutes from the start you climb a rocky gully before the first break in the protection, where you zigzag up a steep wooded slope to the next cable. Now the route traverses back to the right and along another well-protected ledge leading back to the large overhanging roof. You may be worried to see that the cable stops before the rightwards traverse under the big roof. Although the ledge is wide, a good head for heights is required here, with the sheer drop on your right and the awesome view of the roof above you!

After about 200m with no cables you reach a 50m cable continuing the rightward traverse and then follow a narrow track through

Ledges on Sentiero Attrezzato Gerardo Sega (ROVER 6)

the steep wood, with stunning views down the gorge to Avio, now almost 1000m below! A short protected climb up to the left, followed by about 10 minutes' walking up a wide, easy gully, leads to the final cable, with about 20 minutes of climbing. It is a good finish on quite nice rock to arrive on the summit edge, where once again there is a splendid panorama of Avio and the Adige valley. Allow 3 hours to this point (a good spot for lunch), then continue following waymarks for 10 minutes to meet a good jeep track (path 685) signed to the left 'Avio ritorno'.

Follow path 685 (generally south-west) to return to Madonna della Neve by a good track on a high-level Alpe. After 30 minutes walking downhill on the jeep track waymarks lead off to the right on a single-file path to cross a stream (this is the stream which feeds Cascata Prefesa). A 15 minute uphill walk now leads to Madonna della Neve.

ROVER 7:
FERRATA DELLE TACCOLE

Grade:	4
Seriousness:	A
Departure point:	Km 34 on the SP3 Monte Baldo high-level road, 1555m (1km north of Satel Cavel di Novezza, 1433m)
Ascent:	700m
Descent:	700m
Via ferrata:	150m
Approximate time:	4½ hours
Highest altitude:	2155m, Vetta delle Buse

You could spend a couple of days in this area and combine this route with ROVER 5 and 6, staying at Madonna delle Neve (see ROVER 6 above). Alternatively, this route could be included with a high-level traverse of Monte Baldo, either by accessing the ridge from Castelletto or Torri del Benaco on the western side of Monte Baldo coming up from Lake Garda, or by using the cabinovia (gondola) from Malcesine and walking along the ridge, though this lift system gets very busy in July and August. The ferrata is situated on the north side of Vetta delle Buse looking towards Rif. Telegrafo. Although not at a high altitude in Dolomitic terms, being north facing means that early in the season it can hold snow.

An excellent, if somewhat remote, route on the eastern flank of the Monte Baldo range.

One approach is to leave the A22 autostrada at Avio and drive up towards San Valentino on the SP208, but the authors' recommended approach (more scenic and taking about the same time) is by road from Mori, following the SP 3 high-level road on Monte Baldo for 34km until, about 1km before Cavallo di Novezza, 'path 652 Rif. Telegrafo' is signed leading up from the side of the road. Although the road is narrow it is metalled throughout, and where the footpath leads up there are small lay-bys either side of the road with parking for six or seven cars. It's a long drive, but both the walk-in and quality of the ferrata make it worthwhile.

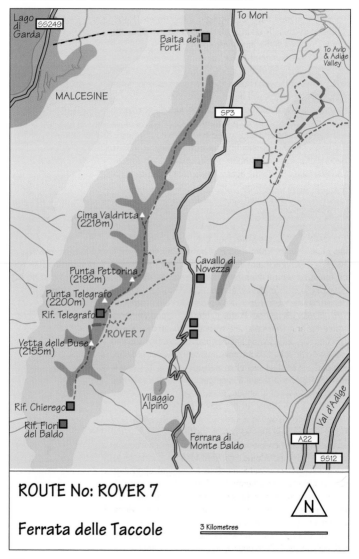

ROUTE No: ROVER 7

Ferrata delle Taccole

3 Kilometres

Follow signed path '652 Rifugio Telegrafo ore 1.40', which climbs steadily up through beech woods. In about 20 minutes you reach the junction of path 66 going uphill to the right; this is signed 'F'lla Val Fontanella ore 1 (per Valdritta)'. Cima Valdritta is the highest peak on the Monte Baldo range, and if you choose to extend your day by climbing it (see below) this will be your return route.

However, approach the ferrata by continuing on path 652 as it goes pleasantly uphill for another 20 minutes or so before it steepens and zigzags up for another 10 minutes then eases off while continuing upwards. After a climb from the road of about 1¼–1½ hours path 652 arrives at a T-junction with path 651. To the right is signed 'Funivia Tredes Pin ore 2.50 Rif M Altissimo 5.30' (note that the 'funivia' referred to here is the old cable car from Malcesine, now replaced with a new gondola system). 'Rif. Telegrafo 651,652 10 minutes' is signed left. Continue on this now wide path (the General Grazziani road in First World War), and in little over 100m it forks. The right fork is to 'Rif Telegrafo 10 minutes', but to continue to the ferrata take the left fork which continues as path 658, Rif. Chierego ore 1.10. This high-level path is at about 2090m; it is also designated Sentiero Europeo 7 (a long-distance path, 4200km in length, stretching from Portugal, through Spain, Andorra, France, Italy and Slovenia, and ending in Romania).

Set off again, passing another path on the right for Rif. Telegrafo, and then two memorial plaques. In about 5 minutes pass yet another memorial plaque and a path coming up from the left (657). Path 658 continues, and in a few minutes arrives at a col at about 2080m, with a view north to Rif. Telegrafo and west all the way down to Lake Garda, almost 2000m below. In a further 5 minutes the path goes through a cutting in the rock, another view appears down to Lake Garda, and on the right are two more plaques. One reads 'CAI Gruppo Alpino Scaligero Verona, Ferrata delle Taccole 1954–1974 Coal Santo 26-6-77'; the other, 'Walter Sartori Non Ti Dimentichermo I Tuoi Amici'.

To get to the start of the ferrata leave path 658 here and follow red waymarks down west into a large bowl, where there may be snow early in the season. Descend the steep scree down to rocks on the left of the bowl (about 2000m) and then waymarks lead down over these rocks to the start of the route at about 1980m; this takes about 2 hours from the start on the SP3 road. Yet another plaque indicates the start of the ferrata, dedicated to Piergiorgio De Rossi Luglio, 1992.

The ferrata goes straight up a wide chimney with good cables, though of the type which run through ringed pegs and are held firm every four or five pegs rather than being fixed at each peg; it helps to climb each 'tied off' section one person at a time to avoid pull on the cable. The chimney is quite steep and strenuous, but the rock is good, and there are some pegs and small stemples as helpful footholds. Be careful at the top of the chimney, as there are some loose small stones where you climb out onto a ledge to complete the first 30m. The cable now traverses right on easy ground for about 50m to a steep impressive wall with a large verti-cal crack (about 2010m). The climbing is superb, with views to Rif. Telegrafo. Note that the crack contains a series of chock-stones, natural higher up but at the bottom cemented in. The cable goes up the wall to the right of the crack for about 20m on excellent rock, with more small stemples occasionally and, of course, the chock-stones to help. The route then crosses over to a corner on the left (with poten-tial drainage) and climbs a further 10m to a ledge (about 30 minutes of climbing so far).

The final climbing pitch is an easier angled 30m wall to the right of a damp cleft. Again there are some small stem-ples for footholds, but there are a couple of awkward moves and some dampness at the top as you move up onto a ledge at about 2070m. The hard climbing is over, but a short walk with intermittent cables leads to the route book in about 5 minutes (2100m). A further 10 minutes' walking leads to the grassy summit of Vette delle Buse, 2155m (the ascent from the start of the ferrata to the summit takes 50–60 minutes). What a summit it is, with commanding views over Lake Garda on the west, the Adige valley on the east, and along the ridge of Monte Baldo to the north and south.

It is possible to descend the ridge eastwards following red waymarks back to path 658 in about 10 minutes, but there are a couple of unprotected awkward down-climbs (one of over 3m). You can avoid this by walking down the grassy slope heading south from Vette Delle Buse for about 150m to rejoin path 658 there. Either way (when back on path 658) look out for a wonderful crest of arms commemorating the centenary of the Verona Section of the CAI 1875–1975. It is topped by an eagle above a capercaille, deer, gentian, edelweiss, ice axe and rope. Return (north-east) along path 658 for about 10 minutes and the path junction up left to Rif. Telegrafo. Now you have some options.

1. To return straight to the start point on the road continue ahead for about 100m and retrace path 652 back down to the road in 1–1½ hours; this is the option as per the summary route timings.
2. Go to Rif. Telegrafo, 2147m; this is open at weekends from the beginning of May until mid-October, and open fully from mid-June to mid-September. Above the *rifugio* is Punta Telegrafo, 2200m, with its summit cross '1950 Anno Santo'. From here you can retrace path 652 to return to the road.
3. You can extend the pleasure of being high up on the Monte Baldo ridge by continuing along path 651 towards Punta Pettorina and the junction of path 66 (signed 'ore 0.30 – Rif Telegrafo 0.45 Funivia 2.15'); this takes about 30 minutes. (If you want to climb Cima Valdritta, 2218m, the return trip from here back to path 66 takes about an hour.) Descend from here on path 66, which is steep but with well-engineered zigzags, for another 30 minutes down to the junction with 652. Another 15 minutes leads back to the SP3 road. Note that 5 minutes down path 66 is a rock carved with a cross and the date 1754.

Whichever option you choose, all paths are well marked and signed.

APPENDIX 1:
GLOSSARY OF MOUNTAIN TERMS

Here is a simple glossary of a few words or expressions that you may find on maps or directional signs, and in guidebooks, weather forecasts, etc.

ITALIAN	GERMAN	ENGLISH
Ago	nadel	needle, pinnacle
Alpe, malga	alp	alp, upland meadow
alta via	hohenweg	high level path
alto	hoch	high
attrezzato	klettersteig	protected
baita	berghutte	mountain hut
bianco	weiss	white
biglietto	fahrkarte	ticket
bivacco	biwak	bivouac hut
bocca	sattel	pass, saddle
bocchetta	kleine scharte	small pass, gap
bosco	wald	forest
cabinovia, telecabina	gondellift	gondola lift
caduta di sassi	steinschlag	stone-fall
camere libre	zimmer frei	rooms to let
canale	rinne	gully
canalone	schlucht	gorge
carta	karte	map
cengia	band	ledge
chiuso	geschlossen	closed
cima	spitze	summit
col, colle	hugel	hill
corda	seil, kabel	rope
cresta	grat	ridge
croce	kreuz	cross
croda	felswand	wall, cliff
curve di livello	hohenlinien	contour lines
destra	rechts	right
difficile	schwierig	difficult
diritto	geradeaus	straight ahead
discesa, giu	absteig	descent, down
dislivello	hohenunterscheid	altitude difference
esposto	exponiert	exposed
est	osten	east

ITALIAN	GERMAN	ENGLISH
estate	sommer	summer
fiume	fluss, strom	river
forcella	scharte	gap, small pass
funivia	seilbahn	cable car
ghiaio	schutt, geroll	scree
ghiacciao	gletscher	glacier
ghiaccio	eis	ice
gradini	klammern	stemples, iron rungs
grande	gross	large
gruppo	gruppe	massif, group
impianti	aufsteigsanlagen	lift system
lago	see	lake
lontano	weit	far
marcia	tritt	foot-hold
montagna	berg	mountain
mugo	latschen	small pine bushes
nebbia	nebel	fog
nord	norden	north
noleggio	verleithen	to hire
occidentale	westlich	western
orientale	orientalisch, ostlich	eastern
ovest	westen	west
parco naturale	naturpark	natural park
parete	wand	wall, cliff
parcheggio	parkplatz	parking
passo	joch	pass
pensione	gasthof	guest house
percorso	wanderweg	path
pericolo	gefahr	danger
pericoloso	gefahrlich	dangerous
piano	ebene,hochflache	level ground, plateau
piccolo	kleine	small
piz, punta	gipfel, spitze	summit
ponte	brucke	bridge
rallentare	langsam	slow down
rifugio	hutte	mountain hut
rio	bach	stream, brook
ripido	steil	steep
rosso	rot	red
salita	aufsteigen	ascent
sasso	fels, stein	stone

ITALIAN	GERMAN	ENGLISH
scala	leiter	ladder
scendere	abstammen	descend
segnalazione	bezeichnung	way-marks
seggiovia	sessellift	chair lift
sella	sattel	saddle
sentiero	fussweg	footpath
sinsistra	links	left
soccorso	bergrettung	rescue
strada	strasse	road
sud	sudden, sud	south
tempo	wetter, zeit	weather or time
torrente	sturzbach	mountain stream
traversata	durchqueren	crossing
ultima	letzte	last
valanga	lawine	avalanche
val, valle	tal	valley
vedretta	gletscher	glacier
vento	wind	wind
via	weg	way, route
vietato	verboten	not permitted

APPENDIX 2:
INDEX OF ROUTES IN GRADE ORDER

This index of routes is arranged in order of difficulty, based on the grading system used in the guide (1 being the easiest grade and 5 the hardest). The commitment of each route is indicated by the 'Seriousness' grade (also detailed at the start of each walk). The route name indicates the section of the book in which each route is found (S.MAR = San Martino, etc). Each section centres on the geographical location that provides the best point of access to the routes in that section.

APPENDIX 3:

INDEX OF ROUTES BY MOUNTAIN GROUP

This index of routes is arranged by mountain group. The route name indicates the section of the book in which each route is found (S.MAR = San Martino, etc). Each section centres on the geographical location that provides the best point of access to the routes in that section.

APPENDIX 4:
MOUNTAIN RESCUE

Hopefully you will never have any cause to call out the rescue services. However, if you do, this checklist, with translations in Italian and German may be of help in a crisis as an aide memoire to providing the rescue services with the appropriate details of your situation.

Call-out for mountain rescue in the Dolomites: Telephone Soccorso Alpino 118

- **Time of Accident/L'Ora/Zeit**

- **Accident Location/Luogo/Platz**

- **Type of Incident/Incidente/Vorfall:**
  Fall/Caduta/Fall
  Heart Attack/Infarto/Herzanfall
  Illness/malattia/Krankheit
  Any Other/Altro/Andere

- **Number of Party at Accident Location/Numero di personne chi rimangono/**
  Zuruckbleibende Personen

- **Number of Casulaties/Numero di personne chi Vittima/Verletzte Personen**

- **Details of Casualty/Vittima/Verletzte:**
  Name/Nome/Name
  Age/Eta/Alter
  Sex/Sesso/Geschlecht: Male/Uomo/Mann or Female/Donna/Frau

- **Level of Consciousness/Livello di Conscinza/Bewusstsein:**
  Alert/Conscienza Normale/Wachsam
  Confused/Conscienza ridotta/Konfus
  Unconscious/Niente/Nichts

- **Symptoms/Sintomi/Symptome:**
  Fracture/Frattura/Bruch
  Sprain/Distorsione/Verrenkung
  Wound/Ferita/Wunde

- **Part of Body/Parte Di Corpo/Korper Teil:**
  Arm/Bracchio/Arm
  Back/Schiena/Rucken
  Chest/Petto/Brust
  Leg/Gamba/Bein
  Hand/Mano/Hand
  Head/Testa/Kopf
  Shoulder/Spalla/Schulter

APPENDIX 5:
USEFUL ADDRESSES

Holidays/Accommodation
See each section introduction for local
tourist board contact details.

ENIT London office: Italian State Tourist
Board
1 Princess Street
London W1B 2AY
Tel: 020 7408 1254
Fax: 020 7399 3567
Email: italy@italiantouristboard.co.uk
Web site: www.enit.it/uk
Italian Tourist Web Guide: www.itwg.com

Trentino Information Service
39 Compton Road
Wimbledon
London SW19 7QA
Tel & fax: 020 8879 1405
Email: trentino.infoservice@virgin.net
Web site: www.trentino.to

Collett's Mountain Holidays
Harvest Mead
Great Hormead
Buntingford
Herts SG9 0PB
Tel: 01763 289660/289680
Fax: 01763 289690
Email: admin@colletts.co.uk
Web site: www.colletts.co.uk

Waymark Holidays Ltd
44 Windsor Road
Slough SL1 2EJ
Tel: 01753 516 477 (international: +44 1753
516 477),
Fax: 01753 517 016 (international +44 1753
517 016)
Email: enquiries@waymarkholidays.co.uk
Web site: www.waymarkholidays.co.uk

Map Suppliers
Edward Stanford Ltd
12 Long Acre
London WC2E 9LP
Tel: 020 7240 3611
Email: sales@stanfords.co.uk
Web site: www.stanfords.co.uk

The Map Shop
15 High Street
Upton on Severn
Worcestershire WR8 0HJ
Tel: 0800 085 40 80
Email: themapshop@btinternet.com
Web site: www.themapshop.co.uk

Special Interest
The Alpine Garden Society
AGS Centre
Avon Bank
Pershore
Worcestershire WR10 3JP
Tel: 01386 554790
Web site: www.alpinegardensociety.org

APPENDIX 6:
BIBLIOGRAPHY

Via Ferratas in the Italian Dolomites, volume 1, John Smith and Graham Fletcher, Cicerone Press, 2002

Treks in the Dolomites: Alta Via 1 and 2, Martin Collins and Gillian Price, Cicerone Press, 2002

Rifugios: Guide to Refuges in Trentino, published by (and available free from) APT Del Trentino

Museums: Guide to the Museums and Collections in Trentino, published by (and available free from) APT Del Trentino

The Italian Alps, D.W. Freshfield, 1875

The Dolomites, C. Douglas Milner, 1951

Dolomites, Selected Climbs, Ron James, Alpine Club

The First World War, John Keegan, Pimlico, 1999

Battleground Europe (Italy) Asiago, F. MacKay, Leo Cooper, 2001

Gebirgskrieg 1915–1918, 3 volumes, Heinz von Lichem (only available in German or Italian)

Contemporary Italy: Politics, Economy and Society since 1945, Donald Sassoon, Longmans, 1986

Concise History of Italy, Peter Gunn, Thames & Hudson, 1971

The Great War on the Little Lagazuoi, Committee Cengia Martini, July 1998 (www.dolomiti.org/lagazuoi)

LISTING OF CICERONE GUIDES